XML

Your visual blueprint for building expert Web pages

by Emily Vander Veer and Rev Mengle

Visual

From

maranGraphics™

&

IDG Books Worldwide, Inc.

An International Data Group Company

Foster City, CA • Indianapolis • Chicago • New York

XML: Your visual blueprint for building expert Web pages

Published by
IDG Books Worldwide, Inc.
An International Data Group Company
919 E. Hillsdale Blvd., Suite 400
Foster City, CA 94404
www.idgbooks.com (IDG Books Worldwide Web Site)

Library of Congress Control Number: 00-109394

ISBN: 0-7645-3477-7

Printed in the United States of America
10 9 8 7 6 5 4 3 2 1

1O/RY/RQ/QQ/IN

Distributed in the United States by IDG Books Worldwide, Inc.

Distributed by CDG Books Canada Inc. for Canada; by Transworld Publishers Limited in the United Kingdom; by IDG Norge Books for Norway; by IDG Sweden Books for Sweden; by IDG Books Australia Publishing Corporation Pty. Ltd. for Australia and New Zealand; by TransQuest Publishers Pte Ltd. for Singapore, Malaysia, Thailand, Indonesia, and Hong Kong; by Gotop Information Inc. for Taiwan; by ICG Muse, Inc. for Japan; by Intersoft for South Africa; by Eyrolles for France; by International Thomson Publishing for Germany, Austria and Switzerland; by Distribuidora Cuspide for Argentina; by LR International for Brazil; by Galileo Libros for Chile; by Ediciones ZETA S.C.R. Ltda. for Peru; by WS Computer Publishing Corporation, Inc. for the Philippines; by Contemporanea de Ediciones for Venezuela; by Express Computer Distributors for the Caribbean and West Indies; by Micronesia Media Distributor, Inc. for Micronesia; by Chips Computadoras S.A. de C.V. for Mexico; by Editorial Norma de Panama S.A. for Panama; by American Bookshops for Finland.

For corporate orders, please call maranGraphics at 800-469-6616.

For general information on IDG Books Worldwide's books in the U.S., please call our Consumer Customer Service department at 800-762-2974.

For reseller information, including discounts and premium sales, please call our Reseller Customer Service department at 800-434-3422.

For information on where to purchase IDG Books Worldwide's books outside the U.S., please contact our International Sales department at 317-572-3993 or fax 317-572-4002.

For consumer information on foreign language translations, please contact our Customer Service department at 800-434-3422, fax 800-550-2747, or e-mail rights@idgbooks.com.

For information on licensing foreign or domestic rights, please phone 650-653-7000 of fax 650-653-7500.

For sales inquiries and special prices for bulk quantities, please contact our Sales department at 650-655-3200.

For information on using IDG Books Worldwide's books in the classroom or for ordering examination copies, please contact our Educational Sales department at 800-434-2086 or fax 317-572-4005.

For press review copies, author interviews, or other publicity information, please contact our Public Relations department at 650-653-7000 or fax 650-653-7500.

For authorization to photocopy items for corporate, personal, or educational use, please contact Copyright Clearance Center, 222 Rosewood Drive, Danvers, MA 01923, or fax 978-750-4470.

Screen shots displayed in this book are based on pre-released software and are subject to change.

Trademark Acknowledgments

U.S. Corporate Sales	**U.S. Trade Sales**
Contact maranGraphics at (800) 469-6616 or fax (905) 890-9434.	Contact IDG Books at (800) 434-3422 or (650) 655-3000.

ABOUT IDG BOOKS WORLDWIDE

Welcome to the world of IDG Books Worldwide.

IDG Books Worldwide, Inc., is a subsidiary of International Data Group, the world's largest publisher of computer-related information and the leading global provider of information services on information technology. IDG was founded more than 30 years ago by Patrick J. McGovern and now employs more than 9,000 people worldwide. IDG publishes more than 290 computer publications in over 75 countries. More than 90 million people read one or more IDG publications each month.

Launched in 1990, IDG Books Worldwide is today the #1 publisher of best-selling computer books in the United States. We are proud to have received eight awards from the Computer Press Association in recognition of editorial excellence and three from Computer Currents' First Annual Readers' Choice Awards. Our best-selling *...For Dummies*® series has more than 50 million copies in print with translations in 31 languages. IDG Books Worldwide, through a joint venture with IDG's Hi-Tech Beijing, became the first U.S. publisher to publish a computer book in the People's Republic of China. In record time, IDG Books Worldwide has become the first choice for millions of readers around the world who want to learn how to better manage their businesses.

Our mission is simple: Every one of our books is designed to bring extra value and skill-building instructions to the reader. Our books are written by experts who understand and care about our readers. The knowledge base of our editorial staff comes from years of experience in publishing, education, and journalism — experience we use to produce books to carry us into the new millennium. In short, we care about books, so we attract the best people. We devote special attention to details such as audience, interior design, use of icons, and illustrations. And because we use an efficient process of authoring, editing, and desktop publishing our books electronically, we can spend more time ensuring superior content and less time on the technicalities of making books.

You can count on our commitment to deliver high-quality books at competitive prices on topics you want to read about. At IDG Books Worldwide, we continue in the IDG tradition of delivering quality for more than 30 years. You'll find no better book on a subject than one from IDG Books Worldwide.

John J. Kilcullen

John Kilcullen
Chairman and CEO
IDG Books Worldwide, Inc.

Eighth Annual Computer Press Awards ➣1992

Ninth Annual Computer Press Awards ➣1993

Tenth Annual Computer Press Awards ➣1994

Eleventh Annual Computer Press Awards ➣1995

IDG is the world's leading IT media, research and exposition company. Founded in 1964, IDG had 1997 revenues of $2.05 billion and has more than 9,000 employees worldwide. IDG offers the widest range of media options that reach IT buyers in 75 countries representing 95% of worldwide IT spending. IDG's diverse product and services portfolio spans six key areas including print publishing, online publishing, expositions and conferences, market research, education and training, and global marketing services. More than 90 million people read one or more of IDG's 290 magazines and newspapers, including IDG's leading global brands — Computerworld, PC World, Network World, Macworld and the Channel World family of publications. IDG Books Worldwide is one of the fastest-growing computer book publishers in the world, with more than 700 titles in 36 languages. The "...For Dummies®" series alone has more than 50 million copies in print. IDG offers online users the largest network of technology-specific Web sites around the world through IDG.net (http://www.idg.net), which comprises more than 225 targeted Web sites in 55 countries worldwide. International Data Corporation (IDC) is the world's largest provider of information technology data, analysis and consulting, with research centers in over 41 countries and more than 400 research analysts worldwide. IDG World Expo is a leading producer of more than 168 globally branded conferences and expositions in 35 countries including E3 (Electronic Entertainment Expo), Macworld Expo, ComNet, Windows World Expo, ICE (Internet Commerce Expo), Agenda, DEMO, and Spotlight. IDG's training subsidiary, ExecuTrain, is the world's largest computer training company, with more than 230 locations worldwide and 785 training courses. IDG Marketing Services helps industry-leading IT companies build international brand recognition by developing global integrated marketing programs via IDG's print, online and exposition products worldwide. Further information about the company can be found at www.idg.com.   1/26/00

**maranGraphics is a family-run business
located near Toronto, Canada.**

At maranGraphics, we believe in producing great computer books — one book at a time.

maranGraphics has been producing high-technology products for over 25 years, which enables us to offer the computer book community a unique communication process.

Our computer books use an integrated communication process, which is very different from the approach used in other computer books. Each spread is, in essence, a flow chart — the text and screen shots are totally incorporated into the layout of the spread. Introductory text and helpful tips complete the learning experience.

maranGraphics' approach encourages the left and right sides of the brain to work together — resulting in faster orientation and greater memory retention.

Above all, we are very proud of the handcrafted nature of our books. Our carefully chosen writers are experts in their fields, and spend countless hours researching and organizing the content for each topic. Our artists rebuild every screen shot to provide the best clarity possible, making our screen shots the most precise and easiest to read in the industry. We strive for perfection, and believe that the time spent handcrafting each element results in the best computer books money can buy.

Thank you for purchasing this book. We hope you enjoy it!

Sincerely,

Robert Maran
President
maranGraphics
Rob@maran.com
www.maran.com
www.idgbooks.com/visual

Please visit us on the Web at:
www.maran.com

CREDITS

Acquisitions, Editorial, and Media Development

Project Editor
Pat O'Brien

Acquisitions Editor
Martine Edwards

Associate Project Coordinator
Lindsay Sandman

Copy Editors
Tim Borek, Paula Lowell

Proof Editor
Teresa Artman

Technical Editor
Heather Williamson

Associate Media Development Specialist
Jamie Smith

Media Development Coordinator
Marisa Pearman

Editorial Manager
Rev Mengle

Media Development Manager
Laura Carpenter

Editorial Assistant
Candance Nicholson

Screen Artists
Craig Dearing, Mark Harris, Jill Johnson

Production

Book Design
maranGraphics©

Project Coordinator
Cindy Phipps

Layout
Joe Bucki, Barry Offringa, Kristin Pickett, Jill Piscitelli

Cover Illustration
Russ Marini

Proofreaders
Vickie Broyles, Corey Bowen, Charles Spencer

Indexer
York Production Services, Inc.

Special Help
Jeanne Criswell

ACKNOWLEDGMENTS

General and Administrative

IDG Books Worldwide, Inc.: John Kilcullen, CEO; Bill Barry, President and COO; John Ball, Executive VP, Operations & Administration; John Harris, CFO

IDG Books Technology Publishing Group: Richard Swadley, Senior Vice President and Publisher; Mary Bednarek, Vice President and Publisher; Walter R. Bruce III, Vice President and Publisher; Joseph Wikert, Vice President and Publisher; Mary C. Corder, Editorial Director; Andy Cummings, Publishing Director, General User Group; Barry Pruett, Publishing Director

IDG Books Manufacturing: Ivor Parker, Vice President, Manufacturing

IDG Books Marketing: John Helmus, Assistant Vice President, Director of Marketing

IDG Books Online Management: Brenda McLaughlin, Executive Vice President, Chief Internet Officer; Gary Millrood, Executive Vice President of Business Development, Sales and Marketing

IDG Books Packaging: Marc J. Mikulich, Vice President, Brand Strategy and Research

IDG Books Production for Branded Press: Debbie Stailey, Production Director

IDG Books Sales: Roland Elgey, Senior Vice President, Sales and Marketing; Michael Violano, Vice President, International Sales and Sub Rights

The publisher would like to give special thanks to Patrick J. McGovern, without whom this book would not have been possible.

About the Authors

Emily A. Vander Veer has written several Internet-related books, including IDG Books' *JavaScript For Dummies* and *JavaBeans For Dummies*. Her work has appeared in numerous online and print publications including *Byte, CNET, Object Magazine,* and *WEBTechniques*.

Emily resides in the hill country of Austin, Texas, where she lives with her husband, Clay (a jazz guitarist nonpareil), and her two-pound pooches, Lochlan and Ceilidh. When she's not hard at work at her keyboard, Emily enjoys traveling, both in the U.S. and abroad.

Rev Mengle is a computer book author with 17 years of editing experience, the last five at IDG Books Worldwide, Inc. Rev has edited books on technology topics as diverse as general business software programs to creating Web pages to database software to programming languages. Rev also was a contributing author for the award-winning *PCs For Kids & Parents*, and was the revision author for the *Internet Directory For Dummies*, 2nd Edition.

XML
Your visual blueprint for
building expert Web pages

4) BUILDING A DTD II: DECLARING DTD ATTRIBUTES

5) BUILDING A DTD III: DECLARING DTD ENTITIES, NOTATIONS, AND MORE

6) BUILDING A SCHEMA I: DECLARING ELEMENTS

7) BUILDING A SCHEMA II: DECLARING ATTRIBUTES AND MORE

8) DISPLAYING DATA IN A BROWSER USING CASCADING STYLE SHEETS (CSS)

XML
Your visual blueprint for
building expert Web pages

9) FORMATTING AND ALIGNING CHARACTERS USING A CSS

10) DEFINING BACKGROUNDS, BORDERS, AND TEXT BOXES USING A CSS

11) DISPLAYING DATA IN A BROWSER USING EXTENSIVE STYLE LANGUAGE (XSL) STLYLE SHEETS

XML
Your visual blueprint for
building expert Web pages

12) CREATING DATA ISLANDS

13) ACCESSING DATA THROUGH THE XML DOCUMENT OBJECT MODEL

14) CREATING XML LINKS

15) TOURING POPULAR XML AUTHORING AND EDITING TOOLS

XML
Your visual blueprint for
building expert Web pages

XML: Your visual blueprint for building expert Web pages uses simple, straightforward examples to teach you how to create powerful, dynamic Web pages and sophisticated Web applications.

To get the most out of this book, you should read each chapter in order, from beginning to end. Each chapter introduces new ideas and builds on the knowledge learned in previous chapters. Once you become familiar with XML, this book can be used as an informative desktop reference.

Who This Book Is For

Because you are interested in authoring XML pages, we assume you have experience using HyperText Markup Language (HTML) to create Web pages. However, if you are not familiar with HTML, you can find the basics you need to get started in this book.

No prior experience with Web server software is required, but familiarity with the Microsoft Windows operating system installed on your computer is an asset.

What You Need To Use This Book

To perform the tasks in this book, you need a computer with a working connection to the Internet. You do not require any special development tools to use XML. All you need is a text editor — we use Notepad in the examples throughout this book — and a Web browser, such as Microsoft Internet Explorer.

The Conventions In This Book

A number of typographic and layout styles have been used throughout *XML: Your visual blueprint for building expert Web pages* to distinguish different types of information.

`Courier Font`

Indicates the use of code.

`Italic Courier Font`

Indicates variables in the code that you must change to match your situation.

Bold

Indicates information that must be typed by you.

Italics

Indicates a new term being introduced.

Apply It

An Apply It section usually contains a segment of code that takes the lesson you just learned one step further. Apply It sections offer inside information and pointers that can be used to enhance the functionality of your code.

Extra

An Extra section provides additional information about the task you just accomplished. Extra sections often contain interesting tips and useful tricks to make working with ASP easier and more efficient.

XML
Your visual blueprint for
building expert Web pages

The Organization Of This Book

XML: Your visual blueprint for building expert Web pages contains 15 chapters.

Chapter 1 shows you how to create a simple page with XML

Chapter 2 demonstrates how a sophisticated page can be created with XML. You may see pages like this on an e-commerce site.

Chapter 3 declares elements (the groups of text and formatting information that make up an XML page) through DTDs (Data Type Documents).

Chapter 4 applies attributes to organize and enhance elements of XML pages.

Chapter 5 uses entities to manage and reuse standard content in XML pages.

Chapter 6 declares elements through the schema process.

Chapter 7 applies the XML schema technique to declare attributes

Chapter 8 uses CSS (Cascading Style Sheets) to format documents with variations of established style sheets.

Chapter 9 expands on the CSS coverage to show you specifics on how to format and align characters with style sheets.

Chapter 10 demonstrates the specifics of backgrounds, borders, and text boxes within a CSS.

Chapter 11 applies XSL (Extensible Style Language) to manage your document formatting information.

Chapter 12 builds XML data islands within HTML documents.

Chapter 13 applies the Document Object Model that can automatically update your XML pages after you create them.

Chapter 14 attaches hyperlinks to your XML page through xLink.

Chapter 15 shows how to use some of the tools that are included on the CD-ROM.

What Is On The CD-ROM

The CD-ROM included in this book contains the sample code from the two-page lessons. This saves you from having to type the code and helps you quickly get started creating ASP code. The CD-ROM also contains several shareware and evaluation versions of programs that can be used to work with XML. An e-version of the book and all the URLs mentioned in the book are also available on the disc.

CREATE YOUR FIRST XML DOCUMENT

Creating an XML document is the first step in creating an XML-based application. The directive you use to create an XML document is

```
<?xml version="version"?>
```

All XML documents, including the one you are about to create, share the following traits:

- They define data in a precise, structured format that follows a simple repeating pattern: **<TAG>**someData**</TAG>**.

- They can include arbitrary amounts of white space for readability, as long as that white space does not appear between tags.

- They are saved as simple text files with the .xml suffix.

- They can be created with a text editor or an XML-supporting editor, like the editors included on the companion CD.

- They are transferred from Web server to Web client via HTTP (HyperText Transfer Protocol), just like HTML files.

- They are an essential component of an XML-based application, which — in addition to an XML file — also includes an optional DTD or schema, an XML parser, and presentation/processing logic.

You can create the file using any text editor. The editor used in this chapter is Microsoft Notepad, a simple text editor that comes bundled with Windows 95/98/NT/2000.

CREATE YOUR FIRST XML DOCUMENT

1 Create a new text file in the text editor of your choice.

■ This example shows a Notepad document.

2 Type the XML directive.

■ The **version="1.0"** attribute/value pair specifies that this document conforms to the XML 1.0 specification.

3 Type the beginning tag for an XML element.

■ In this example, the beginning XML tag is **<GREETING>**.

Extra

XML applications typically include multiple documents, such as XML, HTML, CSS, and DTD documents. Organizing these documents in a single directory is a good idea.

XML parsers identify a file as an XML document as long as the XML declaration tag appears at the top of the file. However, saving XML files using the .xml extension is good programming practice.

XML imposes relatively few syntax rules. All of them are described in this book.

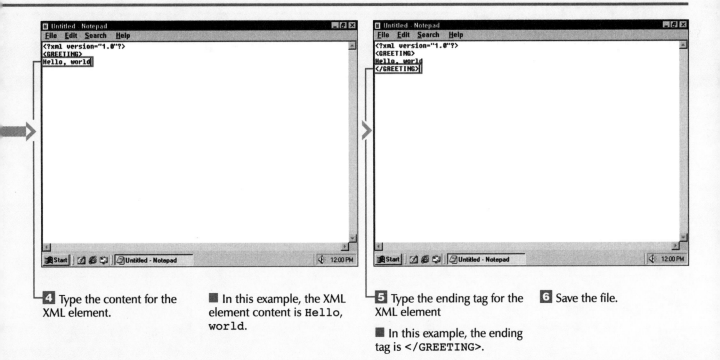

■4 Type the content for the XML element.

■ In this example, the XML element content is Hello, world.

■5 Type the ending tag for the XML element

■ In this example, the ending tag is </GREETING>.

■6 Save the file.

VERIFY YOUR FIRST XML DOCUMENT

This section shows you how to test your first XML file for syntax errors by running it through an XML parser. Two types of XML parsers exist — validating and nonvalidating.

Validating parsers check XML document syntax. They also confirm that XML data matches predefined validation rules, if any, by comparing XML documents to document type definitions (DTDs) and schemas. Validating parsers currently available include

- The Scholarly Technology Group at Brown University's online XML Validation Form at www.stg.brown.edu/service/xmlvalid/.

- Microstar's Aelfred at www.opentext.com/services/ content_management_services/xml_sgml_solutions. html#aelfred_and_sax-.

- Textuality's Larval at www.textuality.com/Lark/.

- IBM's XML Parser for Java at www.alphaworks. ibm.com/tech/xml4j.

Nonvalidating parsers check XML document syntax, but they do not match XML documents against DTDs or schemas. Nonvalidating parsers currently available include

- XML.com's RUWF, which is based on the Lark parser; go to www.xml.com/pub/tools/ruwf/ check.html.

- James Clark's expat at www.jclark.com/xml/ expat.html.

In this section, you test your XML document against MSXML, the validating parser built into Internet Explorer 5.0.

VERIFY YOUR FIRST XML DOCUMENT

1 Run Internet Explorer.

■ Be sure that you have established an Internet connection.

2 Click File.

3 Click Open.

■ The Open dialog box appears.

Extra

The MSXML parser only displays your XML document if the document is well formed. If you attempt to parse a document that is not well formed — in other words, a document containing XML syntax errors — you see an error instead of the XML document data.

The sole job of the MSXML parser is to verify that your XML document is well formed. To display the data intelligently — without the XML tags and in an attractive, easy-to-read format — you must create an XML processor that describes how you want the data to appear. Find out how to create a simple XML processor later in the section, "Create a Simple XML Processor." A stand-alone version of the MSXML parser was provided for use with Internet Explorer 4.*x*, but it has been upgraded significantly for use with Internet Explorer 5. MSXML ships with Internet Explorer 5.0*x* and is also available separately from www.msdn.microsoft.com/downloads/tools/xmlparser/xmlparser.asp.

4 Type the name of the XML document you want to parse.

■ This example uses an XML document called first.xml.

5 Examine the results.

■ If the XML document is well formed, it appears in the browser window, as shown in this example.

EXPLORE MSXML ERROR REPORTS

Before you can process an XML file, ensure that it is well formed.

In the future, you may be able to create your XML file using an XML-generating tool. Until such tools appear on the market, the only way to create XML documents is to type XML tags and data directly into a text editor. This process is error-prone, so you must be able to detect and correct any errors you make while creating your XML files.

After finishing this section, you can

- Recognize when the MSXML parser generates a parsing error.
- Use the error information generated to detect and correct that error.

First, you introduce an intentional error into an XML file. Then you load this new XML file into Internet Explorer and examine the error information generated by the MSXML parser.

EXPLORE MSXML ERROR REPORTS

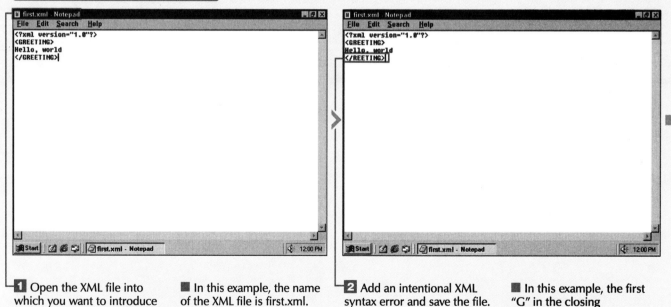

1 Open the XML file into which you want to introduce an error into a text editor.

■ In this example, the name of the XML file is first.xml.

2 Add an intentional XML syntax error and save the file.

■ In this example, the first "G" in the closing `</GREETING>` tag is removed.

Extra

Currently, no online manual exists that describes MSXML's warning or error messages. For now, the only way to decipher error messages is by trial and error. One way to learn MSXML's error reporting scheme is to load one of the working examples from the companion CD into a text editor and make an intentional change to the document. Then save the test document and note the error message your change causes MSXML to generate.

Internet Explorer 5 recognizes the .xml extension, and its built-in MSXML parser understands how to interpret and display a well-formed XML document. Navigator 4.0 does not support XML, although the beta release of Navigator 6.0 does. Some independent browsers, such as Jumbo, support XML.

3 Run Internet Explorer.

4 Open the newly saved file.

5 Examine the error that results.

■ In this example, the XML parser generates the line and character positions of the XML syntax error.

VERIFY WELL-FORMEDNESS

Support for XML is restricted neither to Microsoft products nor to any commercial Web browser. In fact, many vendors are in the process of developing XML-supporting tools and applications, including XML parsers and browsers.

Because Microsoft's MSXML parser is bundled with the freely available Internet Explorer 5.x, it is the easiest parser to obtain and use for prototype applications, such as those described in this book.

However, because parser support for XML varies so widely — and it will vary until the XML specification is complete and mature — you may not want to use MSXML for every development effort. Instead, you may want to use an independent parser to verify that your document is well-formed.

After you complete this section, you can

- Locate and experiment with third-party XML parsers.
- Test your XML document using an online XML validation service.

VERIFY WELL-FORMEDNESS

1 Start Internet Explorer 5.0 or higher (after establishing a working Internet connection).

2 Load the URL of a Web-enabled validating parser.

■ In this example, the validating parser shown is the STG XML Validation Form, which is at www.stg.brown.edu/service/xmlvalid/.

Extra

XML parsers currently available vary based on

- **Implementation.** Some, like the STG validation service shown in this example, are implemented as online services; others, as separate, downloadable utilities; still others, as add-ons to other tools.

- **Reporting schemes.** The error reports generated by different parsers can vary substantially.

- **Stringency.** A line that one parser flags as an error may be flagged as a warning by another parser.

- **Syntax versus syntax-and-semantic-rule checking.** Nonvalidating parsers check XML syntax only. Validating parsers check XML syntax in addition to any semantic validation rules an XML document references.

Expat, Aelfred, and XML for Java are included on the companion CD. To find other XML parsers, visit the following:

- Café con Leche — XML News and Resources (http://metalab.unc.edu/xml/)

- Builder.com's Spotlight on XML (http://builder.cnet.com/Authoring/XmlSpot/)

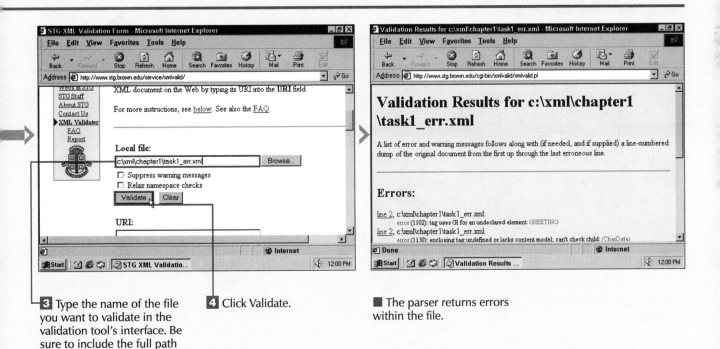

3 Type the name of the file you want to validate in the validation tool's interface. Be sure to include the full path of the file.

4 Click Validate.

■ The parser returns errors within the file.

CREATE A SIMPLE XML PROCESSOR

To process XML data, you must create an *XML processor* (code that accessses, manipulates, or displays XML data intelligently). You can choose from four general categories of XML processors:

- **Cascading style sheets.** Simple XML data display. The easiest type of processor to create, and the most limited. You see examples of cascading style sheets in Chapters 8, 9, and 10.

- **XSL style sheets.** Sophisticated, dynamic XML data display. Chapter 11 provides examples of XSL style sheets.

- **Data island plus script.** Incorporates XML data into an HTML presentation and performs some processing (such as error checking or data manipulation) in addition to display. You see examples of creating and accessing data islands in Chapter 12.

- **Data object model plus script or client-side program.** Create a full-blown XML application. Chapter 13 provides examples of this approach.

In this section, you find out how to

- Create a cascading style sheet.
- Attach a cascading style sheet to an XML document.

CREATE A SIMPLE XML PROCESSOR

```
GREETING
{
    display: block;
    color: red
}
```

```
<?xml version="1.0"?>

<GREETING>Hello, world!</GREETING>
```

■1 Create a cascading style sheet.

■2 Save the cascading style sheet, using a .css extension.

■ In the example, the styles surrounded by curly braces ({ }) are applied to an XML element named GREETING.

■ In this example, the name of the cascading style sheet document is style.css.

■3 Create the XML element you want to display using cascading style sheet rules.

■ This example shows the creation of a single XML element named GREETING.

Extra

Because both XML and HTML were derived from a single specification — the Standard Generalized Markup Language, or SGML — you can use cascading style sheets to format both HTML and XML documents.

Cascading style sheets enable you to control the color, font, and placement of all the elements in an XML document, either individually or in groups.

To find out more about cascading style sheets, check out the following:

■ Chapters 8, 9, and 10

■ An evaluation copy of StyleMaker, a cascading style sheet editor, included on the companion CD.

To find additional utilities — many of which are available for free download — visit ZDNet's Web site at www.zdnet.com/devhead/filters/0,,2133212,00.html.

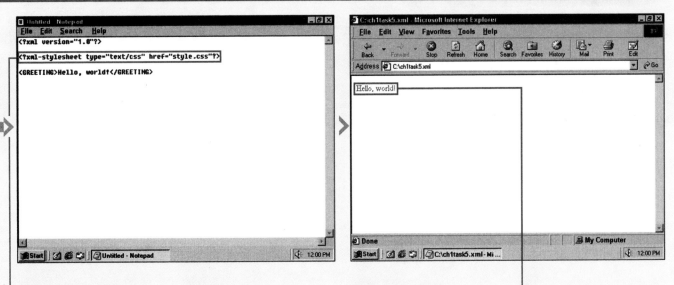

4 Add a cascading style sheet directive to the XML document, specifying the cascading style sheet you want to apply.

5 Save the XML file.

■ In this example, the cascading style sheet document named style.css is applied to the XML data.

6 Launch the Internet Explorer browser.

7 Open XML file.

■ The XML data displays based on the specified cascading style sheet rules.

CREATE AN XML DOCUMENT DECLARATION

You can create an XML document using a special kind of processing instruction called the *XML declaration*. The XML declaration must be the first line in any XML document. The syntax is

```
<?xml version="versionNumber"
[encoding="encodingValue"]
[standalone="yes | no"] ?>
```

versionNumber is the number of the XML specification to which this XML document conforms. Double quotes or single quotes may surround the versionNumber, which is the case with all attribute values.

encodingValue is an optional value. XML processors assume that XML documents are written in the UTF-8 character set, a compressed version of Unicode optimized for American English; providing an encoding value changes the assumption that the XML processors make.

The optional standalone attribute can be set to either *no* or *yes*, depending on whether the document depends on other XML files in order to be valid or not, respectively. (The default is *yes*, meaning that the XML file does not depend on other XML files.)

CREATE AN XML DOCUMENT DECLARATION

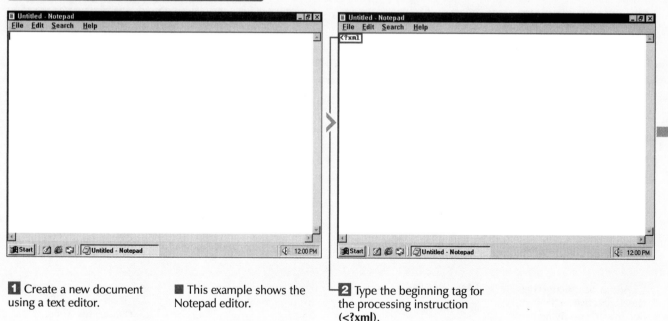

1 Create a new document using a text editor.

■ This example shows the Notepad editor.

2 Type the beginning tag for the processing instruction (**<?xml**).

Extra

You can select from a number of encoding values in your XML declaration:

- UTF-8: Compressed Unicode; the XML default
- UTF-16: Compressed UCS (Universal Character System); may provide more support for non-English characters.
- ISO-10646-UCS-2: Raw, or uncompressed, Unicode.
- ISO-10646-UCS-4: Raw UCS (Universal Character System).
- ISO-8859-1: Latin-1; Western European languages.
- ISO-8859-2: Latin-2; Eastern European languages.
- ISO-8859-3: Latin-3; Southern European languages.

- ISO-8859-4: Latin-1; Northern European languages.
- ISO-8859-5: Cyrillic; Bulgarian, Russian, Serbian, and so on.
- ISO-8859-6: Arabic.
- ISO-8859-7: Greek.
- ISO-8859-8: Hebrew.
- ISO-8859-9: Latin-5; supports Turkish.
- ISO-2022-JP: Japanese.
- Shift_JIS: Japanese, Windows.
- EUC-JP: Japanese, UNIX.

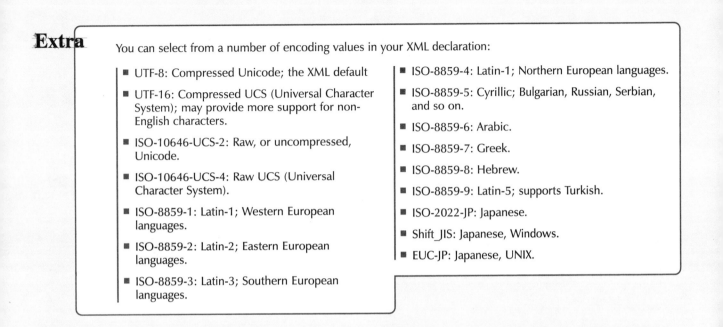

3 Type **version=** and then the number of the XML specification inside quotes.

■ In this example, the value 1.0 is used to denote that this XML document conforms to the XML 1.0 standard.

■ Type in values for the `encoding` and `standalone` attributes, if desired.

4 Type in the ending tag for the processing instruction (**?>**).

5 Save the file.

DECLARE YOUR ROOT ELEMENT

Every valid XML document contains one — and only one — *root* element. A root element is an element that contains all the other elements in a document; in other words, the root element is at the top of the XML data hierarchy, both conceptually and syntactically. Defining a root element enables you to encapsulate all data in an XML document for easy access and manipulation.

Root elements are declared the same way as any other element, with one difference: Root elements must appear at the top of the XML document, after the XML declaration but before any other element declarations.

The syntax for declaring a root element is

```
<rootElementName>
</rootElementName>
```

rootElementName is the name of the root element you want to declare. Keep in mind that XML is case-sensitive and that opening and closing tags must match exactly.

DECLARE YOUR ROOT ELEMENT

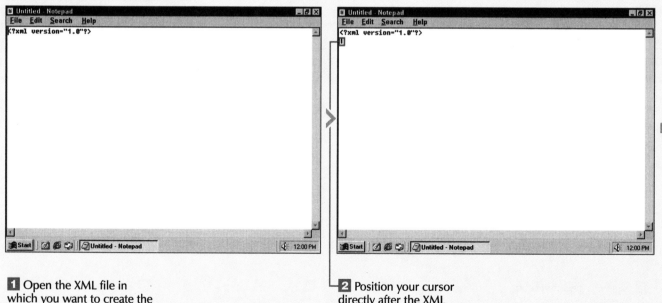

1 Open the XML file in which you want to create the root element.

2 Position your cursor directly after the XML declaration.

Extra

Deciding which XML element should be a root element is a two-step process.

First, understand your data before you begin the implementation phase. XML files should correspond to data requirements; in other words, model your data first and select as your XML root element the element that lies conceptually at the top of your data hierarchy.

Second, choose a naming convention and stick with it. XML syntax enables you to define tags containing both uppercase or lowercase letters, so the following are valid tag names:

- `jamcracker_product_info`
- `JamcrackerProductInfo`
- `JAMCRACKERPRODUCTINFO`
- `jAmCrAcKeRpRoDuCtInFo`

The first two alternatives are probably the most readable from a human standpoint, but ultimately the choice lies with you, the developer.

Untitled - Notepad
File Edit Search Help

```
<?xml version="1.0"?>

<jamcracker_product_info>
```

Start | Untitled - Notepad | 12:00 PM

Untitled - Notepad
File Edit Search Help

```
<?xml version="1.0"?>

<jamcracker_product_info>

</jamcracker_product_info>
```

Start | Untitled - Notepad | 12:00 PM

3 Add the beginning root element declaration tag.

■ In this example, the name of the root element being declared is `jamcracker_product_info`.

4 Add the ending root element declaration tag.

5 Save the file.

ADD A COMMENT TO YOUR XML FILE

Adding comments to your XML documents is an indispensable component of any production-level application. Comments enable you to

- Describe non-intuitive document structure. While XML document structure overall is fairly intuitive to human readers, specific details of your particular XML document may not be. Including a detailed comment helps ensure that readers, from developers to third-party integrators, understand your reasons for modeling the data the way you have.

- Provide additional processing description. XML provides all the constructs necessary for conveying processing information to the client-side

parser or custom processor. However, comments enable you to include information useful to human readers, such as developers processing your XML document for the first time.

Here is the syntax for creating a comment in an XML file:

```
<!- comment ->
```

comment is any text comment, including breaking white space such as a return, that does not contain a double hyphen (--). Keep in mind that comments must be placed after the XML declaration, cannot be placed inside XML tags, and cannot be nested.

ADD A COMMENT TO YOUR XML FILE

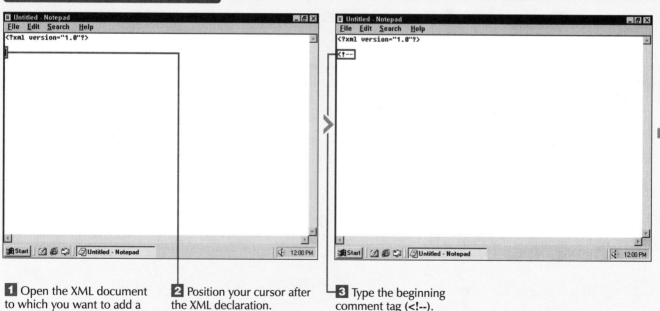

1 Open the XML document to which you want to add a comment.

2 Position your cursor after the XML declaration.

3 Type the beginning comment tag (<!--).

Extra

Because developers can name their own tags and arrange them in an easy-to-read structure, XML is considered a self-documenting language. However, by itself, this self-documenting feature is insufficient for any but the most trivial XML applications. In other words, commenting your XML documents thoroughly is strongly encouraged.

You should always use comments when you

- Begin an XML file.

- Add container elements.

- Add repeating elements.

- Add elements of type ID or IDREF, both of which define logical relationships between elements, or groups of elements.

- Add elements whose names and positioning within the XML data structure aren't completely obvious within the context of your application.

- End an XML file.

Untitled - Notepad
File Edit Search Help
<?xml version="1.0"?>
<!-- Comments may span lines.

4 Type your comment.

Untitled - Notepad
File Edit Search Help
<?xml version="1.0"?>
<!-- Comments may span lines. -->

5 Type the ending comment tag (-->).

DECLARE NON-ROOT DATA ELEMENTS

I n XML, you describe the structure of data elements by nesting contained elements within container elements. All non-root data elements are contained inside the document's root element. Non-root data elements, which you use to define the bulk of your XML data, are the "meat" of your XML document.

Here is the syntax for declaring non-root data elements:

```
<containerElement [attributeInfo]>
[<containedElement [attributeInfo]>
</containedElement>]
</containerElement>
```

containerElement is the name of a data element that contains one or more additional data elements.

containedElement (optional) is the name of a data element that is contained by another data element.

attributeInfo (optional) is a string of attribute-value pairs that specify the attributes associated with a given data element.

No white space can appear inside tags. For example, <price per unit> is an illegal tag declaration.

DECLARE NON-ROOT DATA ELEMENTS

1 Open the XML file in which you want to create non-root data elements.

2 Position your cursor between the beginning and ending root element tags.

■ In this example, the root element is named `jamcracker_product_info`.

Extra

Because elements define individual pieces, or *fields*, of data, they form the bulk of any XML document. In real life, data does not exist in a vacuum; it exists in relationship to other data.

Consider an automobile, for example. An automobile contains an engine, which contains a piston, which contains a rod. In order to represent these items meaningfully, a language must provide a way not just to describe the items themselves, but also their structural relationship to each other. In XML, you might model an automobile like this:

```
<automobile>
    <engine>
        <piston>
            <rod>
            </rod>
        </piston>
    </engine>
</automobile>
```

While no white space can appear *inside* a tag, white space can appear *between* tags or inside the value for an attribute. White space is treated differently depending on whether the value between the tags is text or another tag:

■ Text value. Spaces within text are considered part of the text. The space between *Huckleberry* and *Jam*, for example, is part of the value associated with the first product's name element.

■ Tag value. If the value is another tag, surround space is ignored.

```
🗎 Untitled - Notepad                          _ 🗗 ✕
File  Edit  Search  Help
<?xml version="1.0"?>

<jamcracker_product_info>

    <product>

    </product>


</jamcracker_product_info>
```

```
🗎 Untitled - Notepad                          _ 🗗 ✕
File  Edit  Search  Help
<?xml version="1.0"?>

<jamcracker_product_info>

|   <product>
        <name>Huckleberry Jam</name>
        <price_per_unit >6.50</price_per_unit>
        <test_field>Warning: this artifact will be phased out after Jamcracke
        <marketing_info>
            <unique_characteristics>fresh huckleberries</unique_characteristics
            <rank>2</rank>
        </marketing_info>
        <nutrition_info/>
    </product>

</jamcracker_product_info>
```

3 Type in one or more container elements.

■ In this example, the product container element is added.

4 Type in one or more contained elements.

■ In this example, marketing_info is both a contained element and a container element.

5 Save the file.

DECLARE A REPEATING DATA ELEMENT

Y ou can model multiple instances of the same type of data element simply by reusing the element name. Reusing elements (declaring repeating elements) enables you to define lists. For example, you can define a list of customers, each of which bears the same element name associated with a unique value.

The value of the XML element, along with optional *attributes* and *data constraints*, combine to identify instances uniquely within an XML document.

The syntax to declare a repeating data element is the same as that required to declare non-root XML data elements:

```
<elementName>elementData1</elementName>
<elementName>elementData2</elementName>
<elementName>elementDataN</elementName>
```

`elementName` is the name of a repeating data element.

`elementData1`, `elementData2`, and `elementDataN` represent unique XML data associated with each repeating element.

DECLARE A REPEATING DATA ELEMENT

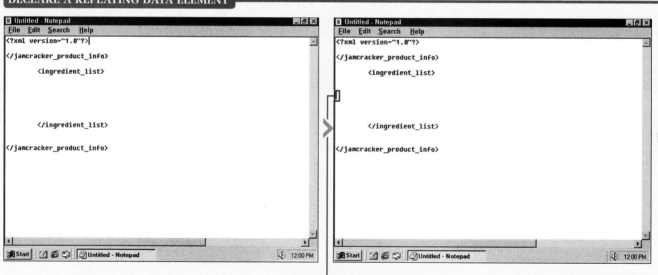

1 Open the XML file in which you want to create a repeating data element.

2 Position your cursor after the XML data element to which you want to add the repeating elements.

■ In this example, the repeating elements to be added (the ingredient elements) are contained by the `ingredient_list` element, which itself is contained by the root element `jamcracker_product_info`.

Extra

XML parsers ignore white space between tag declarations, so developers can arrange tags however they like. For easy readability, a good development practice to follow is to indent nested tags. For example, while both the XML examples below are well formed, seeing the nested relationships between elements is easier using this tag arrangement

```
<product>
    <name>
    <retailers>
            <name>
            </name>
    </retailers>
    </name>
</product>
```

Than this one:

```
<product><name><retailers><name></name></ retailers>
</name></product>
```

Creating long data lists — for example, a customer list containing hundreds or even thousands of entries — increases the possibility of introducing errors into your XML document. One solution is to use an XML editor to create your XML documents. XML editors are tools that generate XML tags and content based on point-and-click selections. At the time of this writing, most XML editors are available in beta form only, but are rapidly maturing. The companion CD includes trial versions of several XML editors.

3 Type in the first instance of the repeating data element.

■ In this example, the first instance of the `ingredient` element is added.

4 Type in any additional instances of the repeating data element.

■ In this example, two additional instances of the `ingredient` element are added.

5 Save the file.

DESCRIBE YOUR DATA ELEMENTS WITH ATTRIBUTES

You can declare attributes and associate them with individual XML elements to model sophisticated data groupings. You must declare an attribute inside the beginning tag of an element. Here is the syntax required to declare attributes in XML:

```
<elementName
[attributeName1="attribute1Value"]
[attributeName2="attribute2Value"]
[attributeNameN="attributeNValue"]
>elementValue</elementName>
```

elementName is the name of the element to which you want to associate an attribute.

attributeName1 is the name of an attribute. Attribute names must begin with a letter or an underscore and may only contain letters, digits, underscores, hyphens, and periods. For example, `currency`, `product_code`, and `deptCode` are all examples of valid attribute names.

attributeValue is the value to associate with that attribute. Attribute values, which must be surrounded by either single or double quotes, can contain any character data, including white space. *elementValue* is the value associated with the XML element.

You cannot associate two identically named attributes with the same element. For example, the following XML declaration causes a parse error:

```
<nutrition_info calories="123"
calories="456">
```

DESCRIBE YOUR DATA ELEMENTS WITH ATTRIBUTES

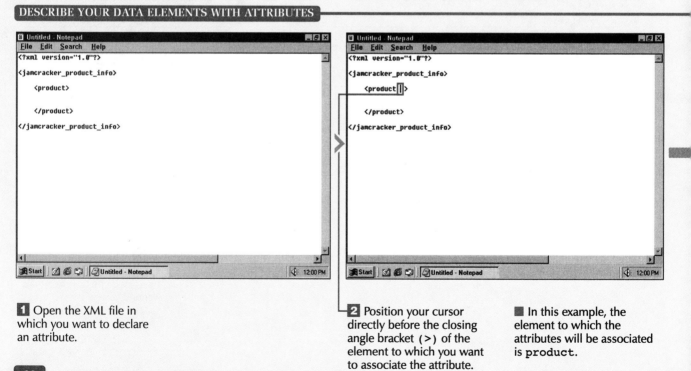

1 Open the XML file in which you want to declare an attribute.

2 Position your cursor directly before the closing angle bracket (`>`) of the element to which you want to associate the attribute.

■ In this example, the element to which the attributes will be associated is `product`.

Apply It

You may choose to create an empty element — such as the `nutrition_info` element described in this section's sample code — that contains nothing but attributes. Or you may also choose to model all of your data, including data descriptions, as separate elements, without any attributes at all.

Good model design rules to follow:

- Model data that is essential to your application — data that you expect to manipulate directly — as elements.

- Model associated data — data that is only meaningful in the context of some element — as attributes.

Attributes describe elements by associating them with additional descriptive information, much like adjectives describe nouns. For example, an automobile is associated with a serial number, a registered owner, and a manufacturer. In XML, you can model this descriptive information as three different attributes associated with the automobile element.

Example:
```
<automobile
serial_number="1234567890"
registered_owner="George Bailey"
manufacturer="Ford"
>
```

Untitled - Notepad

File Edit Search Help
```
<?xml version="1.0"?>

<jamcracker_product_info>

    <product image="P1" >

    </product>

</jamcracker_product_info>
```
Start | Untitled - Notepad   12:00 PM

Untitled - Notepad

File Edit Search Help
```
<?xml version="1.0"?>

<jamcracker_product_info>

    <product image="P1" product_code="A">

    </product>

</jamcracker_product_info>
```
Start | Untitled - Notepad   12:00 PM

3 Type in the attribute declaration for the attribute.

■ In this example, the attribute declaration is `image="P1"`.

4 Type in any additional attribute declarations.

■ In this example, the attribute `product_code` is also declared.

5 Save the file.

DEFINE A NAMESPACE

You can create a namespace to uniquely identify elements within an XML document. Consider an element named `name`, for example. Many XML application developers could reasonably incorporate a `name` element into their documents, representing everything from the name of a product to the name of a customer. Without a method for uniquely identifying which XML document defines which `name`, an application would be unable to make use of any `name`-related data. Namespaces enable XML developers to resolve these potential conflicts.

Here is the syntax required to create a namespace:

```
<namespace:elementName
xmlns:namespace="globallyUniqueURI">
```

```
[<namespace:containedElement
[namespace:attributeName="attributeValue
"]>
</namespace:containedElement>]
</namespace:elementName>
```

namespace is a unique name for the namespace. *elementName* is the name of an XML element to which the namespace will apply.

globallyUniqueURI is a globally unique uniform resource identifier. *containedElement* is the name of an element contained within *elementName*.

attributeName and *attributeValue* are the name and associated value, respectively, of an attribute associated with *containedElement*.

DEFINE A NAMESPACE

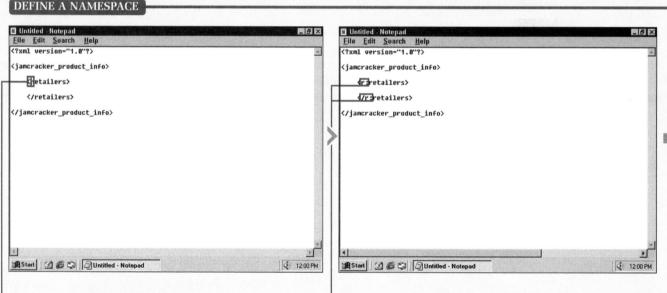

1 Open the XML file in which you want to define the namespace.

2 Position your cursor directly before the name of the element for which you want to define the namespace.

■ In this example, a namespace is being defined for all the elements and attributes contained in the `retailers` element.

3 Append the element name in both the beginning and ending declaration tag with the name of the namespace, followed by a colon.

■ In this example, the name of the namespace is `r`.

Extra

URI, which stands for *uniform resource identifier*, is a generic term meaning "any unique identifier." URL, or *uniform resource locator*, is one common type of URI, but the World Wide Web Consortium is considering other types. A URI can be represented by any unique string of characters, underscores, hyphens, and numbers.

Because the sole purpose of a namespace value is to identify an element, or a group of elements and attributes, uniquely, the value of the namespace does not have to "point" to a resource — although it certainly may. The XML parser's job is to generate an error in the event that two namespaces referenced in an XML application bear the same name.

Namespace names:

■ Begin with a letter or underscore and contain only letters, underscores, digits, hyphens, and periods

■ Cannot be named *xml* or *xmlns*, which are reserved names

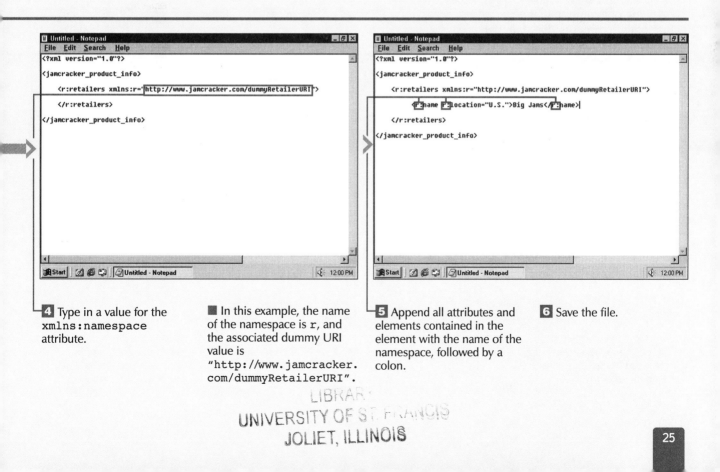

4 Type in a value for the `xmlns:namespace` attribute.

■ In this example, the name of the namespace is `r`, and the associated dummy URI value is `"http://www.jamcracker.com/dummyRetailerURI"`.

5 Append all attributes and elements contained in the element with the name of the namespace, followed by a colon.

6 Save the file.

USE PREDEFINED XML ENTITIES

You can incorporate special characters into XML data using predefined XML entities.

XML parsers make certain assumptions about XML document syntax — for example, that a left angle bracket (<) begins a tag. However, you may reasonably need to include a left angle bracket in an element's value, like this:

```
<err_desc>If the system fails, you will
see this message: <<error
101>></err_desc >
```

Because an XML parser has no way of determining that the second left angle bracket shown above is not the beginning of another tag, it generates an error when attempting to process this statement.

To enable you to define data containing special characters like angle brackets, XML defines predefined *entities* to differentiate between symbols that have special meaning in XML — such as the left angle bracket — and those same symbols embedded in a text string.

XML supports five predefined entities:

- <, which stands for the less-than character (<)
- >, which stands for the greater-than character (>)
- &, which stands for an ampersand (&)
- ', which stands for an apostrophe (')
- ", which stands for a quotation mark (")

USE PREDEFINED XML ENTITIES

```
Untitled - Notepad
File   Edit   Search   Help
<?xml version="1.0"?>

<jamcracker_product_info>

    <r:retailers xmlns:r="http://www.jamcracker.com/dummyRetailerURI ">

        <r:name r:location="Canada"
                r:bestseller="2">The Int</r:name>

    </r:retailers>

</jamcracker_product_info>
```

```
Untitled - Notepad
File   Edit   Search   Help
<?xml version="1.0"?>

<jamcracker_product_info>

    <r:retailers xmlns:r="http://www.jamcracker.com/dummyRetailerURI ">

        <r:name r:location="Canada"
                r:bestseller="2">The Int▮/r:name>

    </r:retailers>

</jamcracker_product_info>
```

1 Open the XML file in which you want to reference a predefined entity.

2 Position your cursor at the point in the text where you want to add the predefined entity.

■ In this example, the reference will be added directly after Int.

Extra

Entities can appear inside attribute declarations as well as inside element values. For example, the following XML code is valid:

```
<wholesalers name="Biggs &amp; Tate"/>
```

The five entities listed in this example are sometimes referred to as predefined *internal* entities. Support for these five entities is included in Internet Explorer, and is available for both XML and HTML documents. Chapter 5 shows you how to define custom entities, including external, parsed, and unparsed.

Entities in XML can take one of four forms:

- **Internal general entities.** Referenced from inside an XML document; substitute text is defined inside a DTD.

- **External general entities.** Referenced from inside an XML document; substitute text is defined inside some external file.

- **Internal parameter entities.** Referenced from inside a DTD document; substitute text is defined inside a DTD.

- **External parameter entities.** Referenced from inside a DTD document; substitute text is defined inside some external file.

```
Untitled - Notepad
File  Edit  Search  Help
<?xml version="1.0"?>

<jamcracker_product_info>

    <r:retailers xmlns:r="http://www.jamcracker.com/dummyRetailerURI ">

        <r:name r:location="Canada"
                r:bestseller="2">The Int&apos;</r:name>

    </r:retailers>

</jamcracker_product_info>
```

```
Untitled - Notepad
File  Edit  Search  Help
<?xml version="1.0"?>

<jamcracker_product_info>

    <r:retailers xmlns:r="http://www.jamcracker.com/dummyRetailerURI ">

        <r:name r:location="Canada"
                r:bestseller="2">The Int&apos;l Pancake House</r:name>

    </r:retailers>

</jamcracker_product_info>
```

3 Type in the entity reference.

■ In this example, the entity referenced is the apostrophe, which you declare using '.

4 Type in any remaining text.

■ The XML parser will interpret the text of this value as *The Int'l Pancake House* at runtime.

5 Save the file.

INCLUDE SPECIAL PROCESSING INSTRUCTIONS

You can pass application-specific instructions from an XML document to an XML processor using a construct called a *processing instruction*.

The syntax for declaring a processing instruction is

`<?spaceDelimitedInstructions?>`

spaceDelimitedInstructions is the name of any valid executable, followed by any required parameters. Because processing instructions are aimed at specific applications, the first word in a processing instruction often represents the name of that specific application, followed by additional words representing parameters

expected by the application. For example

- `<?gcc myProgram.c?>` is a processing instruction that references a C compiler (gcc.exe) and passes to that compiler a C source file (myProgram.c)

- `<?doit.exe parameter1="12345" parameter2="23456" parameter3="33">` is a processing instruction that references some in-house executable (doit.exe), passing three parameters (12345, 23456, and 33).

- `<?xml-stylesheet type="text/xsl" href="task5.xsl"?>` invokes a module that provides XSL style sheet support.

INCLUDE SPECIAL PROCESSING INSTRUCTIONS

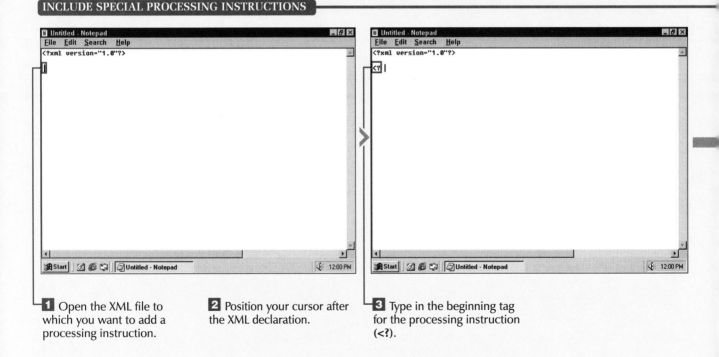

1 Open the XML file to which you want to add a processing instruction.

2 Position your cursor after the XML declaration.

3 Type in the beginning tag for the processing instruction (**<?**).

Extra

Each word contained in a processing instruction must begin with a letter or underscore and can only contain the following:

- Letters
- Digits
- Underscores
- Hyphens
- Periods

The first word in a processing instruction cannot be xml, which is a reserved word.

With a few exceptions, XML parsers ignore processing instructions. Processing instructions are recognized and executed by the processor — the application that extracts, manipulates, and displays XML.

The exceptions are

- The XML declaration itself (<xml version="1.0">). This processing instruction is recognized and handled by all XML parsers.

- The third example shown previously (<?xml-stylesheet type="text/xsl" href="task5.xsl"?>). This processing instruction invokes a module that provides XSL style sheet support and is recognized by some XML parsers, including Internet Explorer's MSXML.

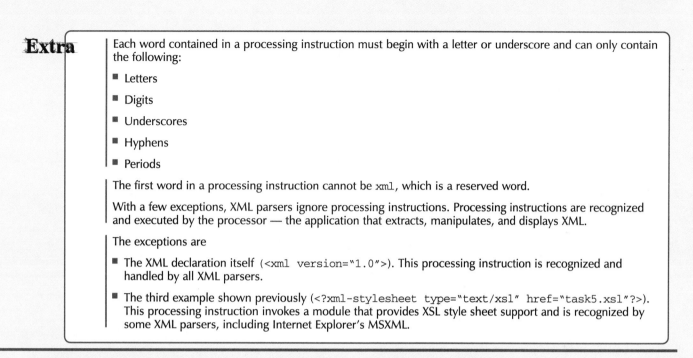

4 Type in the text for the processing instruction.

■ In this example, the processing instruction is iexplore.exe, which is an executable file that runs Internet Explorer.

5 Type in the ending tag for the processing instruction (?>).

6 Save the file.

INCLUDE NONSTANDARD TEXT

The "Use Predefined XML Entities" section earlier in this chapter shows you how to include special characters in your XML documents using predefined entities. Entities are fine for occasional use, but if you need to incorporate a large number of special characters, you can use another construct designed specifically for that use: the CDATA section.

The CDATA section enables you to incorporate large blocks of text containing special characters into an XML document without replacing each special character with an entity reference.

Here is the syntax:

```
<![CDATA[text]]>
```

text is a string of text containing special characters. This text will not be checked by the XML parser; instead, the text is "passed through." The XML processor application has the responsibility to parse and/or otherwise use this text in a meaningful way.

INCLUDE NONSTANDARD TEXT

1 Open the XML document in which you want to declare a CDATA section.

2 Position your cursor where you want to declare the CDATA section.

■ In this example, the CDATA section will be declared directly below the `<js_function>` opening element tag.

3 Type the beginning CDATA tag (**<![CDATA[**).

Extra

Because the purpose of the CDATA section is to hold unrestricted character data, few syntax rules apply to CDATA contents. These rules are

- CDATA sections must be represented as element values.

- Only one string —]] — cannot occur between the beginning and ending CDATA tags.

Using a CDATA section is a good idea if you want to pass a large block of text to your XML processing application containing several special characters.

The following is an example of incorporating a block of scripting code, which contains many special characters, into an XML document.

```
<![CDATA[
<SCRIPT LANGUAGE="JavaScript">
// Jamcracker, Inc. is providing this code as a service only; no warranties
// or fitness for use are implied. Please check our service manual for instructions
// on coding additional necessary functions and parameters.
function isUpToDate(downloadDate) {
// This function queries Jamcracker, Inc.'s database to determine if
// there have been product updates since the last XML file download.
var connectionUp=pingDatabase();
lastUpdated = queryDatabase();
if (downloadDate < lastUpdated && connectionUp) {
        display("Please download the latest XML file to ensure up-to-date product
information.")
    }
}
</SCRIPT>
]]>
```

4 Type in the special character text.

■ In this example, several lines of scripting code, beginning with `<SCRIPT>` and ending with `</SCRIPT>`, form the text of the CDATA section.

5 Add the ending CDATA tag (]]>).

DECLARE AN INLINE DTD

Y ou can define specific data types for each of the components of an XML document by using a document type definition, or DTD.

DTDs are sometimes referred to as *vocabularies* because they define a common set of structured elements and attributes, much like human vocabularies establish common words and syntax rules. For example, you can use a DTD to restrict the value of an XML element to contain only character data. You can implement DTDs two ways:

- You can include the text for a DTD inside your XML document, as shown on this page. So-called inline DTDs are most appropriate for short XML documents and all XML documents during the

development process, and if you do not intend your DTD to be applied to other XML documents.

- You can save the text for a DTD as a separate file and refer to this file inside your XML document. This external DTD approach is covered in "Declare and Save an External DTD File," next in this chapter.

The syntax required to create an inline DTD is

```
<!DOCTYPE rootElement [
dtdRules
]>
```

rootElement is the root element of the XML document in which this DTD is included. *dtdRules* is one or more XML statements that define DTD rules for individual elements within *rootElement*.

DECLARE AN INLINE DTD

1 Open the XML file to which you want to add an inline DTD.

2 Position the cursor directly below the XML declaration and directly above the root element declaration.

■ In this example, the root element is GREETING.

3 Type **<!DOCTYPE** and the root element of the XML document.

■ In this example, the root element is named GREETING.

Extra

All elements defined in an XML file must be associated with a corresponding declaration in the DTD. In this example XML document, only one element, named GREETING, is defined. The element declaration in this DTD describes the semantic validation rule for the GREETING element. #PCDATA is an XML reserved keyword that specifies that a valid value for the GREETING element can only contain characters (as opposed to other elements, such as predefined values). You can declare the type of an XML element using any of the following:

ELEMENT	DESCRIPTION TYPE
(#PCDATA)	Character data
(#PCDATA)*	Zero or more characters
(anElement)	One instance of anElement
(anElement+)	One or more instances of anElement
(anElement?)	Zero or more instances of anElement
(anElement, anotherElement)	One instance each of anElement and anotherElement
(anElement | anotherElement)	One instance of anElement *or* one instance of anotherElement
(#PCDATA | anElement)*	Either an instance of anElement *or* multiple characters (When used as one of multiple options, #PCDATA must appear first.)
EMPTY	No content
ANY	Any content (Because ANY disables type-checking, you should use it only during document conversion, if ever; never in production.)

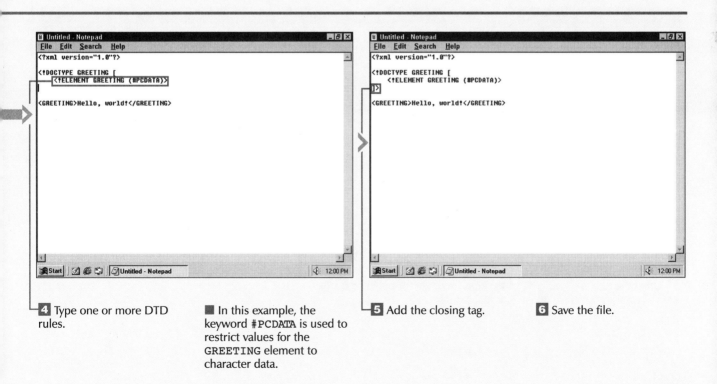

4 Type one or more DTD rules.

■ In this example, the keyword #PCDATA is used to restrict values for the GREETING element to character data.

5 Add the closing tag.

6 Save the file.

DECLARE AND SAVE AN EXTERNAL DTD FILE

I f you intend your DTD to be applied to other XML documents, you can save the text for a DTD as a separate, external file and refer to the DTD file inside your XML document using the DOCTYPE declaration in conjunction with the SYSTEM keyword.

Because it separates validation rules from XML data, this external DTD approach promotes document reusability. Multiple XML documents can refer to the same DTD file without having to replicate validation rules physically.

The syntax required to create an external DTD file is

```
<!DOCTYPE rootElement SYSTEM "dtdFile">
```

rootElement is the root XML element to which the DTD file is to be applied. *dtdFile* is the name of the external DTD file.

The name of any existing DTD file is valid for the DTD filename parameter of the DOCTYPE declaration. By convention, all DTD files end in the .dtd suffix.

DECLARE AND SAVE AN EXTERNAL DTD FILE

1 Open the XML file to which you want to attach an external DTD file.

2 Position your cursor below the XML declaration.

3 Type **<!DOCTYPE**.

Extra

The XML parser assumes that an unqualified filename resides in the same directory as the referring XML document. If the DTD file resides in another directory, the value for this parameter must reflect the qualified DTD filename. For example, if the `task1.xml` file resides in the `c:\xml\chapter2` directory, and the `task2.dtd` file resides one directory beneath it in the `c:\xml\chapter2\DTDs` directory, the DOCTYPE declaration must appear as follows:

`<!DOCTYPE jamcracker_product_info SYSTEM "/DTDs/task2.dtd">`

You can declare the type of XML attribute using any of the following:

ATTRIBUTE DECLARATION TYPE	DESCRIPTION
CDATA	Character data (string)
ID	Unique identifier
IDREF/IDREFS	Value must match a previously defined ID or multiple IDs separated by white space
ENTITY/ENTITIES	A predefined entity or multiple entities separated by white space (see `<!ENTITY>`)
NMTOKEN/NMTOKENS	A restricted form of CDATA (no spaces allowed) or multiples, separated by white space
a | b | c | ...	A pipe-separated list of previously defined attributes

4 Type the root element to which you want to begin applying the DTD.

■ In this example, the root element is `jamcracker_product_ info`.

5 Type **SYSTEM**.

6 Type the quote-delimited name of the DTD file.

■ In this example, the DTD file is `master.dtd`.

7 Type the closing angle bracket (>).

8 Save the file.

COMMENT YOUR DTD FILE

You can add comments to a DTD file to increase readability and maintenance of your DTD code.

You can apply a single DTD to multiple XML documents; in fact, many expect standard DTDs for use across all major industries to evolve over the next several years. This possibility for reuse by third-party developers — coupled with the non-intuitive nature of DTD syntax — makes commenting DTD files an essential part of the DTD development process.

The syntax to add comments to a DTD file is

```
<!-- comment-->
```

comment can include any text except a double hyphen (--). comment can, however, include breaking white space, such as a return (useful for readability).

DTD comments can appear anywhere in a DTD document except inside another DTD comment (in other words, DTD comments cannot be nested). For example, the following is illegal and will cause a parse error:

```
<!-- a comment <!-- another comment -->
-->
```

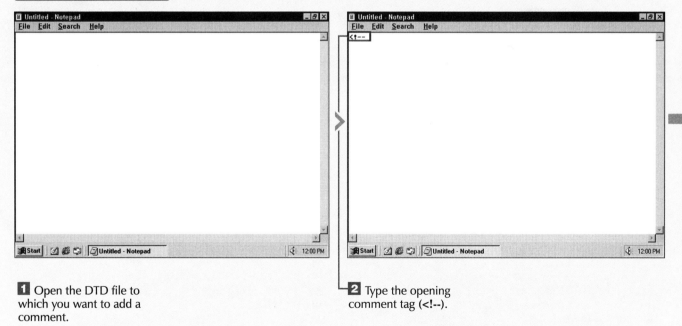

1 Open the DTD file to which you want to add a comment.

2 Type the opening comment tag (<!--).

Extra

Formal DTD comments enable you to:

- Describe validation rules in human terms. If DTDs are to become widespread, developers must be able to understand and work with them easily. Including appropriate comments inside a DTD file, rather than in a separate document or manual, ensures that vital documentation isn't separated from the physical DTD file.

- Organize validation rules for readability. DTDs are typically long and fairly complex documents. Separating the DTD into sections — for example, into entity and element declaration sections — makes the DTD much easier to read and modify.

A good application development design strategy to follow is to include a DTD comment before each of the following:

- The element declaration section. Group all element declarations together and precede this section, which typically forms the bulk of the DTD document, with a section heading comment.

- The entity declaration section. Follow the element declaration section with an entity declaration section. Define all the entities for a DTD in this section and precede it with a section heading comment.

- Any specific element or entity declaration that may not be intuitive to the casual reader of the DTD. Add descriptive comments within sections as necessary.

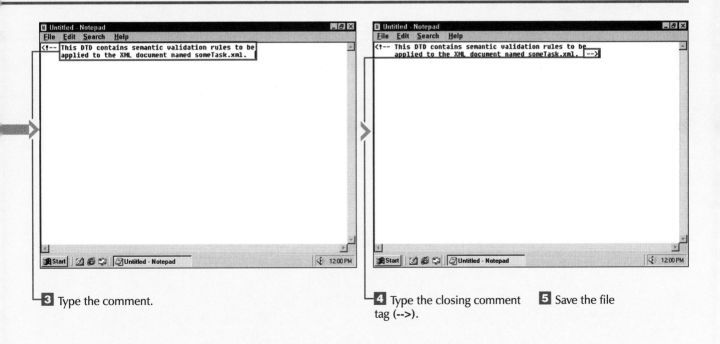

3 Type the comment.

4 Type the closing comment tag (-->).

5 Save the file

DECLARE A CONTAINER ELEMENT

You can enforce container relationships on XML data at runtime. Containers are elements that consist entirely of other, predefined elements.

The ability to enforce container relationships enables you to model complex relationships between XML data. For example, you can model relationships between repeating, related groups of elements, such as employees and projects, customers and orders, products and retailers.

Here is the syntax required to create a container element:

```
<!ELEMENT containerElement
(containedElement1, containedElement2...
containedElementN)>
```

containerElement is the name of the XML element you want to define as a container element

containedElement1, *containedElement2*, and *containedElementN* are the names of XML elements you want to be contained in *containerElement*.

DECLARE A CONTAINER ELEMENT

1 Open the DTD file to which you want to add a container relationship rule.

2 Type **<!ELEMENT**.

Extra

While contained elements need not be declared in the same order in the DTD as they are in the XML document, doing so is good programming practice. Indenting each contained element makes identifying the relationships between elements much easier.

Elements that belong to namespaces must be referenced in DTDs by their fully qualified names. For example, the following specifies that the `retailers` element associated in the corresponding XML file with the `r` namespace is contained by the `marketing_info` element:

```
<!ELEMENT marketing_info
(unique_characteristics, rank, r:retailers)>
```

Attribute declarations can have four possible default values:

ATTRIBUTE DEFAULT VALUE	DESCRIPTION
#REQUIRED	The attribute must contain a value at runtime.
#IMPLIED	The attribute need not contain a value at runtime.
"someValue"	If a value for the attribute is not supplied at runtime, "someValue" will be assigned.
#FIXED "someValue"	The value for the attribute is assigned "someValue".

Untitled - Notepad
File Edit Search Help
```
<!ELEMENT jamcracker_product_info (product, js_function)
```
Start   Untitled - Notepad   12:00 PM

Untitled - Notepad
File Edit Search Help
```
<!ELEMENT jamcracker_product_info (product, js_function)>
```
Start   Untitled - Notepad   12:00 PM

3 Type the name of the container element.

■ In this example, the container element is `jamcracker_product_info`.

4 Type the name of the contained elements, separated by commas and surrounded by parentheses.

■ `Product` and `js_function` are declared in the XML document that applies this DTD document.

5 Type the closing angle bracket (>) for the `<!ELEMENT` tag.

6 Save the file.

DECLARE A REQUIRED ELEMENT

You can create a validation rule to ensure that a given element is associated with one — and only one — value at runtime. Elements so declared are referred to as *required* elements, because they are required to exist at runtime. Because all XML elements are contained in a root element (and some elements may be contained in other elements, as well), required elements are typically defined as contained elements.

Some examples of the type of data elements usually modeled as required include

- Customer name

- Social Security number

- Product identification number

- Account number

Here is the syntax for a required element:

```
<!ELEMENT containerElement
([requiredElementN])>
```

containerElement is the name of the XML element you want to define as a container element.

requiredElementN is the name of one or more XML elements you want to ensure, at runtime, contains one and only one value.

DECLARE A REQUIRED ELEMENT

1 Open the DTD file to which you want to add a required data rule.

2 Type **<!ELEMENT**.

Extra

Contained elements may take one of the three following forms:

- `element`: One — and only one — value for this element is required to exist.
- `element+`: One or more values for this element are required to exist.
- `element*`: Zero or more values for this element are required to exist

For example, the following DTD syntax declares a contained element, `product`, for which exactly one value must exist:

`<!ELEMENT jamcracker_product_info (product)>`

The following DTD syntax declares a contained element, `product`, for which one element must exist, and for which many elements may exist:

`<!ELEMENT jamcracker_product_info (product+)>`

The following DTD syntax declares a contained element, `product`, for which no element must exist, but for which many elements may exist:

`<!ELEMENT jamcracker_product_info (product*)>`

*Note: The + or *, if it exists, must appear inside the parentheses as shown in the preceding examples.*

```
<!ELEMENT product (
        name,
        price_per_unit,
        test_field,
        marketing_info,
        ingredient_list,
        nutrition_info)
```

```
<!ELEMENT product (
        name,
        price_per_unit,
        test_field,
        marketing_info,
        ingredient_list,
        nutrition_info)
>
```

3 Type the name of the container element.

■ In this example, the container element is `product`.

4 Type the required elements, separated by commas and surrounded by parentheses.

■ In this example, the required elements are `name`, `price_per_unit`, `test_field`, `marketing_info`, `ingredient_list`, and `nutrition_info`.

5 Type the closing angle bracket (>) for the `<!ELEMENT` tag.

DECLARE AN OPTIONAL ELEMENT

Y ou can create a data validation rule that enables an element to be associated with zero or more values at runtime — in other words, you can model an *optional* element.

You can define optional elements in conjunction with required elements; for example, you can declare a container element that contains both required and optional elements.

You use a question mark to denote an optional element, as shown in the following syntax:

```
<!ELEMENT
containerElement([optionalElementN?])>
```

containerElement is the name of the XML element you want to define as a container element.

optionalElementN is the name of one or more XML elements you want to allow, at runtime, to be associated with zero or more values. Multiple elements must be separated by commas, like this: (*aRequiredElement+*, *anotherRequiredElement*, *anOptionalElement?*)

DECLARE AN OPTIONAL ELEMENT

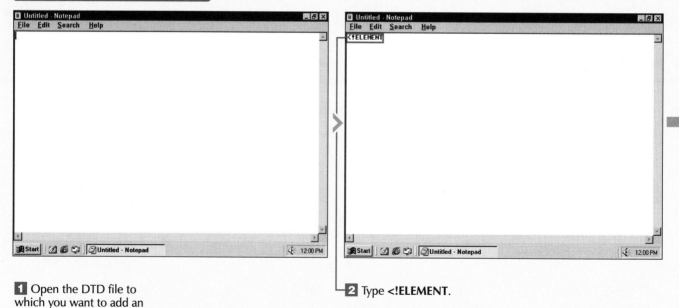

1 Open the DTD file to which you want to add an optional element declaration.

2 Type **<!ELEMENT**.

Extra

The question mark (?) that enables you to define optional elements essentially enables you to define zero-to-many relationships between data elements. Zero-to-many relationships are very familiar to developers of database applications; they occur quite often in real-world data models.

In effect, the combination of XML documents and DTDs enables developers to create database applications, complete with flat-file databases (the XML documents), data definition files (the DTDs), and query capability (processing code).

In the example in this section, you may associate one product with zero or more instances of marketing_info. Using the document object model, or DOM, you can loop through all the instances of marketing_info associated with a given product at runtime (if any). You do so by creating an XML processor, as described in Chapter 13.

Don't confuse the optional element declaration (?) with the punctuation required to declare zero-to-many characters for a given element (#PCDATA)*.

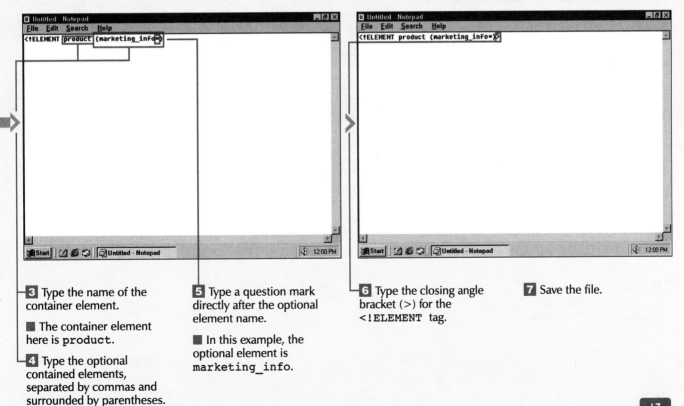

3 Type the name of the container element.

■ The container element here is product.

4 Type the optional contained elements, separated by commas and surrounded by parentheses.

5 Type a question mark directly after the optional element name.

■ In this example, the optional element is marketing_info.

6 Type the closing angle bracket (>) for the <!ELEMENT tag.

7 Save the file.

DECLARE A MULTIPLE OCCURRING ELEMENT

You can create a data validation rule to ensure that an element is associated with one or more values at runtime. This type of declaration is similar to the required element declaration; however, the required element declaration allows a single value at runtime, rather than multiple values.

You use the plus sign (+) to declare a multiple occurring element, as shown in the following syntax:

```
<!ELEMENT containerElement
([containedElementN+])>
```

containerElement is the name of the XML element you want to define as a container element.

containedElementN is the name of one or more XML elements you want to ensure, at runtime, are associated with one or more values.

DECLARE A MULTIPLE OCCURRING ELEMENT

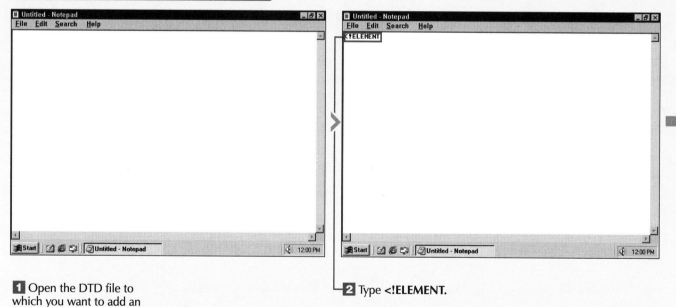

1 Open the DTD file to which you want to add an optional element declaration.

2 Type **<!ELEMENT.**

Extra

The plus sign (+) that enables you to define required elements essentially enables you to define one-to-many relationships between data elements, as well. One-to-many relationships are very familiar to developers of relational database-based applications. In effect, the combination of XML documents and DTDs enables developers to create database applications, complete with flat-file databases (XML documents), data definition files (DTDs), and query capability (XML processing code).

In the example in this section, one `jamcracker_product_info` element must be associated with one or more product elements at runtime.

You can model two other useful database constructs, primary and foreign keys, in XML using the `ID` and `IDREF` keywords. Chapter 4 shows you how to define attributes of type `ID` and `IDREF`, respectively.

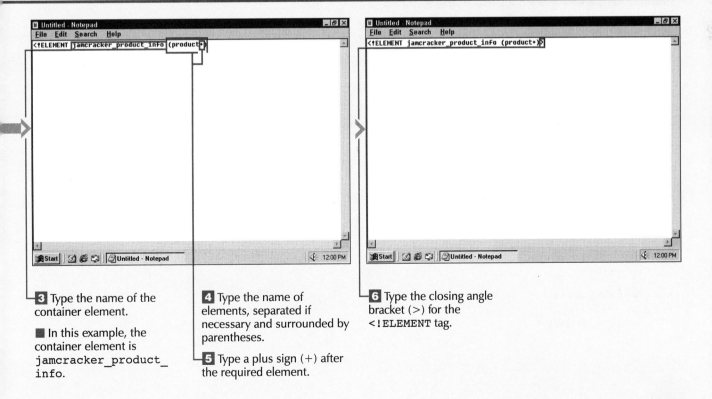

3 Type the name of the container element.

■ In this example, the container element is `jamcracker_product_info`.

4 Type the name of elements, separated if necessary and surrounded by parentheses.

5 Type a plus sign (+) after the required element.

6 Type the closing angle bracket (>) for the `<!ELEMENT` tag.

DECLARE AN ELEMENT THAT HOLDS CHARACTER DATA

You can create a data definition rule to ensure that the value for an element contains only character data at runtime (as opposed to predefined elements or a combination of the two).

You use the #PCDATA keyword to declare the data type for an XML element as a *character*. #PCDATA is a case-sensitive reserved word that stands for *parseable character data*. #PCDATA represents a single parseable, or non-special, character. Elements that are defined as type #PCDATA can only hold character data; they cannot contain other predefined elements.

Here is the syntax:

`<!ELEMENT elementName (#PCDATA)*>`

elementName is the name of the element that you want to constrain to character data.

The asterisk (*) that appears outside the (#PCDATA) data type declaration is required. The asterisk specifies that the value for the name element can contain zero or more parseable characters at runtime. Leaving off the asterisk restricts the element value to a single character.

DECLARE AN ELEMENT THAT HOLDS CHARACTER DATA

1 Open the DTD file in which you want to create a character constraint rule.

2 Type **<!ELEMENT**.

Extra

The only illegal values for an element of type #PCDATA are markup tags. A markup tag is a series of characters that includes a left-angle bracket followed by a right-angle bracket.

Example:

"<This is an example of an illegal value for an element declared as type #PCDATA. It is illegal because it contains <>>"

If you need to define an XML element that can accept markup tags as a valid value, use the CDATA section as shown in "Constrain Attributes to an External Data Source" in Chapter 4.

Numbers are considered characters in the #PCDATA data type. To declare a more specific character-based data type, such as integer or date or time, you must either use a schema or include detection and manipulation code in your XML processor. Chapters 6 and 7 describe how to create a schema. Chapter 13 describes how to create an XML processor.

3 Type the name of the element that you want to constrain.

■ In this example, the name of the constrained element is name.

4 Type (#PCDATA)* directly after the name of the element.

5 Type the closing angle bracket (>).

6 Save the file.

DECLARE AN EMPTY ELEMENT

You can create a data definition rule to ensure that the value for an element contains no data at runtime. Although this may sound odd at first, empty elements do make sense in certain situations.

Some elements serve conceptually to aggregate data, rather than to define specific values themselves. As an example, consider an element named `productDescription`. Depending on the application and product involved, no single value may be appropriate for this element. However, multiple attributes may exist that, when taken together, define a suitable `productDescription`. In this case (and others like it), you can declare the element as empty and

then declare multiple attributes, such as height, weight, color, price, and so on, that — taken together — define a particular product's description. Attributes associated with an empty element need not be empty at runtime. (You see how to declare attributes in Chapter 4.)

Here is the syntax required to model an empty element:

`<!ELEMENT elementName EMPTY>`

`elementName` is the name of the element you want to define as an empty element.

DECLARE AN EMPTY ELEMENT

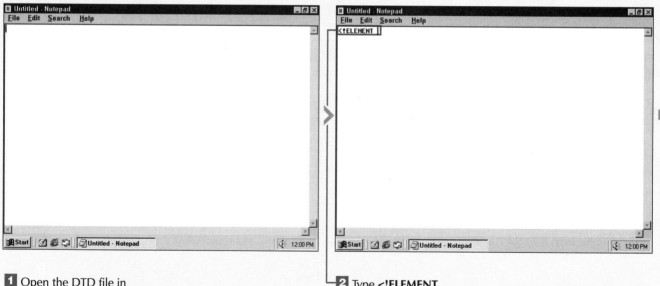

1 Open the DTD file in which you want to create an empty element rule.

2 Type **<!ELEMENT**.

Extra

Empty elements cannot logically be associated with a single, meaningful value. They can, however, serve as an aggregator for multiple attributes. ("Constrain Attributes to an External Data Source" in Chapter 4 shows you how to define attributes for an element.)

Developers are free to choose whether to model data as elements or attributes. One thing to keep in mind is that elements are more easily accessed and manipulated by a processing application than attributes. Elements are best used for describing data that must be accessed and manipulated frequently; attributes are best used for describing metadata, or data about the data.

Following is an example of an empty element, called `nutrition_info`, associated with non-empty attributes (`calories_per_tbsp` and `high_in`). In this example, the values for `calories_per_tbsp` and `high_in help` define the nutrition information for a particular product.

```
<!ELEMENT nutrition_info EMPTY>
<!ATTLIST nutrition_info
    calories_per_tbsp CDATA #REQUIRED
    high_in CDATA #IMPLIED
>
```

3 Type the name of the element that you want to constrain.

■ In this example, the name of the empty element is `nutrition_info`.

4 Type the keyword **EMPTY** directly after the name of the element.

5 Type the closing angle bracket (>).

6 Save the file.

DECLARE ATTRIBUTES THAT HOLD CHARACTERS

You can declare a validation rule that constrains the value of an XML attribute to hold character data only at runtime.

You use the CDATA keyword to declare an attribute of type *character*. Here is the syntax:

```
<!ATTLIST elementname attributeName
CDATA (#REQUIRED/#IMPLIED)>
```

<!ATTLIST is the opening tag to define an attribute list.

elementName is the name of an XML element.

attributeName is the name of an attribute associated with *elementName*.

#REQUIRED specifies that data for this XML attribute is present at runtime.

#IMPLIED specifies that data for this XML attribute may not be present at runtime.

Note: You use the #PCDATA keyword to declare a DTD *element* of type character. See Chapter 3 for details.

This section shows you how to create a data definition rule to constrain an attribute to accept only character data.

DECLARE ATTRIBUTES THAT HOLD CHARACTERS

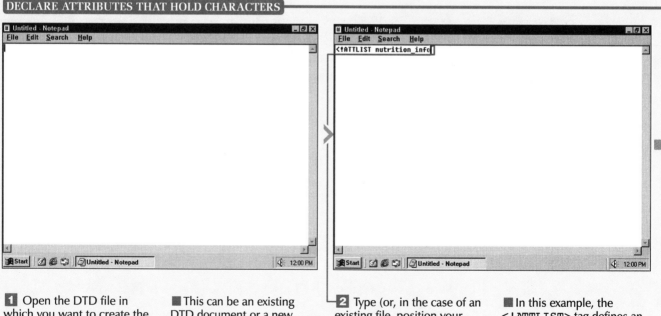

1 Open the DTD file in which you want to create the attribute constraint rule.

■ This can be an existing DTD document or a new Notepad file.

2 Type (or, in the case of an existing file, position your cursor beneath) the appropriate attribute list tag.

■ In this example, the <!ATTLIST> tag defines an attribute list for an XML element called nutrition_info.

Extra | The word directly following the ATTLIST keyword must match the name of a previously defined element. A good design practice to follow is to declare an element's attribute list directly following the element declaration itself.

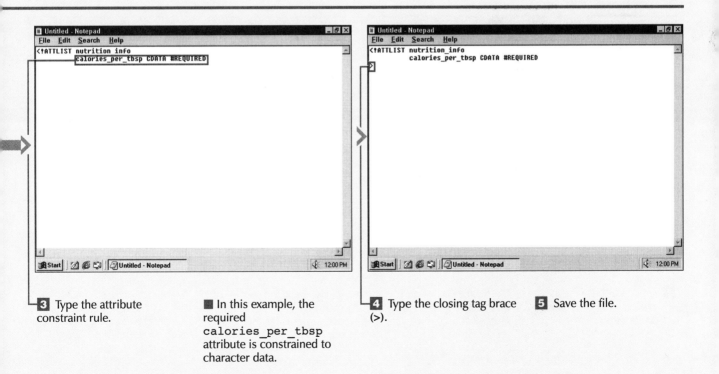

3 Type the attribute constraint rule.

■ In this example, the required `calories_per_tbsp` attribute is constrained to character data.

4 Type the closing tag brace (>).

5 Save the file.

DEFINE AN ENTITY

You can define a validation rule to constrain the value of an XML attribute to a developer-defined external data source. Doing so enables you to organize XML code in multiple files and pull the XML code together at runtime.

You use the ENTITY keyword to declare an attribute of *external* type. At runtime, the only data types allowed for an element declared as type ENTITY are those data types defined in the DTD file using the <!ENTITY> declaration. Here is the syntax:

```
<!ATTLIST elementName attributeName
ENTITY #REQUIRED/#IMPLIED >
```

<!ATTLIST is the opening tag to define an attribute list.

elementName is the name of an XML element.

attributeName is the name of an attribute associated with *elementName*. ENTITY is an XML keyword denoting a developer-defined external data source.

#REQUIRED specifies that data for this XML attribute be present at runtime. #IMPLIED specifies that data for this XML attribute may not be present at runtime.

For example, the steps in this section show you how to ensure that an attribute contains values representing GIF files at runtime. You could constrain an attribute or element to any other type of external file — whatever type makes sense for your application.

DEFINE AN ENTITY

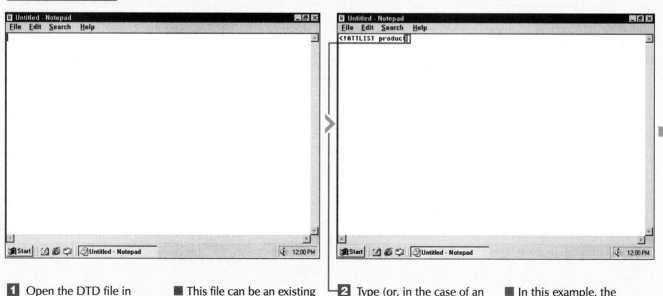

1 Open the DTD file in which you want to create the entity constraint.

■ This file can be an existing DTD document or a new Notepad file.

2 Type (or, in the case of an existing file, position your cursor beneath) the appropriate attribute list tag.

■ In this example, the <!ATTLIST> tag defines an attribute list for an XML element called product.

Apply It

You use an <!ENTITY> tag to declare an entity data type in a DTD file. You use the ENTITY keyword to reference a data type defined with the <!ENTITY> tag.

For example, take a look at the following DTD file snippet, which defines an entity named P1 (a GIF image file) and defines the image attribute associated with the product element as an entity:

```
<!ENTITY P1 SYSTEM "product1.gif" NDATA
GIF>
<!ATTLIST product image ENTITY
#IMPLIED>
```

The associated XML file might include this valid data:

```
<product image="P1">
```

For more information on defining an entity for reference from an attribute constraint rule, see "Declare an Entity" in Chapter 5.

The value of an attribute declared with the ENTITIES keyword may contain multiple ENTITY values separated by white space.

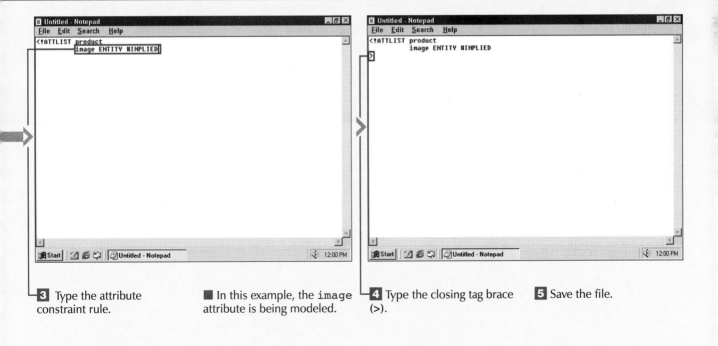

3 Type the attribute constraint rule.

■ In this example, the image attribute is being modeled.

4 Type the closing tag brace (>).

5 Save the file.

DECLARE ATTRIBUTES AS WORDS

You can define a validation rule using the NMTOKEN keyword to constrain the value of an XML attribute to a single word, or *token*. To constrain a value to a collection of individual tokens, you can use the NMTOKENS keyword.

Here is the syntax:

```
<!ATTLIST elementName attributeName
NMTOKEN (#REQUIRED | #IMPLIED)>
```

<!ATTLIST is the opening tag to define an attribute list.

elementName is the name of an XML element.

attributeName is the name of an attribute associated with *elementName*.

NMTOKEN is an XML keyword denoting a single-word token.

#REQUIRED specifies that data for this XML attribute be present at runtime.

#IMPLIED specifies that data for this XML attribute may not be present at runtime.

DECLARE ATTRIBUTES AS WORDS

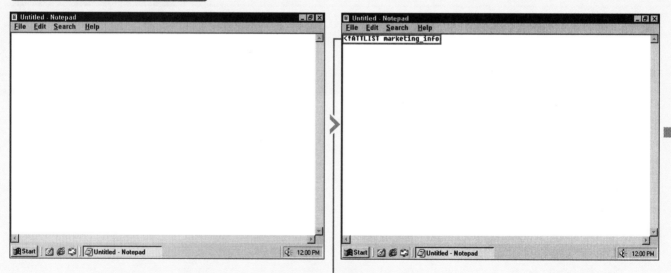

1 Open the DTD file in which you want to create the attribute constraint rule.

■ This file can be an existing DTD document or a new Notepad file.

2 Type (or, in the case of an existing file, position your cursor beneath) the appropriate attribute list tag.

■ In this example, the <!ATTLIST> tag defines an attribute list for an XML element called marketing_info.

Extra

Use of the #REQUIRED keyword depends on your design requirements. Because tokens are often used to create or reference unique identifiers, you usually use the NMTOKEN and #REQUIRED keywords together.

The word directly following the !ATTLIST keyword — in this case, marketing_info — must match the name of a previously defined element. It is this matching that associates an attribute, or a list of attributes, with an element.

A good design practice is to declare all attributes directly below the element to which they are associated, as shown in the following code snippet:

```
<!ELEMENT marketing_info
(unique_characteristics, rank,
r:retailers)>
<!ATTLIST marketing_info     dept_code
 NMTOKEN #REQUIRED>
```

The case-sensitive NMTOKEN keyword specifies that a value for a given attribute contain no white space at runtime. The following examples represent valid values for the dept_code attribute:

- Department_A20

- A20

- departmentA20

In contrast, the following examples represent invalid values for the dept_code attribute:

- Department A20

- A 20

- department A 2 0

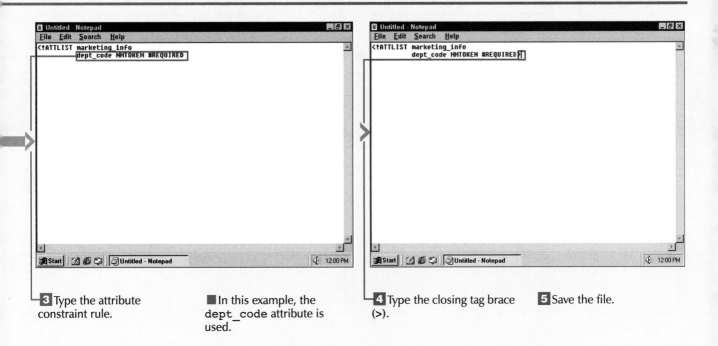

3 Type the attribute constraint rule.

■ In this example, the **dept_code** attribute is used.

4 Type the closing tag brace (>).

5 Save the file.

RESTRICT ATTRIBUTES TO LISTS OF OPTIONS

You can define a validation rule to constrain the value of an XML attribute to one in a list of predefined options. In other words, you can declare an attribute of type *enumerated list*.

Declaring attributes in this way helps reduce input errors and is a good approach for fields where all possible values are known at design time — for example, state or province codes, internally developed codes, or any other finite options. The syntax is:

```
<!ATTLIST elementName
attributeName (option1 | option2 |
optionN) (#REQUIRED | #IMPLIED)
```

`<!ATTLIST` is the opening tag to define an attribute list.

`elementName` is the name of an XML element. `attributeName` is the name of an attribute associated with `elementName`.

`option1`, `option2`, and `optionN` are possible valid values for this attribute separated by the pipe symbol (|).

`#REQUIRED` specifies that data for this XML attribute is present at runtime.

`#IMPLIED` specifies that data for this XML attribute may not be present at runtime.

In this section, you see how to open a DTD file and create an attribute constraint rule.

RESTRICT ATTRIBUTES TO LISTS OF OPTIONS

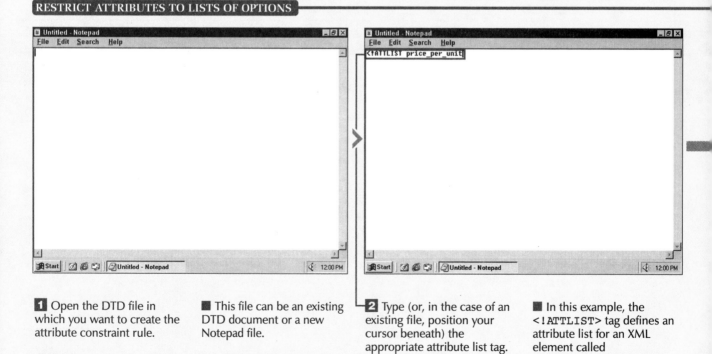

1 Open the DTD file in which you want to create the attribute constraint rule.

■ This file can be an existing DTD document or a new Notepad file.

2 Type (or, in the case of an existing file, position your cursor beneath) the appropriate attribute list tag.

■ In this example, the `<!ATTLIST>` tag defines an attribute list for an XML element called `price_per_unit`.

Extra

To declare an attribute of type enumerated list, you specify a pipe-delimited list of all acceptable values. The values themselves are not surrounded by quotes, even if they represent strings; the list, however, is surrounded by parentheses.

You can add as many values to an enumerated list as you need. To add values to an enumerated list, separate each addition with a pipe symbol (|), as shown here:

```
<!ATTLIST price_per_unit currency (USD
| CD | MP | DM) #REQUIRED >
```

The values between the parentheses cannot be surrounded by quotes.

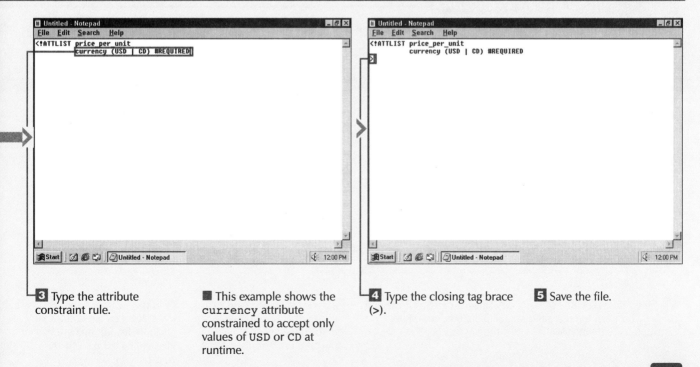

3 Type the attribute constraint rule.

■ This example shows the currency attribute constrained to accept only values of USD or CD at runtime.

4 Type the closing tag brace (>).

5 Save the file.

DECLARE UNIQUE-IDENTIFIER ATTRIBUTES

You can constrain an attribute to accept unique values across an XML application at runtime. You do so using the ID keyword.

The syntax is as follows:

```
<!ATTLIST elementName attributeName ID
#REQUIRED>
```

<!ATTLIST is the opening tag to define an attribute list.

elementName is the name of an XML element.

attributeName is the name of an attribute associated with *elementName*.

ID is the keyword that types this attribute as a unique identifier.

#REQUIRED specifies that data for this XML attribute be present at runtime.

Unique identifiers, or *primary keys*, are an essential component of virtually all database systems, including the flat-file databases that XML documents represent. Unique identifiers are associated with identifier references, called IDREFs in XML, to model logical relationships between XML data records.

DECLARE UNIQUE-IDENTIFIER ATTRIBUTES

1 Open the DTD file in which you want to create the attribute constraint rule.

■ This file can be an existing DTD document or a new Notepad file.

2 Type (or, in the case of an existing file, position your cursor beneath) the appropriate attribute list tag.

■ In this example, the <!ATTLIST> tag defines an attribute list for an XML element called product.

Extra

The ID keyword constrains the values for the product_code attribute to unique identifiers; in other words, no two ID values may be identical for any given XML document at runtime. Unique identifiers may contain letters, spaces, or underscores, but must begin with a letter or an underscore.

The value for an attribute defined as type ID must be previously defined using the IDREF keyword. You see how to define an IDREF later this chapter.

Because attributes declared as type ID must exist to be unique, the #REQUIRED keyword must accompany the ID keyword.

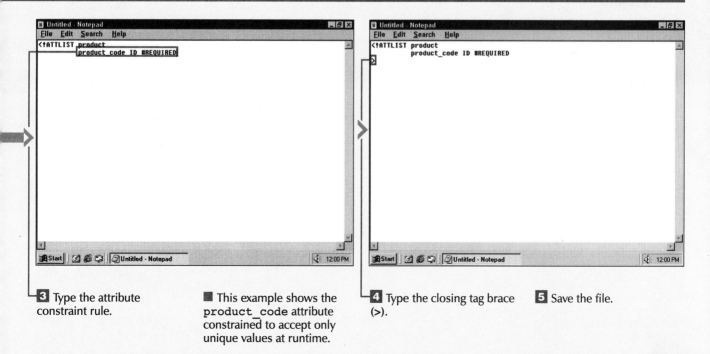

3 Type the attribute constraint rule.

■ This example shows the product_code attribute constrained to accept only unique values at runtime.

4 Type the closing tag brace (>).

5 Save the file.

REFERENCE EXISTING IDENTIFIERS

Using the IDREF keyword, you can define a validation rule to ensure that the value of an XML attribute matches the value of a previously defined attribute.

The syntax is as follows:

```
<!ATTLIST elementName attributeName
IDREF (#IMPLIED | #REQUIRED)>
```

<!ATTLIST is the opening tag to define an attribute list.

elementName is the name of an XML element.

attributeName is the name of an attribute associated with elementName.

IDREF is the keyword that types this attribute as an identifier reference.

#IMPLIED specifies that data for this XML attribute may not be provided at runtime.

#REQUIRED specifies that data for this XML attribute must exist at runtime.

Identifier references, or *foreign keys*, are an essential component of virtually all database systems, including the flat-file databases that XML documents represent. You can associate identifier references with unique identifiers, or IDs, to model logical relationships between XML data records.

REFERENCE EXISTING IDENTIFIERS

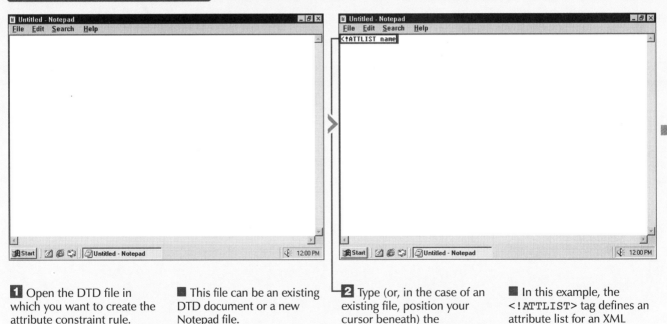

1 Open the DTD file in which you want to create the attribute constraint rule.

■ This file can be an existing DTD document or a new Notepad file.

2 Type (or, in the case of an existing file, position your cursor beneath) the appropriate attribute list tag.

■ In this example, the <!ATTLIST> tag defines an attribute list for an XML element called name.

Apply It

The IDREF keyword specifies that a valid value for the associated attribute must match another value in the XML document previously defined as type ID.

Here is an example of a DTD snippet that demonstrates the relationship between attributes of type ID and IDREF:

```
<!ATTLIST product
product_code ID #REQUIRED>
<!ATTLIST name
bestseller IDREF #IMPLIED>
```

In the preceding DTD code:

- Only unique values are accepted as valid for the product_code attribute.

- A valid value for the bestseller attribute must match a value previously provided for the product_code attribute.

3 Type the attribute constraint rule.

■ In this example, the bestseller attribute is being modeled.

4 Type the closing tag brace (>).

DEFINE AND REUSE TEXT WITHIN DTDS

You can describe a single chunk of text, called a *parameter entity*, and reference the chunk repeatedly inside a DTD file.

Parameter entities enable you to create shorthand notations for lengthy or complex text strings that must be reused repeatedly within a DTD file, thus helping reduce errors introduced by retyping. You must declare entities before you can use them. Declaring entities at the top of the DTD file is good programming practice.

To create a parameter entity, you use the <!ENTITY> keyword inside brackets and a % sign with a space on both sides. The % sign denotes that this entity is a parameter entity. For an internal parameter entry, the complete syntax is

```
<ENTITY! % name "what is being
replaced">
```

For an external parameter entity, you must add the URL where the content is located. The syntax for an external parameter is

```
<!ENTITY % name SYSTEM "URL">
```

DEFINE AND REUSE TEXT WITHIN DTDS

1 Open the DTD file in which you want to create the parameter entity.

■ This file can be an existing document or a new file.

2 Type any comments.

■ This example comment declares that the next line will be an entity declaration. Such comments are helpful when troubleshooting code.

3 Type the opening <!ENTITY tag and a % sign.

4 Type the entity reference name (in this case, YN).

5 Type the replacement text inside quotes.

■ The replacement text shown is (yes | no).

■ For an external parameter entity, type the SYSTEM keyword and substitute a quote-delimited URL containing replacement text (for example, "some.dtd") for the replacement text string.

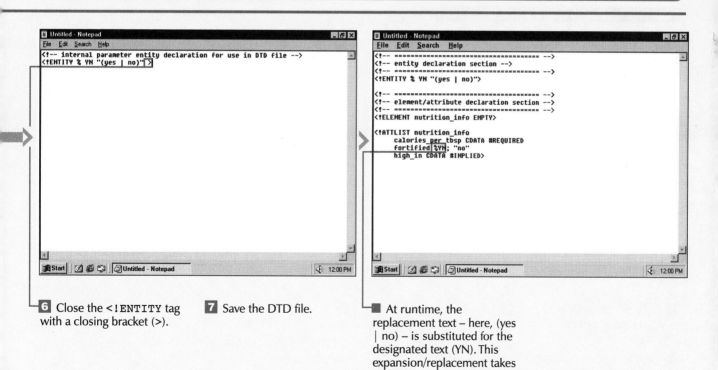

Apply It

Imagine a design team that expects to model many person-related attributes in a given XML project. To streamline their DTD file and define standard values for these attributes (for example, employee, reseller, and customer), the design team can

- Create an internal parameter entity that contains all the text necessary to define an enumerated list of type *employee | reseller | customer*.

- Give the entity a short, meaningful name.

- Reference this short name inside the DTD every time they want to define an enumerated list of type *employee | reseller | customer*. In the following example, the entity named PERSON is defined using the <ENTITY> keyword, then used to define the employee, customer, and reseller attributes.

```
<!ENTITY % PERSON "(employee | reseller | customer)">
...
<!ATTLIST element1
    attr1 PERSON employee
    attr2 PERSON customer
    attr3 PERSON employee
    attr4 PERSON employee
    attr5 PERSON employee
    attr6 PERSON reseller
    ...>
```

6 Close the `<!ENTITY` tag with a closing bracket (>).

7 Save the DTD file.

■ At runtime, the replacement text – here, (yes | no) – is substituted for the designated text (YN). This expansion/replacement takes place internally, when the DTD file is being parsed.

DEFINE REUSABLE TEXT INSIDE XML FILES

You can describe a single chunk of data, called a *general entity*, that can be referred to repeatedly inside an XML document. Defining entities saves you from having to repeat long or difficult passages of text inside an XML file. The syntax of an internal general entity is

```
<!ENTITY name "replacement text in
quotes">
```

These two pages cover internal general entities.

The example figures focus on an attribute named `high_in`, which is intended to hold the name of a vitamin, and how a design team that wants to allow data values of common vitamin references (such as C and B1) might use an internal general entity to expand those references to the more descriptive names *ascorbic acid* and *thiamin* for use in their application.

DEFINE REUSABLE TEXT INSIDE XML FILES

1 Open the XML document in which you want to create the general entity.

■ This file can be an existing XML document or a new Notepad file.

2 Type any comments.

■ This example comment declares that the next line will be a general entity declaration. Such comments are helpful when troubleshooting code.

3 Type the entity tag opening – `<!ENTITY`.

4 Type the elements to be substituted for (in this case, C).

5 Type the replacement text (in this case, "ascorbic acid").

6 Type the closing bracket (>).

Extra

The different types of XML entities — what they are, where you define them, where you reference them, and why you use them — can be confusing.

In a nutshell, XML supports four different types of entities:

- Internal general entities.

- External general entities.

- Internal parameter entities.

- External parameter entities.

You define all four types of entities in a DTD file (or in the `<!DOCTYPE>` section inside the physical XML file) using the `<!ENTITY>` tag. The four types of entities differ in these ways: General entities are referenced inside XML files using an ampersand and a semicolon (`&entityName;`). Parameter entities are referenced inside DTD files using a percent sign and a semicolon (`%entityName;`). Internal entities define replacement text in the same physical document that references those entities; external entities use the `SYSTEM` keyword to reference replacement text that exists in an external document.

```
Untitled - Notepad
File  Edit  Search  Help
<!-- general entity declaration for use inside the XML document -->
<!ENTITY C "ascorbic acid">
<!ENTITY B1 "thiamin">
```

```
Untitled - Notepad
File  Edit  Search  Help
<?xml version="1.0"?>

<!-- XML data excerpt -->

<nutrition_info
    calories_per_tbsp="13"
    fortified="no"
    high_in="&B1;"
/>

<!-- XML data excerpt -->

<nutrition_info
    calories_per_tbsp="13"
    fortified="no"
    high_in="&C;"
/>
```

7 Repeat Steps 3-6 as needed for additional entries.

8 Save the file.

9 Open the XML document in which you want to reference the general entity.

10 Where desired, type the new reference name in quotes, with a semicolon (here, `&B1;` and `&C;`).

USE NON-XML DATA IN XML APPLICATIONS

By declaring an attribute of type *notation*, you can reference an external data type associated with an *external general entity*. An *external data type* is any non-XML data type, such as a picture or word-processing format. An external general entity is a DTD construct used to resolve external data types for use in XML documents.

The declaration syntax is as follows:

`<!NOTATION name SYSTEM "dataType">`

name is the name of the notation.

dataType is any value that an XML processor application can recognize and process at runtime.

The figures in this example show you how to declare a notation that describes the external GIF format, although you can apply the steps to any situation. The next section — "Embed Other Data in XML Applications," which deals with declaring an external entity — builds on this section. In order to declare an external entity, a description of the external format must already be defined as shown next.

USE NON-XML DATA IN XML APPLICATIONS

1 Open the DTD document in which you want to create the notation.

■ This file can be an existing DTD document or a new Notepad file.

2 Type any comments.

■ This example comment declares that the next line will be a notation. Such comments are helpful when maintaining or troubleshooting code.

3 Enter the notation tag opening – `<!NOTATION`.

Extra

Notations are similar to XML entities and processing instructions in that they enable developers to incorporate non-XML data into XML applications. The difference among these three approaches is as follows:

- *Entities* provide links to the physical location of non-XML data; for example, `<!ENTITY name SYSTEM "http://www.someDomain.com/someURL">`.

- *Processing instructions* provide programmatic instructions for accessing and viewing non-XML data; for example, `<?gcc helloWorld.c ?>`.

- *Notations*, in contrast, describe the format of non-XML data files; for example, `<!NOTATION PDF SYSTEM "application/pdf">` or `<!NOTATION PDF PUBLIC "someUrl">`.

No standard approach to specifying non-XML data using notations exists currently. Some programmers favor MIME types (as shown in the example in this section). Others suggest URLs that point to standards documents: for example, a resource maintained by the World Wide Web Consortium or some other standards body. At this point in the evolution of XML, programmers are free to choose the approach that works best for their specific applications.

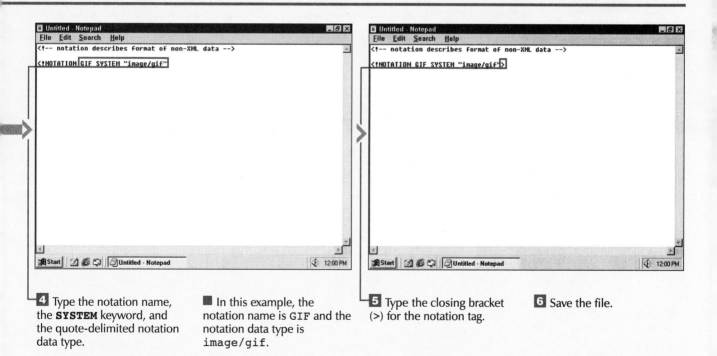

4 Type the notation name, the **SYSTEM** keyword, and the quote-delimited notation data type.

■ In this example, the notation name is `GIF` and the notation data type is `image/gif`.

5 Type the closing bracket (>) for the notation tag.

6 Save the file.

EMBED OTHER DATA IN XML APPLICATIONS

Y ou can declare an *external general entity* to include an external data source, such as a JPG or PDF file, in your XML-based application. An external data type is any non-XML data type, such as a picture or word-processing format.

In order to declare an external general entity to include an external data source, you must first declare a notation attribute.

The external general entity syntax is

```
<!ENTITY stringname SYSTEM "fileName"
NDATA notationName>
```

Stringname refers to the name of the entity being declared; the entity name can contain letters, numbers, or underscores, but it must begin with a letter or underscore.

fileName, which must be surrounded by quotes, represents the name of the external data source.

notationName is the name of a notation previously defined in the DTD.

EMBED OTHER DATA IN XML APPLICATIONS

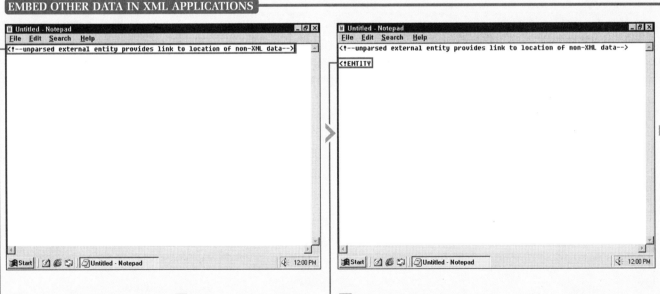

1 Open the DTD file in which you want to create the external entity.

■ This file can be an existing DTD file or a new Notepad file.

2 Type any comments.

■ This example comment declares that the next line will be an unparsed external entity. Such comments are helpful when maintaining and troubleshooting code.

3 Enter the opening entity tag – **<!ENTITY**.

68

Extra

You can specify an external filename using absolute or relative URLs. For example, the following are all valid entity declarations:

```
<!ENTITY P1 SYSTEM "product1.gif" NDATA GIF>
<!ENTITY P1 SYSTEM "http://www.someDomain/product1.gif" NDATA GIF>
<!ENTITY P1 SYSTEM "../product1.gif" NDATA GIF>
<!ENTITY P1 SYSTEM "/xml/product1.gif" NDATA GIF>
```

Notation attributes describe non-XML data formats, while external entities reference notation attributes and describe the logical location of a non-XML data file. You must define a notation attribute before you can reference it. A good design practice is to define both notation attributes and notation references (entity declarations) in the same DTD file, such as:

```
<!NOTATION GIF SYSTEM "image/gif">
<!ENTITY P1 SYSTEM "../product1.gif" NDATA GIF>
```

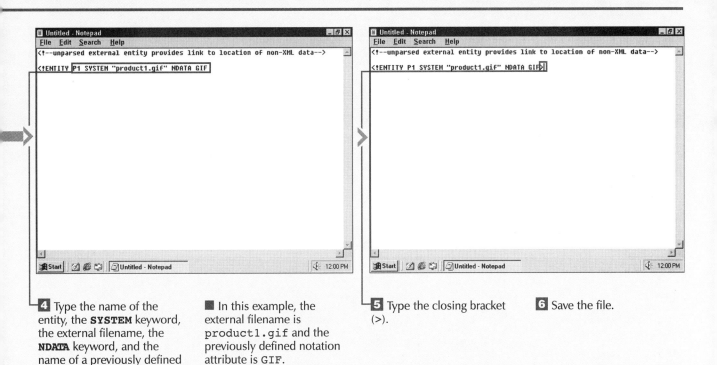

■ **4** Type the name of the entity, the **SYSTEM** keyword, the external filename, the **NDATA** keyword, and the name of a previously defined notation attribute.

■ In this example, the external filename is `product1.gif` and the previously defined notation attribute is `GIF`.

■ **5** Type the closing bracket (>).

■ **6** Save the file.

DESCRIBE NAMESPACE-VALIDATION RULES

You can create validation rules for namespace-qualified elements and attributes declared in an XML document.

Namespace-qualified elements and attributes are identically named elements and attributes that are uniquely identified across an XML application. Namespaces are useful when incorporating externally defined XML elements into your XML application. For example, if you incorporate an XML element called <NAME> into your application, which already defines an XML element called <NAME>, you must be able to distinguish between these two elements.

Associating each of these two <NAME> attributes with a namespace, as described in Chapter 2 ("Incorporate predefined XML elements and attributes by declaring a namespace"), enables you to distinguish between them.

You refer to a namespace-qualified element or attribute in a DTD by appending the name of the namespace, followed by a colon (:), to beginning of the name of the element or attribute, for example r:retailers (where r is the name of a previously defined namespace and retailers is the name of a previously defined element)

DESCRIBE NAMESPACE-VALIDATION RULES

1 Open the DTD file in which you want to create the namespace validation rule.

■ This file can be an existing DTD document or a new Notepad file.

2 Type any comments.

■ Comments such as the one shown are helpful when maintaining or troubleshooting code.

3 Type the appropriate opening tag for the validation rule you want to create.

■ In this example, the opening <!ATTLIST tag is shown.

Extra

xmlns is a reserved keyword that associates a namespace (r, in this example) with a fixed character value (in this example, "http://www.someDomain.com/someURL"). This value is a dummy value, because no file named someURL exists at www.someDomain.com. Furthermore, such a file doesn't need to exist in order for the namespace declaration to be valid. Namespaces need not reference a valid document at this time (although as XML matures, this will almost certainly change). All that is required is that a URL bound to a namespace in an XML file be identical to the URL bound to a namespace in the corresponding DTD file.

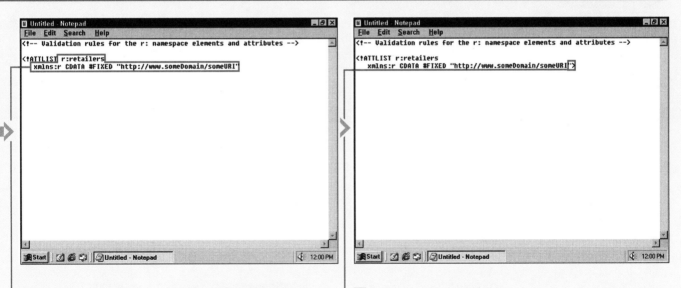

4 Type the appropriate namespace reference.

5 Type a colon (:).

6 Type the element reference.

7 Type the **xmlns** keyword, followed by a colon (:)

8 Type the namespace reference.

9 Type **CDATA #FIXED "URI"** where URI is the name of the unique resource defined in the corresponding XML file.

10 Type the closing tag brace (>).

71

DECLARE A SCHEMA FILE

A schema is a collection of semantic validation rules designed to constrain XML data values. As an alternative to document type definitions, schemas are growing in popularity. Two reasons for choosing schemas over DTDs for XML validation are

- Unlike DTDs, schemas are implemented in standard XML syntax. You must still learn a schema *vocabulary*, such as Microsoft's, in order to develop schemas, but you do not have to learn an additional language syntax.

- Also unlike DTDs, schemas allow you to validate sophisticated data types like `integer`, `date`, and `time`.

Unfortunately, the World Wide Web Consortium's schema recommendation is far from mature, and few schema-supporting tools are available. At the time of this writing, Microsoft's MSXML offers the most advanced support for schemas. Schema development is currently appropriate for prototyping efforts only. Here is the syntax for creating a schema:

```
<Schema
name="schemaName"
xmlns="urn:schemas-microsoft-com:xml-data"
xmlns:dt="urn:schemas-microsoft-com:datatypes">
```

schemaName is the name you want to assign to the schema.

DECLARE A SCHEMA FILE

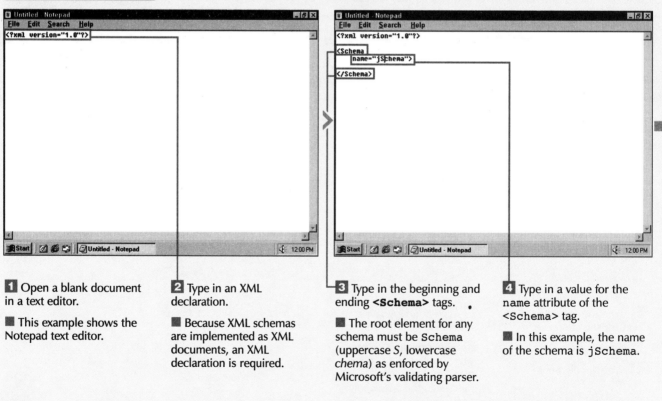

1 Open a blank document in a text editor.

■ This example shows the Notepad text editor.

2 Type in an XML declaration.

■ Because XML schemas are implemented as XML documents, an XML declaration is required.

3 Type in the beginning and ending **<Schema>** tags.

■ The root element for any schema must be `Schema` (uppercase *S*, lowercase *chema*) as enforced by Microsoft's validating parser.

4 Type in a value for the name attribute of the `<Schema>` tag.

■ In this example, the name of the schema is `jSchema`.

Extra

Schemas:

- Represent an alternative to DTDs. Developers can create schemas to specify structure and semantic rules for XML data, just as they can create DTDs.

- Are implemented as XML documents. Unlike DTDs, schemas are implemented using XML syntax.

- Are being defined by the World Wide Web Consortium. The World Wide Web Consortium released the latest working draft in April, 2000, at www.w3.org/TR/xmlschema-1/.

- Are not yet stable enough for production development. The World Wide Web Consortium expects the schema specification to be finalized in late 2000. Until then, vendors are providing schema support that may or may not conform to the latest (if any) working draft.

- Are partially supported by Microsoft's MSXML validating parser. While support for schemas in MSXML is currently incomplete, new versions of the MSXML are expected to keep pace with the World Wide Web Consortium's schema specifications. See http://msdn.microsoft.com/xml/reference/schema/start.asp for detailed information on Microsoft's schema support.

Left screenshot — Untitled - Notepad

```
<?xml version="1.0"?>

<Schema
    name="jSchema"
    xmlns="urn:schemas-microsoft-com:xml-data"


</Schema>
```

Right screenshot — Untitled - Notepad

```
<?xml version="1.0"?>

<Schema
    name="jSchema"
    xmlns="urn:schemas-microsoft-com:xml-data"
    xmlns:dt="urn:schemas-microsoft-com:datatypes">

</Schema>
```

5 Type in a value for the `xmlns` attribute of the `<Schema>` tag.

■ Include a Microsoft schema resource ("urn:schemas-microsoft-com:xml-data") as an implicit namespace. Doing so allows you to reference the special elements you need to create a schema, including `ElementType`, `Element`, `AttributeType`, and `Attribute`.

6 Type in a value for the `xmlns:dt` attribute of the `<Schema>` tag.

■ Include a Microsoft data typing resource ("urn:schemas-microsoft-com:datatypes") as an explicit namespace. Doing so allows you to reference Microsoft's built-in data types, including `string`, `integer`, and `boolean`.

ADD A COMMENT

Because you can apply a single schema to multiple XML documents — and because a single XML document may incorporate multiple schemas — commenting a schema file thoroughly and appropriately is a very important part of the XML application development process.

Comments allow you to describe validation rules so that human readers can easily understand the intent and purpose of each rule. If schemas are to offer a viable alternative to DTDs, developers must be able to understand and work with them easily. Including

appropriate comments inside a schema file, rather than in a separate document or manual, ensures that vital documentation isn't separated from the physical schema file.

Here is the syntax required to comment a schema:

```
<!-- comment   -->
```

comment can include any text except "--". (*comment* can, however, include breaking white space, such as a return — which is useful for readability.)

---

1 Open the schema file to which you want to add a comment.

2 Position your cursor beneath the XML declaration.

3 Type in the opening comment tag (**<!--**).

Extra

Be careful where you place your comments in the document. Comments cannot appear

■ Before the XML declaration. For example, the following XML generates a parse error:

```
<!-- Schema description  -->
<?xml version="1.0"?>
```

■ Inside XML tags. For example, the following XML generates a parse error:

```
<?xml <!-- Jamcracker, Inc. product
information --> version="1.0"?>
```

Other than these two restrictions, comments can appear anywhere in an XML schema document. You cannot nest comments.

In addition to the commenting approach shown in this example, Microsoft's schema implementation supports a specific element named *description* you can use to comment your schema code.

Example:

```
<jamcracker_product_info>
<description>jamcracker_product_info
contains all the validation rules for
Jamcracker, Inc.'s extensive line of
wholesale products.</description>
</jamcracker_inc_product_info>
```

The `description` element provides developers with a convention for describing complex data structures.

Untitled - Notepad
File Edit Search Help

```
<?xml version="1.0"?>

<!-- This schema was developed for use with the some.xml data file. |

<Schema
    name="jSchema"
    xmlns="urn:schemas-microsoft-com:xml-data"
    xmlns:dt="urn:schemas-microsoft-com:datatypes">

</Schema>
```

Start   Untitled - Notepad   12:00 PM

4 Type in the comment.

Untitled - Notepad
File Edit Search Help

```
<?xml version="1.0"?>

<!-- This schema was developed for use with the some.xml data file. -->

<Schema
    name="jSchema"
    xmlns="urn:schemas-microsoft-com:xml-data"
    xmlns:dt="urn:schemas-microsoft-com:datatypes">

</Schema>
```

Start   Untitled - Notepad   12:00 PM

5 Type in the closing comment tag (**-->**).

6 Save the file.

CONTAIN OTHER ELEMENTS

You can enforce container/contained relationships using a schema. Container elements are sometimes referred to as *aggregate* elements because they define no original values; instead, they consist of one or more other, predefined elements.

Here is the syntax required to define an XML element as a container element:

```
<ElementType name="containerElementName"
content="eltOnly" model="closed">
    <element
type="containedElementName1">
```

```
    <element
type="containedElementName2">
    <element
type="containedElementNameN">
</ElementType>
```

containerElementName is the name of the element you want to define as a container element

containedElementName1, *containedElementName2,* and *containedElementNameN* are one or more elements you want to define as contained inside *containerElementName*.

CONTAIN OTHER ELEMENTS

1 Open the schema file in which you want to define a container/contained relationship.

2 Position your cursor between the beginning and ending **<Schema>** tags.

3 Type in the beginning and ending **<ElementType>** tags.

4 Type in a value for the name attribute of the **<ElementType>** tag.

■ In this example, the name of the container element is **marketing_info**.

Extra

When declaring container relationships in schemas, follow these guidelines for reliable code:

- Declare an `ElementType` in your schema for each data element in your XML data document. The names must match exactly; for example, if you declared an element called `jamcracker_product_info` in your XML document, you must declare an `ElementType` element called `jamcracker_product_info` in your schema.

- Contain elements defined with `ElementType` using *element*. After you declare an element using the `ElementType` element, you can reference it inside a container element using the `element` element. For example,

```
<ElementType name="retailers"/>
...
<ElementType name="marketing_info">
    ...
     <element type="retailers"/>
    </ElementType>
```

- Build the data structure from the bottom up. You declare the root element near the bottom of the schema file and the elements it contains above it.

You can find up-to-date syntax for the `ElementType` element, including examples, at http://msdn.microsoft.com/xml/reference/schema/ElementType.asp.

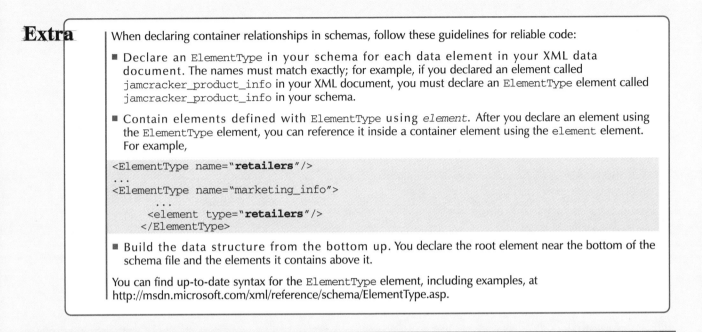

5 Type in the `eltOnly` value for the `content` attribute of the `<ElementType>` tag.

6 Specify one or more elements you want to be contained, using the `<element>` tag.

■ In this example, the `unique_characteristics`, `rank`, and `retailers` elements are defined as contained elements.

7 Type in a value of **"closed"** for the `model` attribute of the `ElementType` tag.

DECLARE ONE-TIME ELEMENTS

You can create a schema validation rule to ensure that a given element is associated with one — and only one — value at runtime. Elements so declared are referred to as *required* elements, because they are required to exist at runtime.

Here is the syntax:

```
<element type="element-type"
[minOccurs="1"]
[maxOccurs="{1 | *}"] >
```

element-type matches the name of a previously defined ElementType.

minOccurs refers to the minimum number of values that may exist for this element at runtime (default is 1).

maxOccurs refers to the maximum number of values that may exist for this element at runtime; can be 1 or * (asterisk denotes "many"; default is 1).

DECLARE ONE-TIME ELEMENTS

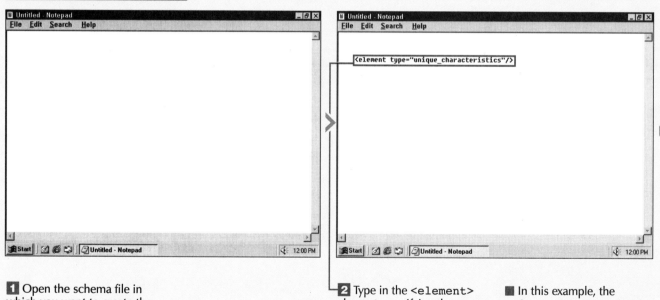

1 Open the schema file in which you want to create the "required" validation rule.

2 Type in the `<element>` element, specifying the name of the required element as the value for the `<element>` type attribute.

■ In this example, the `unique_characteristics` element is being defined as required.

Extra

Some examples of the type of data elements usually modeled as required include

- Customer name

- Social security number

- Product identification number

- Account number

Because the schema standard — as well as Microsoft's implementation of that standard — is still in flux, explicitly defining values for minOccurs and maxOccurs as shown in this section is good programming practice.

You can find updated syntax for the *element* element, including examples, at http://msdn.microsoft.com/xml/reference/schema/Element.asp.

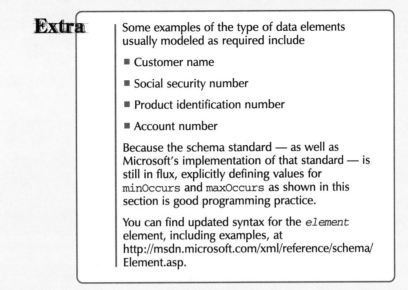

3 Type in a value of **1** for the minOccurs attribute.

4 Type in a value of **1** or ***** for the maxOccurs attribute.

DECLARE OPTIONAL ELEMENTS

Y ou can create a data validation rule that allows an element to be associated with any number of values at runtime. In other words, you can model an *optional* element in a schema.

Here is the syntax required to model an optional element:

```
<element type="element-type"
[minOccurs="0"]
[maxOccurs="{1 | *}"] >
```

element-type is a required attribute; its value must match the name of a previously defined ElementType.

minOccurs refers to the minimum number of values that may exist for this element at runtime.

maxOccurs refers to the maximum number of values that may exist for this element at runtime; can be 1 or * (asterisk denotes "many").

DECLARE OPTIONAL ELEMENTS

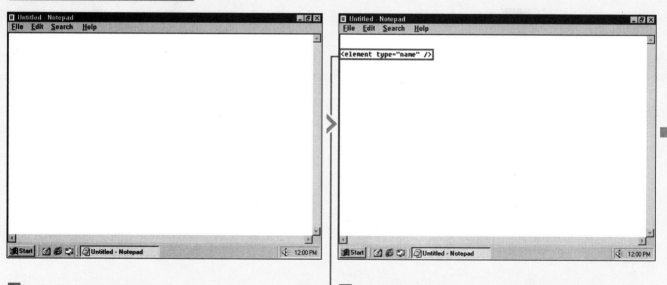

1 Open the schema file in which you want to create the "optional" data validation rule.

2 Type in the `<element>` element, specifying the name of the optional element as the value for the `<element>` type attribute.

■ This example shows the name element as being defined as optional.

Extra

You may find, when gathering data requirements for your XML application, that values for certain elements do not always exist. For example, in the case of an XML application that processes products, newly introduced products may not be associated with complete information at the time of introduction. (A product name and price might exist, but information such as units sold may not.) In such cases you need to define optional elements as described in this section.

You can find up-to-date syntax for the *element* element, including examples, at http://msdn. microsoft.com/xml/reference/schema/Element.asp.

3 Type in a value of **0** for the minOccurs attribute.

4 Type in a value of **1** (exactly one) or * (more than one) for the maxOccurs attribute.

DECLARE REPEATABLE ELEMENTS

You can create a schema validation rule to ensure that an element is associated with one or more values at runtime.

Here is the syntax required to define an element as required and allow that element to contain multiple values at runtime:

```
<element type="element-type"
[minOccurs="1"]
[maxOccurs="*"]  >
```

element-type is a required attribute; its value must match the name of a previously defined ElementType.

minOccurs refers to the minimum number of values that may exist for this element at runtime.

maxOccurs refers to the maximum number of values that may exist for this element at runtime. The asterisk symbol (*) denotes an unspecified number of values.

DECLARE REPEATABLE ELEMENTS

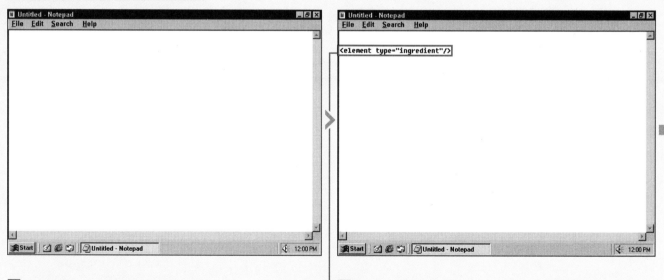

■1 Open the schema file in which you want to create the data validation rule.

■2 Type in the <element> element, specifying the name of the required element as the value for the <element> type attribute.

■ This example shows the ingredient element being defined as required.

Extra

Limiting the number of values that may exist for an element allows you to enforce cases where an upper limit (or *cap*) exists but need not be met, such as the following:

- A class may contain up to 50 students, but no more.

- A manager can only be responsible for 20 or fewer employees.

- A product must contain 99 or fewer ingredients.

To limit the number of values that may exist for an element, set the maxOccurs attribute to an integer, such as 99.

You can find up-to-date syntax for the element element, including examples, on Microsoft's Web site at http://msdn.microsoft.com/xml/reference/schema/Element.asp.

3 Type in a value of **1** for the minOccurs attribute.

4 Type in a value of * for the maxOccurs attribute.

CONTAIN CHARACTER DATA

Y ou can create a data definition rule to ensure that the value for an element contains only character data (text) at runtime.

You use the content attribute of the ElementType element to declare the data type for an XML element as *textOnly* in a schema. Elements declared as type textOnly can only hold character data; they cannot contain other predefined elements.

Here is the syntax:

```
<ElementType name="elementName"
content="textOnly" model="closed"/>
```

elementName is the name of the element you want to define as type text.

(Unlike DTDs, schemas offer more specific data types than a simple character type. To specify a more constrained data type, such as a real number, time, or date, you can add a value for the dt:type attribute to your element declaration.)

CONTAIN CHARACTER DATA

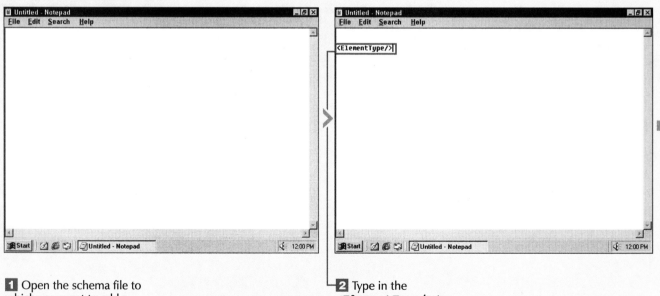

1 Open the schema file to which you want to add a **text** element definition.

2 Type in the **<ElementType/>** tag.

Extra

The value for the content attribute of the ElementType attribute can be any of the following:

- **empty**: Elements of this type cannot contain any content.

- **textOnly**: Elements of this type cannot contain any elements — only text, or *character-based*, content.

- **elementOnly**: Elements of this type can contain other elements only; they cannot contain text content.

- **mixed**: Elements of this type can contain both text and element content. This value is the default. If you do not explicitly declare a value for an ElementType's content attribute, elements of that type will be able to contain both text and element content.

```
Untitled - Notepad
File  Edit  Search  Help

<ElementType name="ingredient"/>
```

```
Untitled - Notepad
File  Edit  Search  Help

<ElementType name="ingredient" content="textOnly" model="closed"/>
```

3 Type in the name of the element you want to define as type text.

■ In this example, the name of the element is ingredient.

4 Type in a value of **textOnly** for the content attribute associated with the ElementType element.

5 Type in a value of **closed** for the model attribute associated with the ElementType element.

DECLARE EMPTY ELEMENTS

You can create a schema validation rule to ensure that the value for an element is empty (contains no data) at runtime.

By assigning the content attribute a value of *empty*, you can model an XML element that cannot contain a corresponding element value. Although this may sound odd, empty elements do make sense in certain situations. For example, some elements serve conceptually to aggregate data, rather than to define specific values themselves. These elements are best modeled as empty elements. You can associate empty

elements with attributes, which need not be empty at runtime.

Here is the syntax required to declare an empty element:

```
<ElementType name="elementName"
content="empty" model="closed"/>
```

elementName is the name of the element you want to define as an empty element.

DECLARE EMPTY ELEMENTS

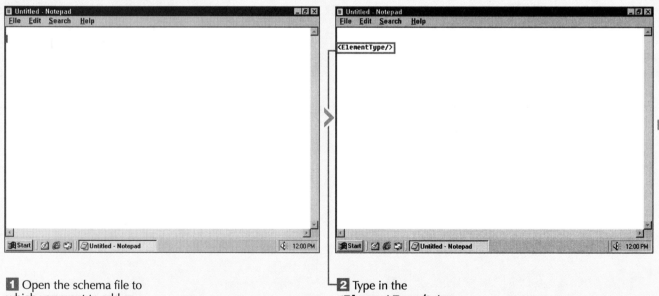

1 Open the schema file to which you want to add an empty element definition.

2 Type in the **<ElementType/>** tag.

Extra

Developers are free to choose whether to model data as elements, attributes, or a combination of both. Conceptually, elements represent data, while attributes represent metadata, or "data about data." In other words, elements model essential information; attributes model descriptive information. Associating attributes with an element defined as *empty* is fairly common practice.

A value of *empty* for the ElementType's content attribute is valid only if the value of that ElementType's model attribute is equal to *closed* (model="closed"). If the value of an ElementType's model attribute is equal to *open*, the value of the content attribute is ignored and elements based on that ElementType can contain virtually anything: text, declared elements, and even non-declared elements. The model is *closed* by default.

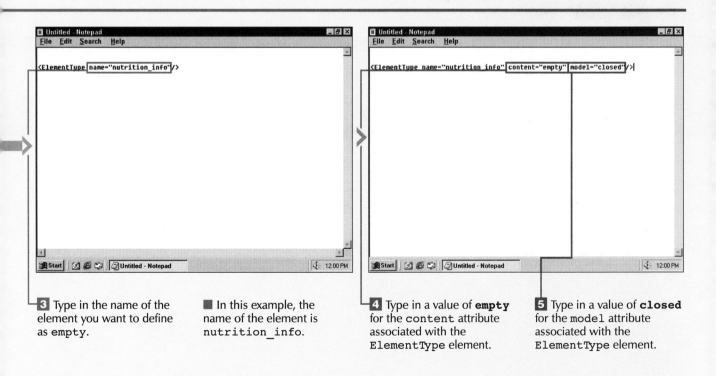

3 Type in the name of the element you want to define as **empty**.

■ In this example, the name of the element is `nutrition_info`.

4 Type in a value of **empty** for the content attribute associated with the ElementType element.

5 Type in a value of **closed** for the model attribute associated with the ElementType element.

CONTAIN MIXED VALUES

You can declare a schema validation rule that allows an XML element to contain, at runtime, both

- Character data
- Other predefined elements

Declaring such a schema rule gives you the flexibility to model rich data structures.

Here is the syntax:

```
<ElementType name="elementName"
content="mixed" model="closed"/>
```

elementName is the name of the element you want to define as a mixed element.

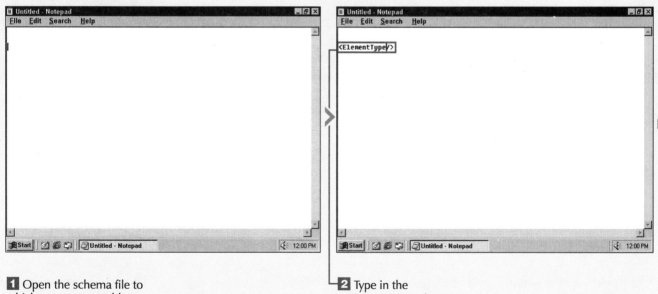

1 Open the schema file to which you want to add a mixed element definition.

2 Type in the **<ElementType/>** tag.

Apply It

The fictional Jamcracker, Inc. design team modeled the unique_characteristics element as a mixed element, as shown next, because they expect it to contain

- Instances of the ingredient element when appropriate

- Other, additional characteristics that don't appear in the XML data model

```
<ElementType
name="unique_characteristics"
content="mixed"

model="closed">
        <element type="ingredient"
minOccurs="1" maxOccurs="1"/>
            </ElementType>
```

To allow the unique_characteristics element to accept additional values at runtime, additional elements could be defined within the unique_characteristics' ElementType declaration, like this:

```
<ElementType name="unique_characteristics"
  content="mixed"
                        model="closed">
        <element type="ingredient"
minOccurs="1" maxOccurs="1"/>
            <element type="nutrient"
minOccurs="1" maxOccurs="1"/>
        <element type="customer_feedback"
                        minOccurs="1"
maxOccurs="1"/>
        ...
        </ElementType>
```

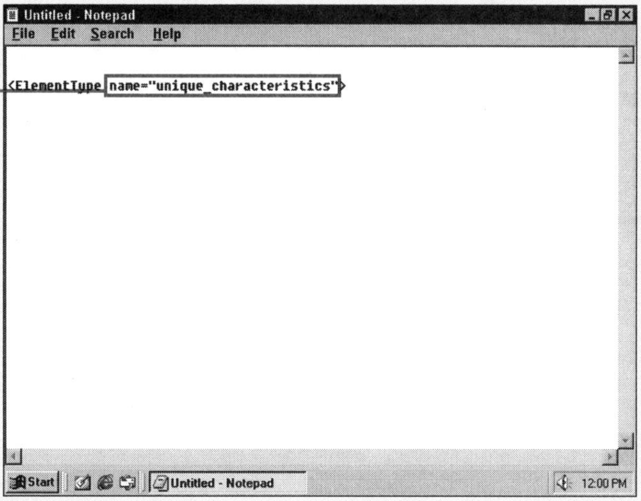

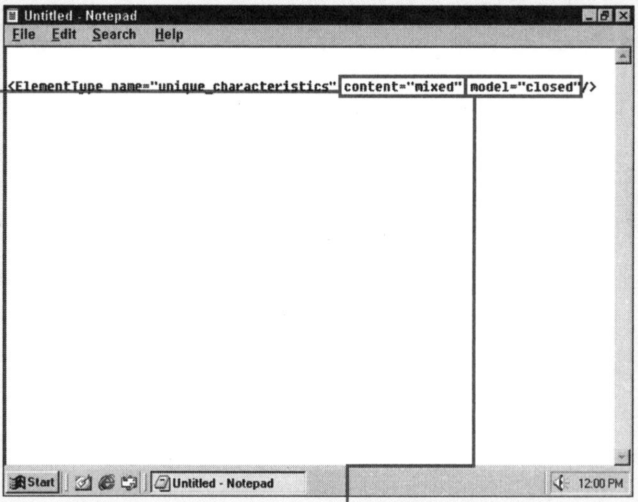

3 Type in the name of the element you want to define as mixed.

■ In this example, the name of the element is unique_ characteristics.

4 Type in a value of **mixed** for the content attribute associated with the ElementType element.

5 Type in a value of **closed** for the model attribute associated with the ElementType element.

DECLARE UNRESTRICTED ELEMENTS

Yoù can declare a schema validation rule to allow an element to contain any of the following at runtime:

- A text value
- One or more predefined elements
- One or more *ad-hoc* elements, or elements that do not appear in the schema

Here is the syntax:

```
<ElementType name="elementName"
model="open"/>
```

elementName is the name of the element for which you want to turn off validation checking.

DECLARE UNRESTRICTED ELEMENTS

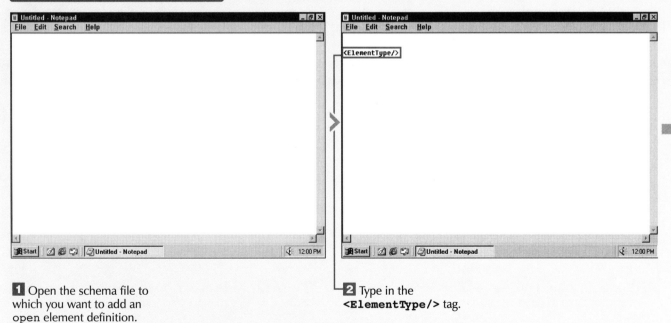

1 Open the schema file to which you want to add an open element definition.

2 Type in the **<ElementType/>** tag.

Extra

To restrict an element's content model and make use of the `content` and `dt:type` attributes of the `ElementType` declaration, you must explicitly set the value for the `model` attribute to `closed`, because the default value for the `ElementType`'s model attribute is `open`.

A closed model mimics the DTD model; only those elements and attributes that you specifically declare are allowed to exist in the XML document at runtime.

The ability to declare `ElementTypes` with open content models is typically useful

- **During application development.** You may want to skip some schema validation checks while you debug other parts of your XML application. After you debug your application, you can then turn on validation checks by setting your elements' `model` attribute to `closed`.

- **If you expect your schema to be used by third parties.** If you are developing a schema for use by third-party developers, you may want to intentionally specify an open model so that they can use your schema with their custom data.

| Untitled - Notepad |
| File Edit Search Help |

```
<ElementType name="test_field"/>
```

| Untitled - Notepad |
| File Edit Search Help |

```
<ElementType name="test_field" model="open"/>
```

3 Type in the name of the element you want to define as **open**.

■ In this example, the name of the element is **test_field**.

4 Type in a value of **open** for the `model` attribute associated with the `ElementType` element.

DECLARE PREDEFINED DATA TYPES

You can declare a schema validation rule to constrain an element to a rich data type, such as boolean, integer, real, time, or date.

Here is the syntax:

```
<Schema name="mySchema"
        xmlns="urn:schemas-microsoft-
com:xml-data"
        xmlns:dt="urn:schemas-microsoft-
com:datatypes">
<ElementType name="elementName"
content="contentType" dt:type="dataType"
model="closed"/>
```

elementName is the name of the element you want to associate with a rich data type.

contentType is a valid content type (`empty`, `textOnly`, `elementOnly`, or `mixed`)

dataType is a valid data type, such as boolean, date, or time. (The `dt:` prefix corresponds to the `xmlns:dt="urn:schemas-microsoft-com:datatypes"` namespace; more valid data types are described in the "Apply It" section.)

DECLARE PREDEFINED DATA TYPES

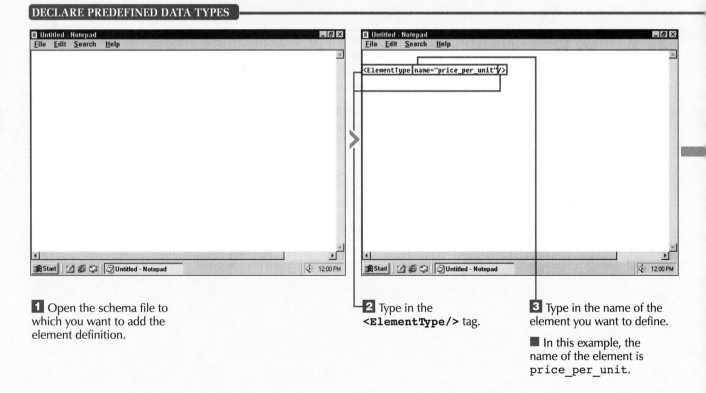

1 Open the schema file to which you want to add the element definition.

2 Type in the **`<ElementType/>`** tag.

3 Type in the name of the element you want to define.

■ In this example, the name of the element is `price_per_unit`.

**Apply
It**

The ability to enforce rich data types is the primary benefit of using schemas in your XML application. Microsoft defines many data types for use in XML schemas. In the future, you may be able to define and integrate your own data types using Microsoft's schema implementation, as well.

Microsoft's MSXML processor supports what Microsoft calls *primitive* data types, which are the data types defined by the XML 1.0 specification and directly enforceable using DTDs. If you need to check a value for a pattern or data type not supported by Microsoft's MSXML parser, you can add validation logic to your XML processing application.

For complete, up-to-date syntax for the built-in data types supported by Microsoft's MSXML, visit http://msdn.microsoft.com/xml/reference/schema/datatypes.asp.

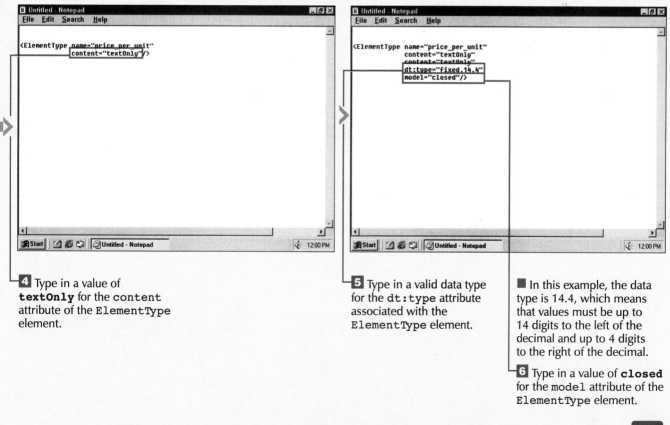

4 Type in a value of **textOnly** for the content attribute of the ElementType element.

5 Type in a valid data type for the dt:type attribute associated with the ElementType element.

■ In this example, the data type is 14.4, which means that values must be up to 14 digits to the left of the decimal and up to 4 digits to the right of the decimal.

6 Type in a value of **closed** for the model attribute of the ElementType element.

DESCRIBE ELEMENTS

You can document the elements and attributes in your XML schema using the `description` element. Microsoft's schema implementation, the MSXML parser, supports the `description` element.

While documenting schema rules using standard XML comments is possible, Microsoft designed the `description` element to provide developers with an alternative, more structured method for documenting schema rules. Using a `description` element in place of a comment can be useful, because

- Unlike comments, `description` values can be accessed at runtime through the document object model, if necessary.
- Unlike comments, the presence of `description` values — and, therefore, of schema documentation — can be determined programmatically.

The MSXML processor does not use the value of a `description` element to validate XML data; it merely passes `description` values on to the XML processing application. Description values are intended for human readers only.

Here is the syntax:

`<description>`*descriptionText*`</description>`

descriptionText is descriptive text.

You can declare a `description` element as part of

- An `ElementType` element
- An `AttributeType` element

DESCRIBE ELEMENTS

1 Open the schema file to which you want to add a descriptive element.

2 Type in the opening **<description>** tag (all lowercase).

Extra

The description element was designed to provide developers with an alternative to comments as a standard way to document schema rules. The MSXML processor does use the value of a description element to validate XML data; description values are intended for human readers only. The contents of a description element can be accessed at runtime through the document object model.

Chapter 7 discusses at length AttributeType elements, which you use with the attribute element to declare attributes in a schema.

To see the latest syntax for the description element, visit Microsoft's Web site at http://msdn.microsoft.com/xml/reference/schema/description.asp.

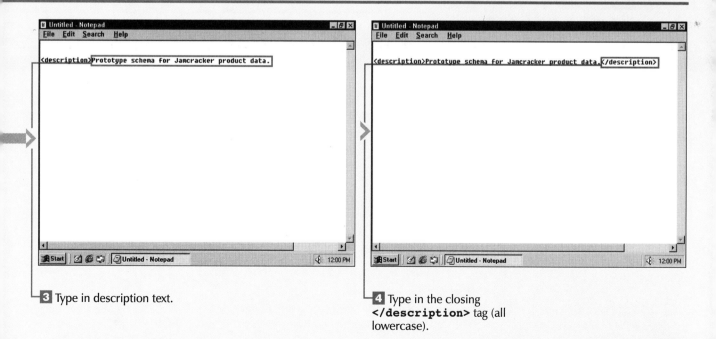

3 Type in description text.

4 Type in the closing **</description>** tag (all lowercase).

DECLARE AN ATTRIBUTE (ATTRIBUTETYPE)

Y ou can declare attributes to describe XML elements. Before you can declare an attribute, you must first declare a type of attribute (an AttributeType).

Here is the syntax:

```
<AttributeType
default="default-value"
dt:type="primitive-type"
dt:values="enumerated-values"
name="idref"
required="{yes | no}" >
<attribute type="idref">
```

default-value refers to the default value for this attribute, if any.

primitive-type specifies the data type for this attribute (one of entity, entities, enumeration, id, idref, idrefs, nmtoken, nmtokens, notation, string).

enumerated-values: when *primitive-type* is set to enumeration, *enumerated-values* specify enumeration values.

idref is the name of the attribute; used for internal reference. *yes | no* specifies whether a value for this attribute is required to exist at runtime.

This section shows you how to declare an attribute using the AttributeType and attribute elements defined and supported in MSXML.

DECLARE AN ATTRIBUTE (ATTRIBUTETYPE)

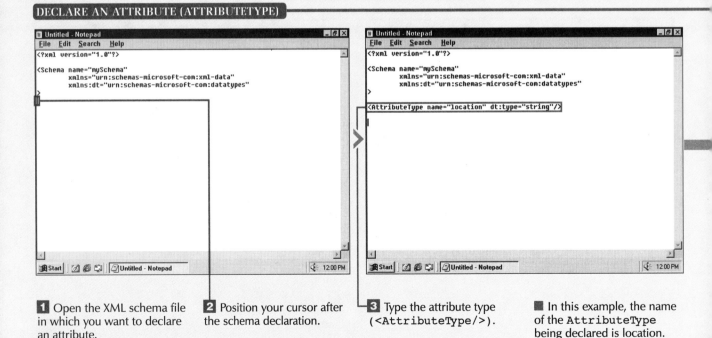

1 Open the XML schema file in which you want to declare an attribute.

2 Position your cursor after the schema declaration.

3 Type the attribute type (<AttributeType/>).

■ In this example, the name of the AttributeType being declared is location.

Extra

This section shows you how to declare an attribute using the *AttributeType* and *attribute* elements defined and supported in MSXML. To declare an attribute, you first declare an attribute *type*.

You use the AttributeType element to declare a type of attribute, specifying

- The default value for this type of attribute
- The data type of this type of attribute
- The enumerated values of this type of attribute, if appropriate
- The name of this type of attribute
- Whether this type of attribute is considered required or optional

After you declare an attribute type, you declare an *instance* of the attribute. You use the attribute element to create a specific instance of the attribute and associate it with a specific element, specifying

- The default value for an instance of this attribute
- The attribute type associated with an instance of this attribute
- Whether an instance of this attribute is considered required or optional

At runtime, you can extract an attribute value and process it.

Untitled - Notepad
File Edit Search Help

```
<?xml version="1.0"?>

<Schema name="mySchema"
        xmlns="urn:schemas-microsoft-com:xml-data"
        xmlns:dt="urn:schemas-microsoft-com:datatypes"
>

<AttributeType name="location" dt:type="string"/>

<ElementType name="name" content="textOnly" model="closed">


</ElementType>
```

Start | Untitled - Notepad | 12:00 PM

Untitled - Notepad
File Edit Search Help

```
<?xml version="1.0"?>

<Schema name="mySchema"
        xmlns="urn:schemas-microsoft-com:xml-data"
        xmlns:dt="urn:schemas-microsoft-com:datatypes"
>

<AttributeType name="location" dt:type="string"/>

<ElementType name="name" content="textOnly" model="closed">
    <attribute type="location"/>
</ElementType>
```

Start | Untitled - Notepad | 12:00 PM

■4 Type a declaration for the ElementType for which you want to declare an attribute.

■ In this example, the name of the ElementType being declared is name.

■5 Type the attribute declaration.

■ In this example, an attribute of type location is being declared.

■6 Save the file.

DECLARE AN ATTRIBUTE FOR CHARACTER DATA

You can declare an attribute in an XML schema that accepts only character data, or *string* values, at runtime.

Here is the syntax:

```
<AttributeType
default="default-value"
dt:type="string"
name="idref"
```

required="{yes | no}" >

```
<attribute type="idref">
```

default-value refers to the default value for this attribute, if any.

idref is the name of the attribute; used for internal reference.

yes | no specifies whether a value for this attribute is required to exist at runtime.

DECLARE AN ATTRIBUTE FOR CHARACTER DATA

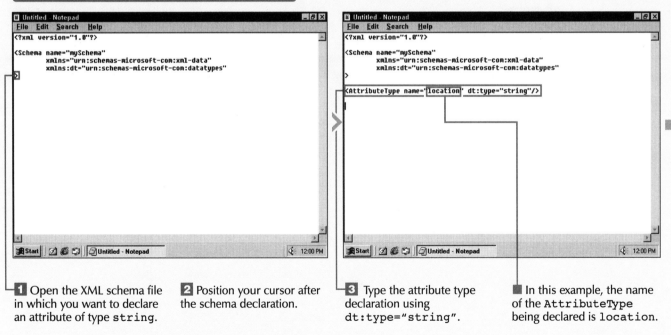

■1 Open the XML schema file in which you want to declare an attribute of type `string`.

■2 Position your cursor after the schema declaration.

■3 Type the attribute type declaration using `dt:type="string"`.

■ In this example, the name of the `AttributeType` being declared is `location`.

Extra

The *string* data type corresponds directly to the CDATA data type supported in DTD syntax. Valid strings can contain

- Letters (a, b, c. . .)
- Numbers (1, 2, 3. . .)
- White space
- Special characters (hyphen, period, colon, and so on)

The string data type is typically used either to enable freeform text entry (such as a comment field) or as the basis for additional validation routines. For example, if your design requirements dictate that you validate an attribute's value by checking for the existence of a specific pattern, you can declare that attribute as type string in the DTD. Then, in a separate XML processing application, you can examine the contents of that attribute and apply additional validation checks. You see an example of creating an XML-processing application in Chapter 13.

For a complete list of the data types MSXML supports, visit http://msdn.microsoft.com/xml/reference/schema/datatypes.asp.

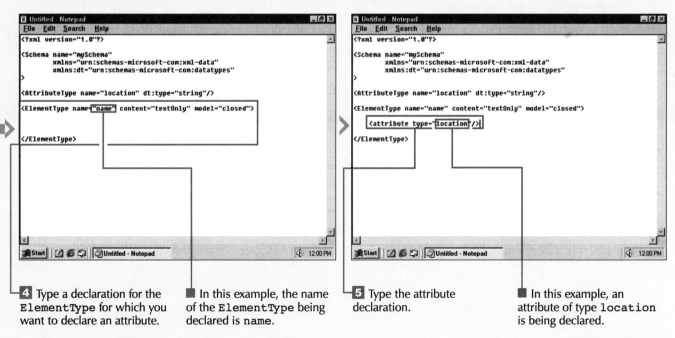

■ 4 Type a declaration for the ElementType for which you want to declare an attribute.

■ In this example, the name of the ElementType being declared is name.

■ 5 Type the attribute declaration.

■ In this example, an attribute of type location is being declared.

DECLARE AN NMTOKEN ATTRIBUTE

Y ou can define a schema validation rule, using the nmtoken data type, to constrain the value of an XML attribute to a single word, or *token*.

Here is the syntax:

```
<AttributeType
default="default-value"
dt:type="nmtoken"
name="idref"
required="{yes | no}" >
<attribute type="idref">
```

default-value refers to the default value for this attribute, if any.

idref is the name of the attribute; used for internal reference.

yes | no specifies whether a value for this attribute is required to exist at runtime.

Department and employee codes typically comprise both letters and numbers, but no white space (in other words, no spaces, tabs, or returns). To model such an application-specific code, you can use the NMTOKEN keyword. Attributes of this type are traditionally used as primary and foreign keys in relational data-based applications because they disallow special characters and white space. To use an attribute as a primary key, type the #REQUIRED keyword; foreign keys can include the #IMPLIED keyword.

DECLARE AN NMTOKEN ATTRIBUTE

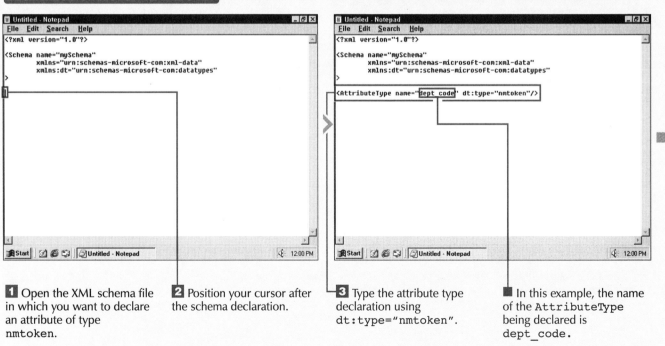

■1 Open the XML schema file in which you want to declare an attribute of type nmtoken.

■2 Position your cursor after the schema declaration.

■3 Type the attribute type declaration using dt:type="nmtoken".

■ In this example, the name of the AttributeType being declared is dept_code.

Extra

Only the following characters can appear in a valid token value:

- Letters (a, b, c. . .)
- Numbers (1, 2, 3. . .)
- Underscore (_)
- Hyphen (-)
- Period (.)

A valid token must begin with one of the following characters:

- A letter
- An underscore

Attributes of type nmtoken are distinguished from attributes of type string by one difference: Valid attributes of type string can contain white space; valid attributes of type nmtoken cannot.

To constrain a value to a collection of tokens, you can use the nmtokens data type.

The nmtoken and nmtokens data types correspond to the NMTOKEN and NMTOKENS keywords supported in DTDs, respectively.

For a complete list of the data types MSXML supports, visit http://msdn.microsoft.com/xml/reference/schema/datatypes.asp.

```
Untitled - Notepad
File  Edit  Search  Help
<?xml version="1.0"?>

<Schema name="mySchema"
        xmlns="urn:schemas-microsoft-com:xml-data"
        xmlns:dt="urn:schemas-microsoft-com:datatypes"
>

<AttributeType name="dept_code" dt:type="nmtoken"/>

<ElementType name="marketing_info" content="eltOnly" model="closed">


</ElementType>
```

```
Untitled - Notepad
File  Edit  Search  Help
<?xml version="1.0"?>

<Schema name="mySchema"
        xmlns="urn:schemas-microsoft-com:xml-data"
        xmlns:dt="urn:schemas-microsoft-com:datatypes"
>

<AttributeType name="dept_code" dt:type="nmtoken"/>

<ElementType name="marketing_info" content="eltOnly" model="closed">
    <attribute type="dept_code"/>
</ElementType>
```

4 Type a declaration for the ElementType for which you want to declare an attribute.

■ In this example, the name of the ElementType being declared is marketing_info.

5 Type the attribute declaration.

■ In this example, an attribute of type dept_code is being declared.

6 Save the file.

RESTRICT AN ATTRIBUTE TO DEFINED OPTIONS

You can declare a schema validation rule to constrain the value of an XML attribute to one in a list of predefined options. In other words, this section shows you how to declare an attribute of type *enumerated list*, or *enumeration*. Declaring attributes in this way helps reduce input errors and is a good approach for attributes where all possible values are known at design time — for example, state or province codes, internally developed codes, or any other finite options.

Here is the syntax:

```
<AttributeType
default="default-value"
dt:type="enumeration"
```

```
dt:values="enumerated-values"
name="idref"
required="{yes | no}" >
<attribute type="idref">
```

default-value refers to the default value for this attribute, if any.

enumerated-values is a list of valid space-delimited values.

idref is the name of the attribute; used for internal reference.

yes | no specifies whether a value for this attribute is required to exist at runtime.

RESTRICT AN ATTRIBUTE TO DEFINED OPTIONS

1 Open the XML schema file in which you want to declare an attribute of type enumeration.

2 Position your cursor after the schema declaration.

3 Type the attribute type declaration using dt:type="enumeration".

■ In this example, the name of the **AttributeType** being declared is **currency**. Valid values include **USD** and **CD**.

Extra

You can specify additional values for an enumerated attribute by separating each value with white space.

Example:

```
dt:values="USD CD MP DM"
```

The enumeration data type provided in Microsoft's schema implementation corresponds with the following DTD syntax:

```
<!ATTLIST price_per_unit
currency (USD | CD | MP | DM)
   >
```

Chapter 4 shows you how to declare an attribute of type enumerated list in a DTD.

For a complete list of the data types MSXML supports, visit http://msdn.microsoft.com/xml/reference/schema/datatypes.asp.

```
<?xml version="1.0"?>

<Schema name="mySchema"
        xmlns="urn:schemas-microsoft-com:xml-data"
        xmlns:dt="urn:schemas-microsoft-com:datatypes"
>

<AttributeType name="currency"
               dt:type="enumeration"
               dt:values="USD CD"/>

<ElementType name="price_per_unit">

</ElementType>
```

```
<?xml version="1.0"?>

<Schema name="mySchema"
        xmlns="urn:schemas-microsoft-com:xml-data"
        xmlns:dt="urn:schemas-microsoft-com:datatypes"
>

<AttributeType name="currency"
               dt:type="enumeration"
               dt:values="USD CD"/>

<ElementType name="price_per_unit">

    <attribute type="currency" required="yes"/>

</ElementType>
```

■ **4** Type a declaration for the ElementType for which you want to declare an attribute.

■ In this example, the name of the ElementType being declared is price_per_unit.

■ **5** Type the attribute declaration.

■ In this example, an attribute of type currency is being declared.

■ **6** Save the file.

DECLARE A UNIQUE IDENTIFIER ATTRIBUTE

Y ou can constrain an attribute to accept only values that are unique across the XML document at runtime. You do so by declaring an attribute as type *id*. Here is the syntax:

```
<AttributeType

default="default-value"

dt:type="id"

name="idref"

required="{yes | no}" >

<attribute type="idref">
```

default-value refers to the default value for this attribute, if any.

idref is the name of the attribute; used for internal reference.

yes | no specifies whether a value for this attribute is required to exist at runtime.

Unique identifiers, or *primary keys*, are an essential component of virtually all database systems, including the flat-file databases that XML documents represent. You can associate unique identifiers with identifier references, called IDREFs in XML, to model logical relationships between XML data records.

DECLARE A UNIQUE IDENTIFIER ATTRIBUTE

```
<?xml version="1.0"?>

<Schema name="mySchema"
        xmlns="urn:schemas-microsoft-com:xml-data"
        xmlns:dt="urn:schemas-microsoft-com:datatypes">
>
```

```
<?xml version="1.0"?>

<Schema name="mySchema"
        xmlns="urn:schemas-microsoft-com:xml-data"
        xmlns:dt="urn:schemas-microsoft-com:datatypes">
>

<AttributeType name="product_code" dt:type="id"/>
```

1 Open the XML schema file in which you want to declare an attribute of type id.

2 Position your cursor after the schema declaration.

3 Type the attribute type declaration using dt:type="id".

■ In this example, the name of the AttributeType being declared is product_code.

Extra

Unique identifiers are an essential component of virtually all database systems — including the flat-file databases that XML documents represent. Using a schema, you can enforce relationships between primary keys (attributes of type *id*) and identifier references, or *foreign keys* (attributes of type *idref*).

Valid values for an attribute declared as type *id* may contain letters, spaces, or underscores, but must begin with a letter or an underscore. Valid *id* values must also be unique within the XML document.

For a complete list of the data types MSXML supports, visit http://msdn.microsoft.com/xml/reference/schema/datatypes.asp.

```
Untitled - Notepad
File  Edit  Search  Help
<?xml version="1.0"?>

<Schema name="mySchema"
        xmlns="urn:schemas-microsoft-com:xml-data"
        xmlns:dt="urn:schemas-microsoft-com:datatypes"
>

<AttributeType name="product_code" dt:type="id"/>

<ElementType name="product" content="eltOnly" model="closed">


</ElementType>
```

```
Untitled - Notepad
File  Edit  Search  Help
<?xml version="1.0"?>

<Schema name="mySchema"
        xmlns="urn:schemas-microsoft-com:xml-data"
        xmlns:dt="urn:schemas-microsoft-com:datatypes"
>

<AttributeType name="product_code" dt:type="id"/>

<ElementType name="product" content="eltOnly" model="closed">

    <attribute type="product_code"/>

</ElementType>
```

4 Type a declaration for the **ElementType** for which you want to declare an attribute.

■ In this example, the name of the **ElementType** being declared is **product**.

5 Type the attribute declaration.

■ In this example, an attribute of type **product_code** is being declared.

6 Save the file.

DECLARE AN IDENTIFIER REFERENCE

You can define a schema validation rule to ensure that the value of an XML attribute matches a previously defined unique identifier. To do so, you declare an attribute of type *idref* and associate it with an attribute of type *id*.

Here is the syntax:

```
<AttributeType

default="default-value"

dt:type="idref"

name="idref"

required="{yes | no}" >
```

```
<attribute type="idref">
```

default-value refers to the default value for this attribute, if any.

idref is the name of the attribute; used for internal reference.

yes | no specifies whether a value for this attribute is required to exist at runtime.

For example, you may want to associate information with a unique department, product, or employee code. You can implement this relationship by declaring one attribute as type *idref* and associating it with another attribute that has been declared as type *id*.

DECLARE AN IDENTIFIER REFERENCE

```
Untitled - Notepad                                          _ 8 X
File  Edit  Search  Help
<?xml version="1.0"?>

<Schema name="mySchema"
        xmlns="urn:schemas-microsoft-com:xml-data"
        xmlns:dt="urn:schemas-microsoft-com:datatypes"
>
```

```
Untitled - Notepad                                          _ 8 X
File  Edit  Search  Help
<?xml version="1.0"?>

<Schema name="mySchema"
        xmlns="urn:schemas-microsoft-com:xml-data"
        xmlns:dt="urn:schemas-microsoft-com:datatypes"
>

<AttributeType name="bestseller" dt:type="idref"/>
```

1 Open the XML schema file in which you want to declare an attribute of type **id**.

2 Position your cursor after the schema declaration.

3 Type the attribute type declaration using **dt:type="idref"**.

■ In this example, the name of the **AttributeType** being declared is **bestseller**.

Extra

Using a schema, you can enforce relationships between primary keys (attributes of type *id*) and identifier references, or *foreign keys* (attributes of type *idref*).

```
Untitled - Notepad
File  Edit  Search  Help
<?xml version="1.0"?>

<Schema name="mySchema"
        xmlns="urn:schemas-microsoft-com:xml-data"
        xmlns:dt="urn:schemas-microsoft-com:datatypes"
>

<AttributeType name="bestseller" dt:type="idref"/>

<ElementType name="name" content="textOnly" model="closed">


</ElementType>
```

```
Untitled - Notepad
File  Edit  Search  Help
<?xml version="1.0"?>

<Schema name="mySchema"
        xmlns="urn:schemas-microsoft-com:xml-data"
        xmlns:dt="urn:schemas-microsoft-com:datatypes"
>

<AttributeType name="bestseller" dt:type="idref"/>

<ElementType name="name" content="textOnly" model="closed">

    <attribute type="bestseller"/>

</ElementType>
```

■ Start ☑ 🥯 ⟶ Untitled - Notepad 🔶 12:00 PM

4 Type a declaration for the **ElementType** for which you want to declare an attribute.

■ In this example, the name of the **ElementType** being declared is **name**.

5 Type the attribute declaration.

■ In this example, an attribute of type **bestseller** is being declared.

6 Save the file.

REFERENCE A BUILT-IN DATA TYPE

You can declare a schema validation rule to ensure that the value of an XML attribute is of a built-in data type, such as integer, boolean, string, or date.

To reference a built-in data type, you must first declare the namespace that Microsoft requires for schema data type support. The namespace declaration looks like this:

```
xmlns:dt="urn:schemas-microsoft-
com:datatypes"
```

After you declare the namespace, you can reference your choice of data type:

```
<AttributeType name="name"
dt:type="dataType"/>
```

name is the name of an attribute type.

dt matches the prefix assigned to the data type's namespace and *dataType* is the name of a supported data type, such as int, bool, notation, or string.

REFERENCE A BUILT-IN DATA TYPE

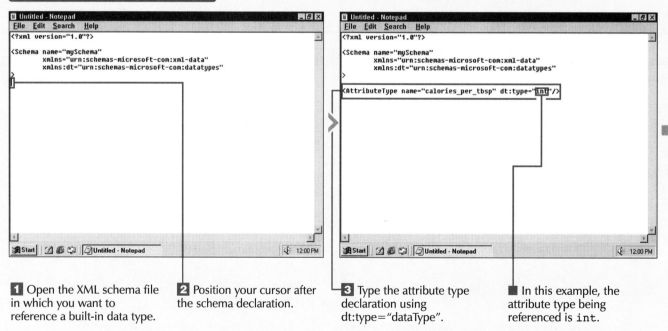

1 Open the XML schema file in which you want to reference a built-in data type.

2 Position your cursor after the schema declaration.

3 Type the attribute type declaration using dt:type="dataType".

■ In this example, the attribute type being referenced is int.

Extra

At runtime, Microsoft's MSXML validating parser resolves the dt namespace and checks the value of the attribute against its predefined rules for the specified *dataType*.

Using a schema, you can enforce sophisticated data typing at runtime without custom processing code. Some of the data types Microsoft's MSXML supports are

- bin.base64 — MIME-style Base64 encoded binary BLOB

- boolean — 0 or 1, where 0 = "false" and 1 = "true"

- dateTime — Date with optional time and optional zone

- float — Floating-point number

- i1 — Integer represented in one byte (-127 to 128)

For a complete list of the data types Microsoft's MSXML supports, visit http://msdn.microsoft.com/xml/reference/schema/datatypes.asp.

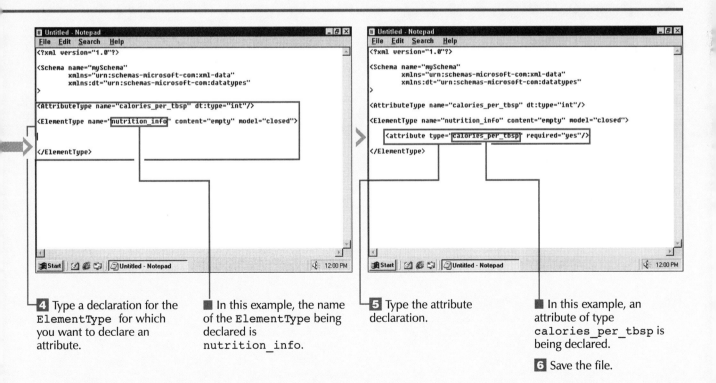

4 Type a declaration for the **ElementType** for which you want to declare an attribute.

■ In this example, the name of the **ElementType** being declared is **nutrition_info**.

5 Type the attribute declaration.

■ In this example, an attribute of type **calories_per_tbsp** is being declared.

6 Save the file.

ATTACH THE SCHEMA TO AN XML DOCUMENT

You can reference a schema from inside an XML document so that, at runtime, a validating parser applies schema rules to the XML data and validates the document.

Here is the syntax:

```
<root_element

    xmlns= "x-schema:URI">
```

root_element is the root element of the XML document to which you want to apply the schema.

URI, or uniform resource identifier, is the name of the schema you want to attach. (The x-schema: prefix is required by the MSXML processor; you cannot substitute your own prefix for x-schema:)

ATTACH THE SCHEMA TO AN XML DOCUMENT

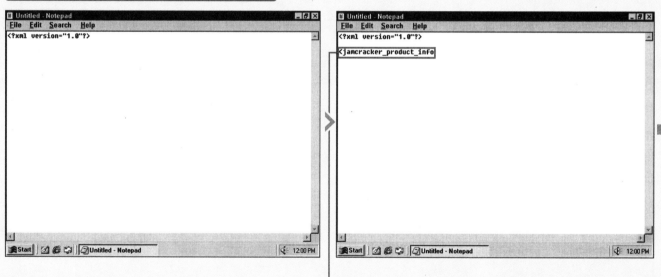

1 Open the XML file to which you want to attach a schema.

■ This file can be an existing XML document or a new Notepad file.

2 Type the opening angle bracket (<) followed by the name of the root element declared in the XML document.

■ In this example, the name of the root element is jamcracker_product_info

Extra

Like DTDs, schemas enable you to separate data (the XML document) from data validation rules (DTDs and schemas). You save a schema in its own file, separate from your XML document; then you incorporate the schema into your XML document using a special namespace declaration supported by Microsoft's MSXML validating parser (as shown in this example).

At runtime, the MSXML processor checks the structure and type of the XML data against the validation rules declared in the schema file and generates either a failure or success message.

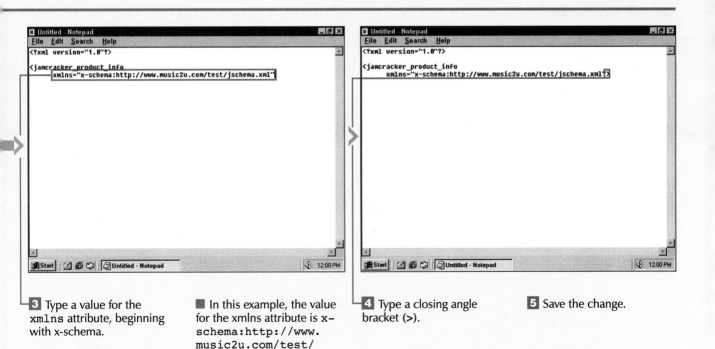

3 Type a value for the xmlns attribute, beginning with x-schema.

■ In this example, the value for the xmlns attribute is x-schema:http://www.music2u.com/test/jschema.xml.

4 Type a closing angle bracket (>).

5 Save the change.

VALIDATE AN XML FILE

Y ou can validate an XML file against a schema using Microsoft's validating parser.

After you create a schema and reference it within an XML document, you are ready to validate your XML document. You do so by loading the XML document into Microsoft's XML Validator and monitoring the failure or success message the XML Validator generates. If the XML Validator generates an error message, you can use the information it provides to correct any errors in the schema, including any discrepancies between the XML and schema files.

At the time of this writing, the XML Validator is the only validating parser that supports schemas. Because the XML Validator is currently available as a demo only, the results you see when you perform this section may differ slightly from those presented here.

Note: Before completing the steps in this section, make sure you have established a working Internet connection.

VALIDATE AN XML FILE

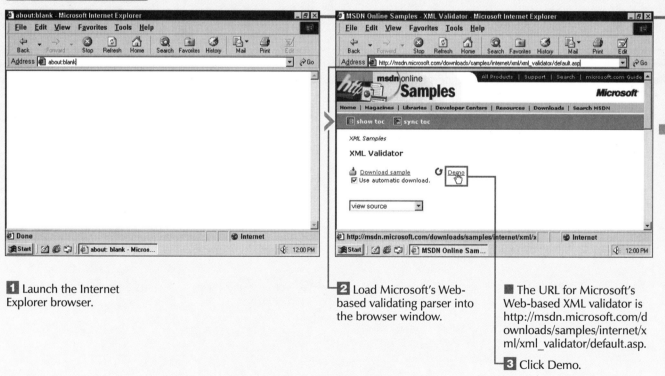

1 Launch the Internet Explorer browser.

2 Load Microsoft's Web-based validating parser into the browser window.

■ The URL for Microsoft's Web-based XML validator is http://msdn.microsoft.com/downloads/samples/internet/xml/xml_validator/default.asp.

3 Click Demo.

Extra

Clicking the root element (in this example, `ELEMENT: jamcracker_product_info`) expands that root element to show you all the contained elements and attributes defined in the XML data file.

Unlike standard DTD support, standard schema support is not available in all validating parsers. The only widely available validating parser that currently supports schemas is Microsoft's validating parser, which is available on the Web in demo form.

By the time you read this, Microsoft's validating parser may appear or behave differently than you see in this section, and new schema-supporting parsers may become available. For details on the latest World Wide Web Consortium activity pertaining to schemas, check out the latest working drafts on schema structures and data types, at www.w3.org/TR/1999/WD-xmlschema-1-19991217 and www.w3.org/TR/xmlschema-2/, respectively.

XML Validator

Close This Sample

Enter a url to load:

`http://www.music2u.com/test/task9.xml`

or paste in some XML:

PASTE

check the "Validation" box if you want to validate your document:

☑ Validation

click the "Validate" button to see if your text is valid XML:

VALIDATE

check the "Validation" box if you want to validate your document:

☑ Validation

click the "Validate" button to see if your text is valid XML:

VALIDATE

Your XML is well formed and is validated

- o PI: xml
- o PI: xml-stylesheet type="text/xsl" href="task9.xsl"
- • ELEMENT: jamcracker_product_info

2000 Microsoft Corporation. All rights reserved. Terms of use.

■ The XML Validator window appears.

4 Type the name of a schema-referencing XML document into the input field.

■ The XML document must reside on a Web server. In this example, the fully qualified name of the XML document is www.music2u.com/test/task9.xml.

5 Click the Validate button.

■ The validation results appear.

CREATE A SIMPLE CASCADING STYLE SHEET

You can create a simple cascading style sheet (CSS) to format and display XML data elements. Using CSS, you can separate data from its presentation details (such as font size, color, and placement; see Chapters 9 and 10). This separation enables

- Experimentation with data presentation techniques without altering (or introducing errors into) a data file.

- Fast application of the same presentation effects in other data files.

- Different presentation of a data file.

Here is the syntax:

```
elementName {
property: value;
...
}
```

elementName is the name of any XML element. *property* is one of many display properties, including font-related, color-related, and text-related properties. *value* is any appropriate CSS value for the specified *property*.

You must separate CSS properties and values with a colon (:) and end each property-value pair with a semicolon (;). You can add white space (spaces, tabs, or returns) to your CSS declarations to improve readability.

CREATE A SIMPLE CASCADING STYLE SHEET

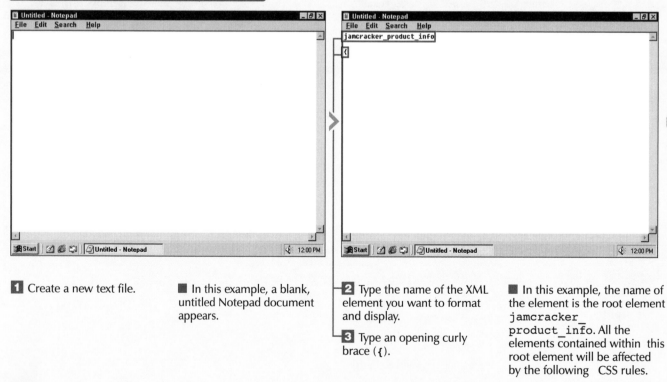

1 Create a new text file.

■ In this example, a blank, untitled Notepad document appears.

2 Type the name of the XML element you want to format and display.

3 Type an opening curly brace ({).

■ In this example, the name of the element is the root element `jamcracker_product_info`. All the elements contained within this root element will be affected by the following CSS rules.

Extra

In theory, CSS is a relatively easy way to format XML data. Unfortunately, it poses drawbacks for real-life XML applications:

- CSS only presents data that appears in the XML document, and only in the order in which the data appears.

- CSS support for XML documents is not complete. For example, in Internet Explorer 5.*x*, default namespaces declared in XML are not recognized by CSS.

For technical specifications, a quick reference guide to CSS properties and values, and Microsoft-specific XML/CSS tips, visit

- www.w3.org/Style/CSS/

- www.builder.com/Authoring/CSS/ss11.html

- http://msdn.microsoft.com/xml/xsluide/browsing-css.asp

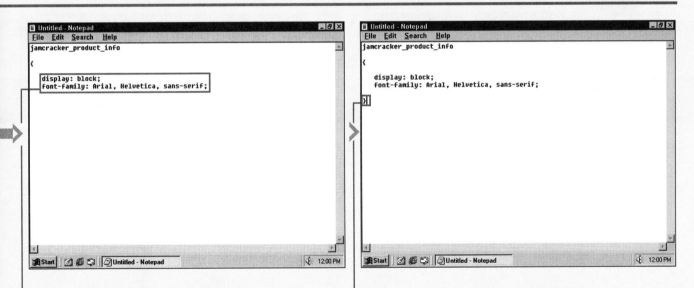

4 Type the CSS rules you want to apply to the XML element(s).

■ In this example, the CSS rules display XML values on separate lines (`display: block`) and in any of three common font styles (`font-family: Arial, Helvetica, sans-serif`).

5 Type the closing curly bracket (`}`).

6 Save the file using the .css extension.

ADD A COMMENT

You can add a comment to a cascading style sheet to improve readability, maintenance, and debugging.

Tool support for CSS and XML is maturing with the CSS and XML specifications. Support for cascading style sheets varies among browsers (even between different browser versions), which makes creating cross-platform CSS/XML applications difficult. In addition, CSS syntax is fairly cryptic; and although the length of a cascading style sheet varies according to the amount of data it can format and display, CSS tend to be quite lengthy.

In light of these challenges, thorough documentation as demonstrated in this section is crucial. Documenting your style sheets makes rules (including browser-specific workarounds) easily understood by human readers. You document a CSS by including a special comment line:

```
/* comment */
```

ADD A COMMENT

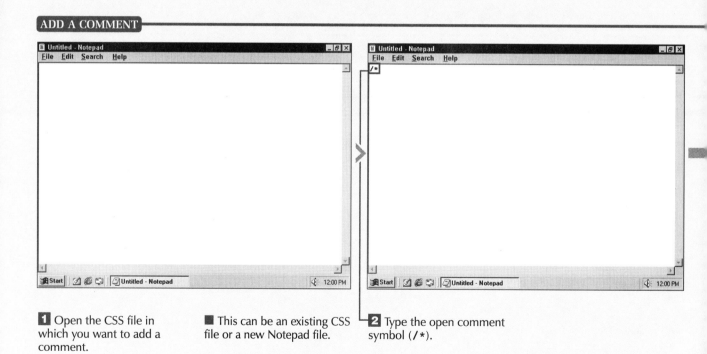

1 Open the CSS file in which you want to add a comment.

■ This can be an existing CSS file or a new Notepad file.

2 Type the open comment symbol (/*).

Extra

A comment can appear anywhere inside a CSS file *except* between property/value pairs. For example, the following comment is *invalid*:

```
jamcracker_product_info
{
    display: /* invalid comment
placement */ block
}
```

Comments can span multiple lines but cannot be nested.

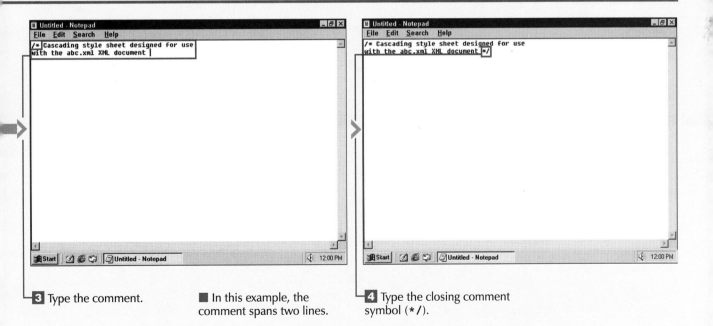

3 Type the comment.

■ In this example, the comment spans two lines.

4 Type the closing comment symbol (***/**).

ADD STYLE RULES TO DISPLAY ELEMENTS

You can add CSS rules to format and display individual XML elements differently. You can specify display options related to font style, color, text appearance, and image placement.

The *cascading* capability of CSS means that the options specified for a container element apply to contained elements. For example, if all text in the root element is specified as bright red, all the text values for the XML document automatically are bright red, as well.

You *override* cascaded options simply by specifying new display options for individual contained elements. Here is the syntax:

```
elementName {
```

```
property: value;...
}
containedElementName {
property: value;...
}
...
```

elementName is the name of any XML element. *containedElementName* is the name of any XML contained in *elementName*.

property is one of many display properties, including font-related, color-related, and text-related properties. *value* is any appropriate CSS value for the specified property (See Chapters 9 and 10.)

ADD STYLE RULES TO DISPLAY ELEMENTS

Untitled - Notepad
File   Edit   Search   Help

Untitled - Notepad
File   Edit   Search   Help
```
jamcracker_product_info
{
        display: block;
        font-family: Arial, Helvetica, sans-serif;
}
```

Start | Untitled - Notepad | 12:00 PM

Start | Untitled - Notepad | 12:00 PM

1 Open the CSS file in which you want to add an element display rule.

■ This can be an existing CSS file or a new Notepad file.

2 Type a CSS rule for a container element.

■ In this example, the container element is the root element (`jamcracker _product_info`) of an XML file.

Extra

CSS enable you to display

- XML elements only. You cannot add descriptions, column headings, or any other display-oriented elements to an XML document using a CSS.

- XML elements in the order in which they appear in the XML document. You cannot display XML elements in any other order than the order they were declared in the XML document.

Given these restrictions, when developing your XML applications you may need to

- Incorporate display-specific data in your XML document.

- Investigate XML style sheets. While they are currently more challenging to develop, XML style sheets offer far more flexibility in formatting and displaying XML data than do CSS. You create an XML style sheet in Chapter 11.

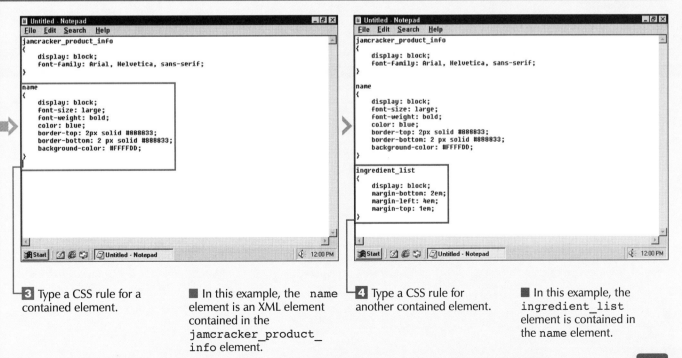

-3 Type a CSS rule for a contained element.

■ In this example, the `name` element is an XML element contained in the `jamcracker_product_info` element.

-4 Type a CSS rule for another contained element.

■ In this example, the `ingredient_list` element is contained in the `name` element.

ADD STYLE RULES TO SUPPRESS ELEMENTS

You can use cascading style sheet rules to prevent specified XML elements from being displayed.

Here is the syntax:

```
elementName [, elementName...]
{
```

```
    display: none;
}
```

elementName is the name of an XML element of which you want to suppress display.

ADD STYLE RULES TO SUPPRESS ELEMENTS

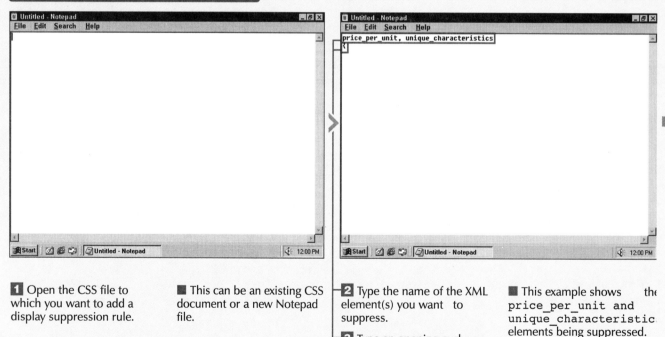

■ **1** Open the CSS file to which you want to add a display suppression rule.

■ This can be an existing CSS document or a new Notepad file.

■ **2** Type the name of the XML element(s) you want to suppress.

■ **3** Type an opening curly bracket (**{**).

■ This example shows the `price_per_unit` and `unique_characteristic` elements being suppressed.

Extra

Any element not explicitly suppressed appears by default. For example, a CSS that contains only

```
jamcracker_product_info
{
    display: block;
}
```

concatenates and displays all the XML elements contained in the root XML element.

Suppressing element display is useful when testing a cascading style sheet.One of the benefits cascading style sheets provide — the ability to separate XML data from the presentation of that data — lies in the ability to apply multiple style sheets to a single XML document.

For example, by developing three different style sheets, you can present the same XML document

- As a sophisticated, colorful document.

- As a pared-down, printer-friendly document.

- In large-size text for sight-impaired visitors.

You can also create separate style sheets for diverse audiences; for example, you can present the same XML document optimized and formatted specifically for

- Company employees.

- Customers.

- Business partners.

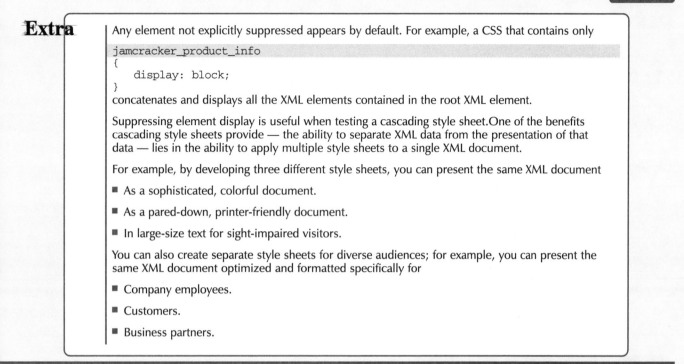

■4 Type the **display: none;** directive.

■5 Type the closing curly bracket (**}**).

■ The Open dialog box appears.

VALIDATE THE CASCADING STYLE SHEET

You can validate (test and debug) your cascading style sheet syntax through an online validation service.

In the future, XML development tools may integrate XML, DTD, schema, and style sheet development. Until then, you must develop and test each component of your XML application separately.

Several tools can help you debug cascading style sheets. In this section, you use an online CSS validation service. Online validation services do not require you to download or configure software; you load the interface for the online service in your Web browser and specify the fully qualified name (which includes the path) of a CSS document to test.

VALIDATE THE CASCADING STYLE SHEET

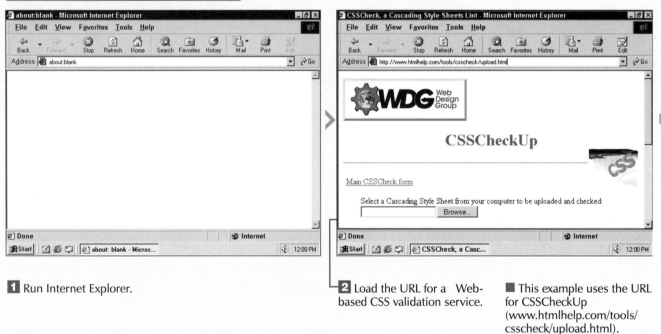

1 Run Internet Explorer.

2 Load the URL for a Web-based CSS validation service.

■ This example uses the URL for CSSCheckUp (www.htmlhelp.com/tools/csscheck/upload.html).

Extra

The World Wide Web Consortium produced the first CSS recommendation in 1996. Cascading style sheets were designed to be applied to many different types of documents; however, in practice, they were applied almost exclusively to HTML documents until the advent of XML.

As a result, most CSS validation tools and services still enforce HTML-based rules rather than XML-based rules. For example, in XML, you can use underscores to define an element; in HTML, you cannot.

3 Type the name of the CSS file you want to validate into the validation interface.

■ In this example, the fully qualified filename of the CSS file to check is c:\xml\chapter8\valid.css.

4 Validate the CSS file.

■ In this example, clicking the Check It! button begins the CSS file validation process.

5 Examine the validation results.

■ In this example, no validation errors were reported.

ATTACH A CASCADING STYLE SHEET TO A FILE

You can attach a cascading style sheet to an XML document. At runtime, when you load the CSS-referencing XML document into Internet Explorer, MSXML applies the style sheet rules to format and display the XML data.

Here is the syntax:

```
<?xml-stylesheet
type="stylesheetType"
href="stylesheetFile"?>
```

stylesheetType is the MIME type of the style sheet to attach to an XML document. Valid MIME type values

for the *stylesheetType* attribute include

`text/css`, which specifies a cascading style sheet

`text/xsl`, which specifies an XML style sheet

stylesheetFile is the name of the cascading style sheet document to attach; for example, abc.css. The CSS file is assumed to reside in the same directory as the XML file to which it is attached unless a fully qualified filename is specified.

ATTACH A CASCADING STYLE SHEET TO A FILE

1 Open the XML document in which you want to create the CSS reference.

■ This file can be an existing XML document or a new Notepad file.

2 Type the beginning xml-stylesheet processing instruction (**<?xml-stylesheet type="text/css"**) after the xml directive.

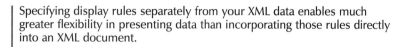
Extra

Specifying display rules separately from your XML data enables much greater flexibility in presenting data than incorporating those rules directly into an XML document.

For example, an XML document can have different CSS documents for

- Wholesale customers
- Retail customers
- Employees

In this case, each CSS displays only that data relevant to the target audience. If a new group — for example, an export cooperative — requested a slightly different report, a design team can simply create a new CSS. They do not have to redesign the XML data representation itself, so their existing audiences are not affected.

■ Untitled - Notepad
File Edit Search Help

```
<?xml version="1.0"?>

<?xml-stylesheet type="text/css" href="master.css"
```

Start Untitled - Notepad 12:00 PM

■ Untitled - Notepad
File Edit Search Help

```
<?xml version="1.0"?>

<?xml-stylesheet type="text/css" href="master.css"?>
```

Start Untitled - Notepad 12:00 PM

3 Specify the name of the cascading style sheet file you want to apply to this XML document at runtime by adding a value for the `href` attribute.

■ In this example, the CSS filename is master.css.

4 Type the closing `xml-stylesheet` processing instruction (`?>`).

DISPLAY A FORMATTED XML EXAMPLE

Y ou can display an XML document formatted with a cascading style sheet using Internet Explorer and the built-in MSXML validating parser.

You do so by loading an XML document that contains a reference to a CSS document into Internet Explorer and examining the results.

If the XML file you load into Internet Explorer references a nonexistent CSS, MSXML does not generate an error. Instead, the XML element values are concatenated and displayed in the browser window without any formatting.

DISPLAY A FORMATTED XML EXAMPLE

1 Run Internet Explorer.

2 Click File.

3 Click Open.

■ The Open dialog box appears.

Extra

Cascading style sheets are useful for displaying XML data, because

- They are fairly easy to construct.

- They are a relatively mature technology, so tools are available to help you debug your CSS syntax.

- They are supported in Internet Explorer 5.

CSS have their drawbacks, however:

- Only those elements declared in the XML document can appear using a CSS.

- The order in which XML elements are declared determines the order in which they can appear using a CSS.

- Most CSS tools do not provide support for integrating CSS with XML.

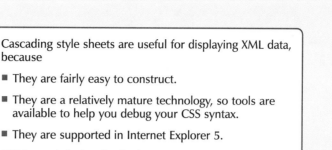

■4 Type the name of the CSS-referencing XML source file you want to open into the Open field.

■ In this example, the fully qualified name of the CSS-referencing XML file is C:\xml\chapter8\task6.xml.

■ You can examine the results.

■ The formatted XML document appears.

USE THE DISPLAY PROPERTY

Using style sheets, you can define exactly how you want text displayed in your document using the `display` property. This allows you more precise control to group together relevant information, or to separate text for special emphasis.

The syntax is

elementName {display:*format*}

elementName is the name of the element to which you want to apply the format. The most common *format* options are:

- `block`: When you specify this format, a line break is placed before and after this element, making it much like a paragraph in a word processor.

- `inline`: The default value, and one that inserts no line breaks. Elements defined as inline line up next to each other.

- `none`: This option tells the browser not to display the specified item. For example, if you are coding a page that retail customers will see, you might use `none` to hide department codes or internal company notes that don't apply to, or won't interest, viewers.

USE THE DISPLAY PROPERTY

```
Untitled - Notepad
File  Edit  Search  Help
/* Cascading style sheet for use with the jamcracker.xml file */

jamcracker product info
{ display: block;}

title

name

price_per_unit, unique_characteristics, rname, rank, test_field, js_function

ingredient_list

ingredient
```

```
Untitled - Notepad
File  Edit  Search  Help
/* Cascading style sheet for use with the jamcracker.xml file */

jamcracker product info
{ display: block;}

title
{ display: block;}

name
{ display: block;}

price per unit, unique_characteristics, rname, rank, test_field, js_function
{ display: none;}

ingredient list
{ display: inline;}

ingredient
{ display: inline;}
```

1 Open or create the style sheet file.

■ See Chapter 8 for details on how to create a basic style sheet.

2 Position the cursor after the item whose display property you want to set.

3 Type **display** and the desired property.

■ This example shows the display set to block.

4 Type `display` properties for the other elements.

Note: The value for the `display` *property is not inherited.*

5 Save the style sheet file.

Extra

The cascading style sheet standards maintained by the World Wide Web Consortium (W3C) are living documents; they change over time as new style sheet elements are proposed, rejected, and accepted. Different versions of Microsoft's Internet Explorer support different versions of the W3C standard. In addition, different versions of Internet Explorer provide additional, non-standard elements called *extensions*.

In terms of the `display` property, Internet Explorer 5.5 provides support for the following format options in addition to `block`, `inline`, and `none`:

FORMAT OPTION	DESCRIPTION
`inline-block`	Object is rendered inline, but the contents of the object are rendered as a `block` element. Adjacent inline elements are rendered on the same line, space permitting.
`list-item`	Object is rendered as a `block` element, and a `list-item` marker is added.
`table-header-group`	Table header always displays before all other rows and row groups, and after any top captions. The header displays on each page spanned by a table.
`table-footer-group`	Table footer always displays after all other rows and row groups, and before any bottom captions. The footer displays on each page spanned by a table.

In contrast, the latest version of the CSS standard (CSS-2, which you can find at `www.w3.org/TR/REC-CSS2/`, suggests the following display options:

`inline`, `block`. `list-item`, `run-in`, `compact`, `marker`, `table`, `inline-table`, `table-row-group`, `table-header-group`, `table-footer-group`, `table-row`, `table-column-group`, `table-column`, `table-cell`, `table-caption`, `none`, and `inherit`.

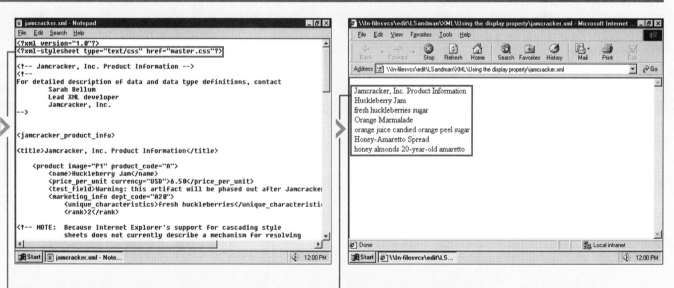

6 If you have not already done so, open up the source code for the Web page you are formatting and attach the style sheet, then close the file.

■ For more information, see Chapter 8.

■ When you open up the Web page in a browser, the page displays the specified type display properties.

USE THE FONT-FAMILY PROPERTY

You can use the `font-family` property to designate which fonts or which font categories your page uses. The basic syntax is

```
elementName {font-family: firstchoice,
secondchoice, thirdchoice}
```

`elementName` is the name of the element to which you want to apply the `font-family` property. The font choices can be of two different kinds, either specific font names (like Arial or Courier or Times New Roman) or generic font categories. Naming a font category as your final choice is good practice, because if the specific font you request is not available but a font family is also specified, the system finds a replacement font from the designated font category.

You can choose from among five font categories:

- `Serif`: Fonts such as Times or Times New Roman that have fine ornamental cross strokes at the edge of the letters.
- `Sans-serif`: Fonts without serifs, such as Arial or Helvetica.
- `Monospace`: Fonts such as Courier that look more like the product of an old typewriter.
- `Cursive`: A script font such as ZapfChancery.
- `Fantasy`: Fonts that are primarily decorative while still containing representations of characters, such as Alpha Geometrique or Western.

USE THE FONT-FAMILY PROPERTY

Untitled - Notepad

```
/* Cascading style sheet for use with the jamcracker.xml file */

jamcracker_product_info
{ display: block; Font-family: Times, Times New Roman, serif}

title
{ display: block}

name
{ display: block}

price_per_unit, unique_characteristics, rname, rank, test_field, js_function
{ display: none}

ingredient_list
{ display: inline}

ingredient
{ display: inline}
```

Untitled - Notepad

```
/* Cascading style sheet for use with the jamcracker.xml file */

jamcracker_product_info
{ display: block; Font-family: Times, Times New Roman, serif}

title
{ display: block; Font-family: Arial, Helvetica, sans-serif}

name
{ display: block}

price_per_unit, unique_characteristics, rname, rank, test_field, js_function
{ display: none}

ingredient_list
{ display: inline}

ingredient
{ display: inline}
```

■1 Open or create the style sheet file.

■ See Chapter 8 for more on how to create a style sheet.

■2 Place the cursor after the item whose `font-family` property you want to set.

■3 Type **font-family:** and the desired choices.

■ In this example, the font used will be first Times, if available, then Times New Roman, then something in the generic serif category.

■4 Type any other desired `font-family` properties for other elements.

Note: `font-family` *properties are inherited, so if another font is not designated, the parent element font will be used.*

■5 Save the style sheet file.

Extra

The font-family property is inherited. What this means is that when you associate a container element with a font-family property of, say, sans serif, any contained elements you specify in your XML document display in sans serif as well unless you specify another font-family property with those contained elements. For example, in the following CSS code, the contained name element will display in sans serif.

Because sans serif and monospace fonts are fairly clean and easy to read, they are a good choice for applications that involve dense paragraphs of displayed text. Serif and cursive fonts are better choices for headlines and other snippets of text you want to stand out.

Example:

```
product_info
{
    display: block;
    font-family:   sans-serif;
}
name
{
    display: block;
    font-size: large;
    font-weight: bold;
}
```

```
jamcracker.xml - Notepad                                    _ 8 X
File  Edit  Search  Help
<?xml version="1.0"?>
<?xml-stylesheet type="text/css" href="master.css"?>

<!-- Jamcracker, Inc. Product Information -->
<!--
For detailed description of data and data type definitions, contact
        Sarah Bellum
        Lead XML developer
        Jamcracker, Inc.
-->


<jamcracker_product_info>

<title>Jamcracker, Inc. Product Information</title>
    <product image="P1" product_code="A">
        <name>Huckleberry Jam</name>
        <price_per_unit currency="USD">6.50</price_per_unit>
        <test_field>Warning: this artifact will be phased out after Jamcracker
        <marketing_info dept_code="A20">
            <unique_characteristics>fresh huckleberries</unique_characteristi
            <rank>2</rank>

<!-- NOTE:  Because Internet Explorer's support for cascading style
            sheets does not currently describe a mechanism for resolving
            namespace prefixes, the r: prefix has been removed from the
```

```
\\In-filesvcs\edit\LSandman\XML\2Using the Font Family Property\jamcracker.xml - Microsoft Int... _ 8 X
File  Edit  View  Favorites  Tools  Help
Back  Forward  Stop  Refresh  Home  Search  Favorites  History  Mail  Print  Edit
Address  \\In-filesvcs\edit\LSandman\XML\2Using the Font Family Property\jamcracker.xml              Go

Jamcracker, Inc. Product Information
Huckleberry Jam
fresh huckleberries sugar
Orange Marmalade
orange juice candied orange peel sugar
Honey-Amaretto Spread
honey almonds 20-year-old amaretto

Done                                                   Local intranet
```

■ 6 If you have not already done so, open up the source code for the Web page you are formatting, attach the style sheet, and then close the file.

■ For more information, see Chapter 8.

■ When you open up the Web page in a browser, the page displays the specified font-family properties.

■ This example shows the title font as Arial, but the body copy as Times.

USE THE FONT-SIZE PROPERTY

Y ou can use the `font-size` property to designate the height of type used by specific elements on your page.

The basic syntax is

elementName {font-size:*sizechoice*}

elementName is the name of the element to which you want to apply the `font-size` property. The *sizechoice*, however, can be any one of four different categories:

■ A value relative to the *browser's* current font. The options are `xx-small`, `x-small`, `small`, `medium`, `large`, `x-large`, or `xx-large`.

■ A value relative to the *parent element's* font size. The options are `smaller` or `larger`.

■ A percentage value of the parent element's font size. For example, `font-size:50%` makes the font half the size of the parent element's font.

■ A specific size value. The most common method is to specify a size in points, such as `font-size: 12pt`.

Keep your target display device (for example, a hand-held device versus a 17-inch monitor) in mind when specifying font sizes.

USE THE FONT-SIZE PROPERTY

```
/* Cascading style sheet for use with the jamcracker.xml file */

jamcracker_product_info
{ display: block; font-family: Times, Times New Roman, serif; font-size:12pt}

title
{ display: block; font-family: Arial, Helvetica, sans-serif}

name
{ display: block}

price_per_unit, unique_characteristics, rname, rank, test_field, js_function
{ display: none}

ingredient_list
{ display: inline}

ingredient
{ display: inline}
```

```
/* Cascading style sheet for use with the jamcracker.xml file */

jamcracker_product_info
{ display: block; font-family: Times, Times New Roman, serif; font-size:
12pt}

title
{ display: block; font-family: Arial, Helvetica, sans-serif; font-size: 36pt}

name
{ display: block}

price_per_unit, unique_characteristics, rname, rank, test_field, js_function
{ display: none}

ingredient_list
{ display: inline}

ingredient
{ display: inline}
```

■1 Open or create the style sheet file.

■ See Chapter 8 for more on how to create a style sheet.

■2 Place the cursor after the item whose **font-size** property you want to set.

■3 Type **font-size:** and the desired choices.

■ This example shows the parent **font-size** set for 12 points.

■4 Type any other desired **font-size** properties for other elements.

Note: **font-size** *properties are inherited, so if another size is not designated, the parent element font size will be used.*

■5 Save the style sheet file.

Extra

Specifying relative font sizes helps display text scale more easily from one medium to another (for example, from a 15-inch monitor to a printer).

You can specify size for any of the following as relative font sizes:

- em: A percentage of the em (a measurement used in traditional print media that spans the width of the "m" in the specified font). For example, 0.5em

- ex: the 'x-height' (a measurement that represents the height of a lowercase "x" in the specified font). For example, 1ex

- px: pixels, relative to the viewing device. For example, 12px

You can use the font-size-adjust property to preserve readability in small font sizes. (Depending on the font you choose, specifying small values for font-size may result in unreadable text. For example, Verdana has an aspect value of 0.58; Times New Roman has an aspect value of 0.46. Verdana therefore tends to remain more legible at smaller sizes than Times New Roman.)

Here is the syntax:

```
font-size-adjust number
```
number is the aspect ratio to which you want to adjust the specified font.

6 If you have not already done so, open up the source code for the Web page you are formatting, attach the style sheet, and then close the file.

■ For more information, see Chapter 8.

■ When you open up the Web page in a browser, the page displays the specified font-size properties.

■ In this example, the title font is 36 points, but the body copy is 12 points.

USE THE FONT-STYLE PROPERTY

You can use the font-style property to craft fonts to meet the needs of groups of elements on your page.

The syntax is

elementName {font-style:style}

elementName is the name of the element to which you want to apply the font-style property. The style can be any one of three different categories:

- Normal: This style displays the text as created and is the default property.

- Italic: This style displays a slanted version of the font.

- Oblique: This style is also a slanted or inclined font, but one generated by computer. Oblique fonts are not always available.

Font-style properties are inherited, so if another font style is not designated, the parent element font style is used.

Keep in mind that because italic and oblique font styles are typically much harder for people to read than normal fonts (especially on computer screens, but in print, as well), these options should be used sparingly.

USE THE FONT-STYLE PROPERTY

```
Untitled - Notepad
File  Edit  Search  Help
/* Cascading style sheet for use with the jamcracker.xml file */

jamcracker_product_info
{ display: block; font-family: Times, Times New Roman, serif; font-size: 12pt
  font-style: normal}

title
{ display: block; font-family: Arial, Helvetica, sans-serif; font-size: 36pt}

name
{ display: block}

price_per_unit, unique_characteristics, rname, rank, test_field, js_function
{ display: none}

ingredient_list
{ display: inline}

ingredient
{ display: inline}

Start   Untitled - Notepad                                      12:00 PM
```

```
Untitled - Notepad
File  Edit  Search  Help
/* Cascading style sheet for use with the jamcracker.xml file */

jamcracker_product_info
{ display: block; font-family: Times, Times New Roman, serif; font-size: 12pt
  font-style: normal}

title
{ display: block; font-family: Arial, Helvetica, sans-serif; font-size: 36pt}

name
{ display: block}

price_per_unit, unique_characteristics, rname, rank, test_field, js_function
{ display: none}

ingredient_list
{ display: inline; font-style: italic}

ingredient
{ display: inline}

Start   Untitled - Notepad                                      12:00 PM
```

1 Open or create the style sheet file.

■ See Chapter 8 for more on how to create a style sheet.

2 Place the cursor after the item with the font-style property you want to set.

3 Type **font-style:** and the desired choices.

■ This example shows the parent font-style set for normal.

4 Type any other desired font-style properties for other elements.

■ This example shows the ingredient_list set for italic.

5 Save the style sheet file.

Extra

"Normal" fonts, such as the text you're reading right now, are sometimes referred to as "upright" or "Roman" fonts. Fonts in this category are nearly always clearer and easier to read than either oblique or italicized versions. Normal fonts also take up less space.

You should reserve use of both oblique and italicized fonts for small sections of text that you want to emphasize. For the same reason, these fonts are best suited for display on large display devices.

Using oblique and italicized fonts is not the only font trick you can use with a CSS. See "Using the Font-Weight Property," next in this chapter, for how you can increase or decrease the boldness of individual letters in a font.

6 If you have not already done so, open up the source code for the Web page you are formatting, attach the style sheet, and then close the file.

■ For more information, see Chapter 8.

■ When you open up the Web page in a browser, the page displays the specified `font-style` properties.

■ In this example, the ingredients list is italic, while the rest of the text is normal.

USE THE FONT-WEIGHT PROPERTY

The font-weight property lets you define how thick you want your letters to appear on the page.

This property is useful for emphasizing or de-emphasizing portions of text. For example, increasing the boldness of a headline can make the item stand out. On the other hand, lightening up something like a company motto can also attract the viewer's eye.

The basic syntax is

elementName {font-weight:value}

elementName is the name of the element to which you want to apply the font-weight property. The value can be any one of 13 different choices in two different categories:

- Relative values: The four options in this category adjust the text's boldness relative to the boldness of the parent text. The values are normal, lighter, bold, and bolder.

- Range values: The nine options in this set — 100, 200, 300, 400, 500, 600, 700, 800, and 900 — display the text in increasing degrees of boldness. You cannot use intermediate values, such as 475.

USE THE FONT-WEIGHT PROPERTY

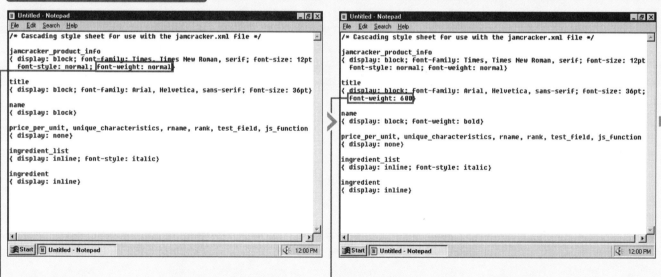

1 Open or create the style sheet file.

■ See Chapter 8 for more on how to create a style sheet.

2 Place the cursor after the item with the font-style property you want to set.

3 Type **font-weight:** and the desired choices.

■ This example shows the parent font-weight set for normal.

4 Type any other desired font-weight properties for other elements.

■ This example shows the title set for 600 and name set for bold.

5 Save the style sheet file.

Extra

The `font-weight` property is inherited. What this means is that when you associate a container element with a `font-weight` property of, say, `bold`, any contained elements you specify in your XML document display in bold as well, unless you specify another `font-weight` property with those contained elements. For example, in the following CSS code, the contained `name` element will display in bold.

Example:

```
product_info
{
    display: block;
  font-family: sans-serif;
    font-weight:   bold;
}
name
{
    display: block;
    font-size: large;
}
```

The relative values `bolder` and `lighter` darken and lighten the associated text based on the parent `font-weight`, with the following absolute weight limits:

- `lighter`: Can't be lighter than 100
- `normal`: 400
- `bolder`: Can't be bolder than 900

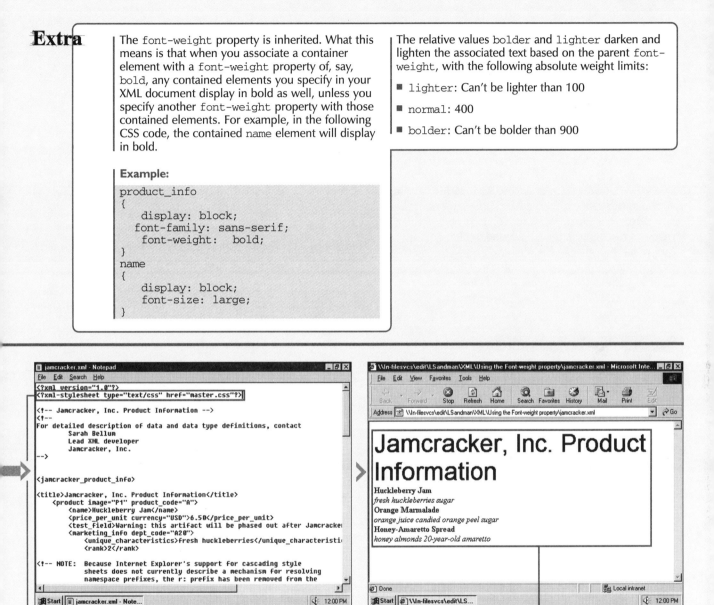

6 If you have not already done so, open up the source code for the Web page you are formatting, attach the style sheet, and then close the file.

■ For more information, see Chapter 8.

■ When you open up the Web page in a browser, the page displays the specified `font-weight` properties.

■ In this example, the page title and the product name reflect bolder type.

USE THE FONT-VARIANT PROPERTY

You can use the font-variant property to add special emphasis to elements on your Web page.

The font-variant property allows you to use all small uppercase letters on elements. This method can be very effective in small doses, such as for headings, subheadings, special instructions, product names — any category of text you want to stand out to the reader. Presenting a mix of bolded, italicized, and otherwise emphasized text isn't a good idea from a design standpoint, because doing so dilutes the eye-catching effect you're trying to achieve.

The basic syntax is

elementName {font-variant:*value*}

elementName is the name of the element to which you want to apply the font-variant property. You have two choices for the *value*:

■ small-caps: This option changes the designated text to all uppercase letters.

■ normal: This option leaves the text in its existing mix of uppercase and lowercase letters.

Font-variant properties are inherited, so if another variant is not designated, the parent element font style will be used.

USE THE FONT-VARIANT PROPERTY

```
/* Cascading style sheet for use with the jamcracker.xml file */

jamcracker_product_info
{ display: block; font-family: Times, Times New Roman, serif; font-size: 12pt
  font-style: normal; font-weight: normal; Font-variant: normal}

title
{ display: block; font-family: Arial, Helvetica, sans-serif; font-size: 36pt;
  font-weight: 600}

name
{ display: block; font-weight: bold}

price_per_unit, unique_characteristics, rname, rank, test_field, js_function
{ display: none}

ingredient_list
{ display: inline; font-style: italic}

ingredient
{ display: inline}
```

```
/* Cascading style sheet for use with the jamcracker.xml file */

jamcracker_product_info
{ display: block; font-family: Times, Times New Roman, serif; font-size: 12pt
  font-style: normal; font-weight: normal; font-variant: normal}

title
{ display: block; font-family: Arial, Helvetica, sans-serif; font-size: 36pt;
  font-weight: 600}

name
{ display: block; font-weight: bold; Font-variant: small-caps}

price_per_unit, unique_characteristics, rname, rank, test_field, js_function
{ display: none}

ingredient_list
{ display: inline; font-style: italic}

ingredient
{ display: inline}
```

■1 Open or create the style sheet file.

■ See Chapter 8 for more on how to create a style sheet.

■2 Place the cursor after the item whose font-variant property you want to set.

■3 Type **font-variant:** and the desired choices.

■ This example shows the parent font-variant set for normal.

■4 Type any other desired font-variant properties for other elements.

■ This example shows the font-variant property of name set for small-caps.

■5 Save the style sheet file.

Extra

In the small-caps font you get using the font-variant property, the glyphs for lowercase letters look similar to the uppercase ones, but in a smaller size and with slightly different proportions. This means that the font-variant property isn't effective for all fonts; only those that are *bicameral* (those whose lowercase letters are represented differently than the uppercase letters, such as with Latin script). The font-variant property has no visible effect for scripts that are *unicameral* (having only one case, as with most of the world's writing systems).

For more information on using global capitalization to emphasize text, check out "Apply Global Capitalization" later in this chapter.

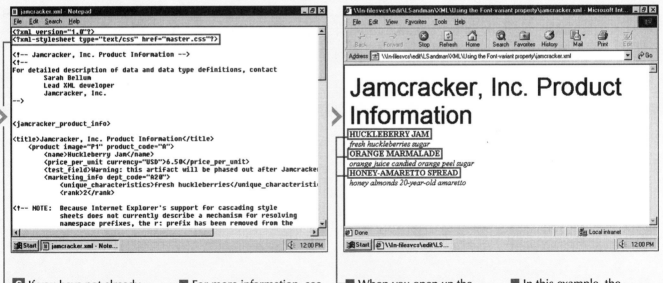

6 If you have not already done so, open up the source code for the Web page you are formatting, attach the style sheet, and then close the file.

■ For more information, see Chapter 8.

■ When you open up the Web page in a browser, the page displays the specified font-variant properties.

■ In this example, the product names are in all uppercase letters.

USE FONT PROPERTY SHORTHAND

The font property is defined as a *shorthand* property by the W3C, meaning that you can combine the font style, variant, weight, size, and family properties into one rule.

The basic syntax is

elementName {font:*style variant weight size family*}

elementName is the name of the element to which you want to apply the font property. The other ingredients follow:

- *style*, *variant*, and *weight* refer to the font style, font variant, and font weight properties, respectively. You can include these values in any order, and they are optional.

- *size* refers to the font size property. This value is *not* optional.

- *family* refers to the font family property. This value is also not optional. You *can* specify specific fonts, just as when you are making a font family declaration. Simply separate the options with commas.

For more information on these individual properties, see their respective sections earlier in this chapter.

USE FONT PROPERTY SHORTHAND

```
/* Cascading style sheet for use with the jamcracker.xml file */

jamcracker_product_info
{ display: block; font: normal normal normal 12pt Times, serif}

title
{ display: block}

name
{ display: block}

price_per_unit, unique_characteristics, rname, rank, test_field, js_function
{ display: none}

ingredient_list
{ display: inline}

ingredient
{ display: inline}
```

```
/* Cascading style sheet for use with the jamcracker.xml file */

jamcracker_product_info
{ display: block; font: normal normal normal 12pt Times, serif}

title
{ display: block; font: 600 36pt sans-serif}

name
{ display: block; font: bold small-caps}

price_per_unit, unique_characteristics, rname, rank, test_field, js_function
{ display: none}

ingredient_list
{ display: inline; font: italic}

ingredient
{ display: inline}
```

1 Open or create the style sheet file.

■ See Chapter 8 for more on how to create a style sheet.

2 Place the cursor where you want to declare your font properties.

3 Type **font:** and the desired choices.

4 Type any other desired font properties for other elements.

5 Save the style sheet file.

Note: Font- properties are inherited, so if another set of properties is not designated, the parent element's will be used.

Extra

The shorthand `font` property allows you to set some, but not all, of the properties associated with fonts (`font-style`, `font-variant`, `font-weight`, `font-size`, `line-height`, and `font-family`). Setting the `font-stretch` and `font-size-adjust` properties is not possible using the `font` shorthand property. If you do not supply values for each of the attributes of the `font` property, the default value of `normal` applies.

Using this shorthand lets you describe fonts in one location in a cascading style sheet, which is useful for XML documents in which not much variation in text display is desired.

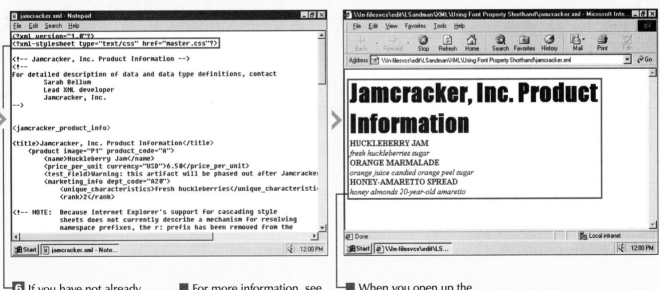

6 If you have not already done so, open up the source code for the Web page you are formatting, attach the style sheet, and then close the file.

■ For more information, see Chapter 8.

■ When you open up the Web page in a browser, the page displays the specified `font` properties.

DEFINE FONT COLOR

You can apply color to font elements very simply by using the `color` property.

`Color` properties are inherited, so if another variant is not designated, the parent element color will be used. The basic syntax is

elementName {color:*color*}

elementName is the name of the element to which you want to apply the `color` property. You can declare the specific *color* any of four ways:

- By a specific color name. Currently, CSS allows for 16 named color keywords: aqua, black, blue, fuchsia, gray, green, lime, maroon, navy, olive, purple, red, silver, teal, white, and yellow.

- By RGB hexadecimal value. For example, black is #000000, while the red represented by the color keyword is #FF0000.

- By RGB decimal value. For example, black is RGB(0,0,0), while red is RGB(255,0,0).

- By RGB percentage. For example, black is RGB(0%,0%,0%), while red is RGB(100%,0%,0%).

In general, using the 16 named colors is the safest programming practice, because they are the most reliably supported.

DEFINE FONT COLOR

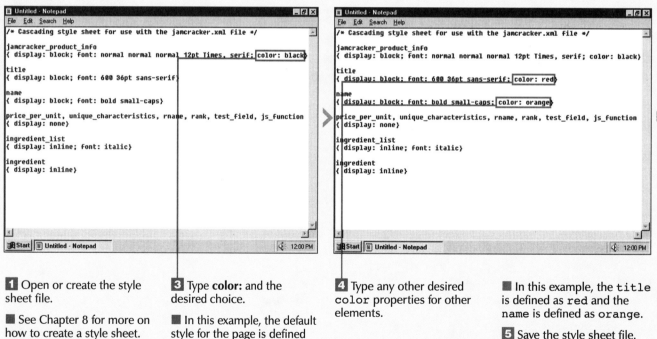

1 Open or create the style sheet file.

■ See Chapter 8 for more on how to create a style sheet.

2 Place the cursor where you want to declare your color properties.

3 Type **color:** and the desired choice.

■ In this example, the default style for the page is defined as black.

4 Type any other desired color properties for other elements.

■ In this example, the title is defined as red and the name is defined as orange.

5 Save the style sheet file.

Extra

Specifying color is a good way to emphasize XML elements and create an attractive user interface. Because monitors and viewing applications may render colors differently, however, make sure you test your code in your target display device. If you apply color to more than one element, make sure that the colors produce the desired effect at runtime (that they don't clash, aren't rendered too similarly, and so forth).

The following are RGB designations for additional colors:

COLOR	RGB TRIPLET
antiquewhite	#FAEBD7
brown	#A52A2A
chartreuse	#7FFF00
crimson	#DC143C
cyan	#00FFFF
forestgreen	#228B22

COLOR	RGB TRIPLET
gold	#FFD700
hotpink	#FF69B4
khaki	#F0E68C
magenta	#FF00FF
midnightblue	#191970
navajowhite	#FFDEAD
orange	#FFA500
pink	#FFC0CB
plum	#DDA0DD
salmon	#FA8072
skyblue	#87CEEB
tan	#D2B48C
tomato	#FF6347
turquoise	#40E0D0
violet	#EE82EE

To see how to specify a background color (as opposed to a font color), check out "Apply Background Color" in Chapter 10.

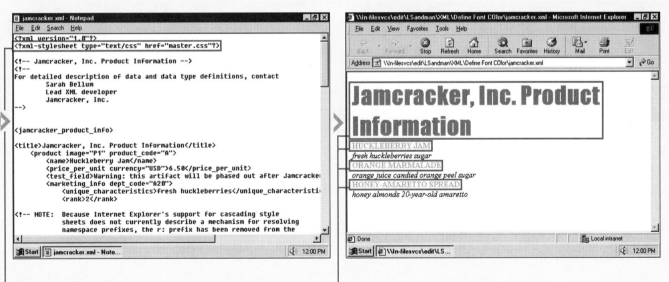

6 If you have not already done so, open up the source code for the Web page you are formatting, attach the style sheet, and then close the file.

■ For more information, see Chapter 8.

■ When you open up the Web page in a browser, the page displays the specified color properties.

APPLY GLOBAL CAPITALIZATION

Y ou can use the `text-transform` property to apply consistent capitalization rules to elements on your Web pages.

This can be very handy if, for example, you have several different people entering categories of information. Rather than having to worry about editing to achieve a consistent style, you can let the style sheet do the editing for you.

The basic syntax is

elementName {text-transform:*style*}
elementName is the name of the element to which you want to apply the `text-transform` property. You have four different values of *style* to choose from:

- `capitalize`, which uppercases the first letter of every word in the element

- `uppercase`, which puts all the element's letters in uppercase

- `lowercase`, which changes all the element's letters to lowercase

- `none`, which makes no changes to the element

`Text-transform` properties are inherited, so if another set of properties is not designated, the parent element's `text-transform` property will be used.

APPLY GLOBAL CAPITALIZATION

```
/* Cascading style sheet for use with the jamcracker.xml file */

jamcracker_product_info
{ display: block; font: normal normal normal 12pt Times, serif; color: black
  text-transform: none}

title
{ display: block; font: 600 36pt sans-serif;  color: red}

name
{ display: block; font: bold small-caps; color: orange}

price_per_unit, unique_characteristics, rname, rank, test_field, js_function
{ display: none}

ingredient_list
{ display: inline; font: italic}

ingredient
{ display: inline}
```

```
/* Cascading style sheet for use with the jamcracker.xml file */

jamcracker_product_info
{ display: block; font: normal normal normal 12pt Times, serif; color: black
  text-transform: none}

title
{ display: block; font: 600 36pt sans-serif; color: red}

name
{ display: block; font: bold small-caps; color: orange}

price_per_unit, unique_characteristics, rname, rank, test_field, js_function
{ display: none}

ingredient_list
{ display: inline; font: italic; text-transform: capitalize}

ingredient
{ display: inline}
```

■1 Open or create the style sheet file.

■ See Chapter 8 for more on how to create a style sheet.

■2 Place the cursor where you want to declare your `text-transform` properties.

■3 Type **text-transform:** and the desired choice.

■ In this example, the default style for the page is defined as `none`.

■4 Type any other desired `text-transform` properties for other elements.

■ In this example, the `ingredient_list` is defined as `capitalize`.

■5 Save the style sheet file.

Extra

The actual transformation in each case is written language dependent. For more information, you can download "Internationalization of the HyperText Markup Language" (RFC2070) from the World Wide Web Consortium at ftp://ds.internic.net/rfc/rfc2070.txt.

Browsers and other conforming user agents may implement the `text-transform` property so that its value is `none` for characters not from the Latin-1 repertoire, and for elements in other languages as well. You can find information on Microsoft's implementation of this property in Internet Explorer at http://msdn.microsoft.com/ workshop/author/dhtml/reference/properties/textTransform.asp and suggested implementation details (from the W3C) at www.w3.org/TR/REC-CSS2/text.html, for which the transformation is different from that specified by the case-conversion tables of ISO 10646 ([ISO10646]).

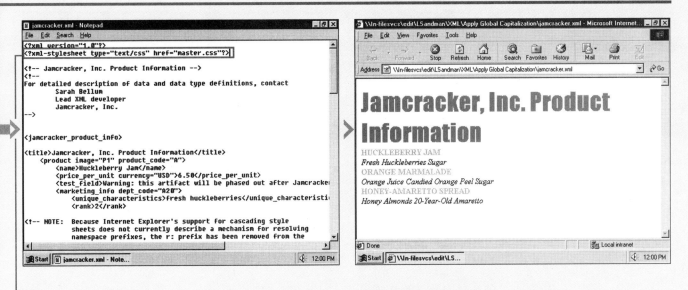

6 If you have not already done so, open up the source code for the Web page you are formatting, attach the style sheet, and then close the file.

■ For more information, see Chapter 8.

■ When you open up the Web page in a browser, the page displays the specified `text-transform` properties.

APPLY THE TEXT-DECORATION PROPERTY

You can decorate text in a number of ways simply by using the text-decoration property.

The text-decoration property lets you place lines above, below, and through text without having to worry about coordinating art elements. Depending on the browser, you can also make your text blink.

The basic syntax is

elementName {text-decoration:style}

elementName is the name of the element to which you want to apply the text-decoration property. You have four different values of style to choose from:

- underline, which puts a line underneath the element text.
- overline, which puts a line above the element text.
- line-through, which puts a line through the middle of each line of the element text.
- none, which makes no changes to the element.
- blink, which can cause the text to appear and disappear. However, support for this feature is not widespread.

The text-decoration property is not inherited.

APPLY THE TEXT-DECORATION PROPERTY

```
/* Cascading style sheet for use with the jamcracker.xml file */

jamcracker_product_info
{ display: block; font: normal normal normal 12pt Times, serif; color: black
  text-transform: none}

title
{ display: block; font: 600 36pt sans-serif; color: red; text-decoration:
underline}

name
{ display: block; font: bold small-caps; color: orange}

price_per_unit, unique_characteristics, rname, rank, test_field, js_function
{ display: none}

ingredient_list
{ display: inline; font: italic; text-transform: capitalize}

ingredient
{ display: inline}
```

```
/* Cascading style sheet for use with the jamcracker.xml file */

jamcracker_product_info
{ display: block; font: normal normal normal 12pt Times, serif; color: black
  text-transform: none}

title
{ display: block; font: 600 36pt sans-serif; color: red; text-decoration:
underline}

name
{ display: block; font: bold small-caps; color: orange}

price_per_unit, unique_characteristics, rname, rank, test_field, js_function
{ display: none}

ingredient_list
{ display: inline; font: italic; text-transform: capitalize; text-decoration:
underline}

ingredient
{ display: inline}
```

1 Open or create the style sheet file.

■ See Chapter 8 for more on how to create a style sheet.

2 Place the cursor where you want to declare your text-decoration property.

3 Type **text-decoration:** and the desired choice.

■ This example shows the title style for the page defined as underline.

4 Type any other desired text-decoration properties for other elements.

■ In this example, the ingredient_list is also defined as underline.

5 Save the style sheet file.

Extra

The `text-decoration` property isn't always inherited, but it can be inherited in some instances (depending on how the browser, or user agent, implements the W3C's cascading style sheet standards):

- If it is specified for a block-level element (a block element is one in which a value of `block` or `list-item` is specified for the `display` property), the `text-decoration` can affect all inline-level descendants of the element.

- If it is specified for (or affects) an in-line level element, a `text-decoration` property can affect all boxes generated by the element.

- If the element has no content or no text content (an example of an element without text content is the HTML `<IMG>` element), the browser may ignore the `text-decoration` property altogether.

A related property, `text-shadow`, enables you to decorate text with a configurable shadow effect. CSS2 defines the `text-shadow` property but it is not widely implemented. For more information on this property, visit www.w3.org/TR/REC-CSS2/text.html.

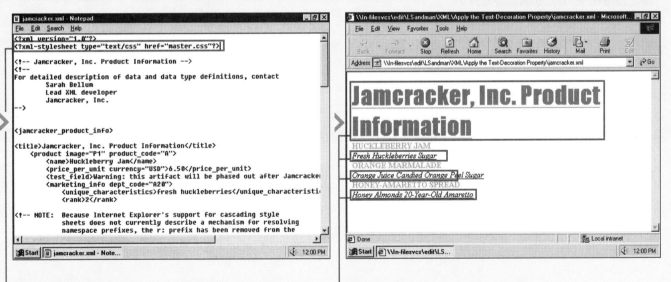

6 If you have not already done so, open up the source code for the Web page you are formatting, attach the style sheet, and then close the file.

■ For more information, see Chapter 8.

■ When you open up the Web page in a browser, the page displays the specified `text-decoration` properties. In this example, both the title and the ingredients are underlined.

USE THE LINE-HEIGHT PROPERTY

Controlling how elements appear vertically is an important component of Web page design. You can use the `line-height` property to adjust the vertical spacing of elements.

When you input a `line-height` property value, you establish the distance between the baselines of the elements. The basic syntax is

elementName {line_height:*value*}

elementName is the name of the element to which you want to apply the `line-height` property. The *value* can be any one of three different categories:

- A number that serves as a multiplier for the parent property. For example, entering 2.5 mandates a

`line-height` property two and a half times that of the parent text.

- A multiplier relative to the parent property, given either as a percentage or in terms of *em* (the width of the letter m in the current font), *ex* (the height of the letter x in the current font), or *px* (the size of a pixel). For example, entering 250% accomplishes the same thing as the number entry 2.5.

- An absolute size value, meaning a number paired with common abbreviations such as *cm, in, mm, pc,* or *pt,* such as 2cm for two centimeters.

The `line-height` property is inherited, so if no value is specified, the value of the parent property will be used.

USE THE LINE-HEIGHT PROPERTY

1 Open or create the style sheet file.

■ See Chapter 8 for more on how to create a style sheet.

2 Place the cursor where you want to place your `line-height` property.

3 Type **line-height:** and the desired choice.

■ In this example, the title element has a `line-height` of 200%.

4 Type any other desired `line-height` properties for other elements.

■ In this example, the `name` has a value of 3.5.

5 Save the style sheet file.

Extra

Line height measures the distance between the descender of the font and the top of the internal leading of the font. You can specify a negative value for the line-height property to achieve various shadowing effects.

If a formatted line contains more than one element, the maximum line height applies to all the elements in that line. In this case, negative values are not allowed.

For more information on specifying relative values for this property, see "Using the Font-Size Property" earlier in this chapter.

For details on Internet Explorer 5.5's implementation of the line-height property, visit http://msdn.microsoft.com/workshop/author/dhtml/reference/properties/lineHeight.asp#lineHeight.

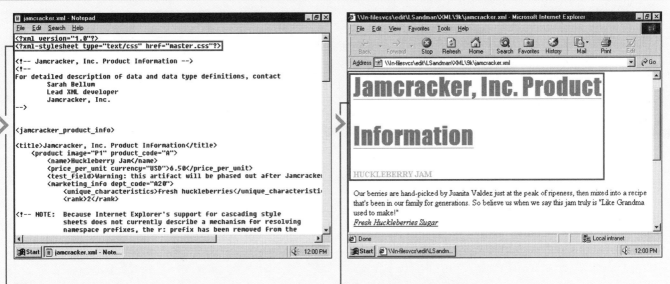

■ **6** If you have not already done so, open up the source code for the Web page you are formatting, attach the style sheet, and then close the file.

■ For more information, see Chapter 8.

■ When you open up the Web page in a browser, the page displays the specified line-height properties. In this example, extra vertical space surrounds both the title and the name.

ALIGN TEXT

You can use the text-align property to control how elements display horizontally on your Web page.

The text-align property affects *block* elements. Block elements are elements formatted visually as blocks and defined by specifying one of the following attributes for the display property: block, list-item, compact, and run-in. (The block value is the most widely supported.)

You define the text-align property with this syntax:

elementName {text-align:value}

elementName is the name of the element to which you want to apply the text-align property. You have four choices for the value, options which should be familiar if you have done much work with a word processor:

- left: The designated element is aligned to the left margin.

- right: The designated element is aligned with the right margin.

- center: The designated element is centered.

- justify: The designated element is aligned with *both* margins. For large blocks of text, this option results in smooth-looking margins along both sides, as opposed to the feathered margins of the other options.

ALIGN TEXT

```
/* Cascading style sheet for use with the jamcracker.xml file */

jamcracker_product_info
{ display: block; font: normal normal normal 12pt Times, serif; color: black
  text-transform: none}

title
{ display: block; font: 600 36pt sans-serif; color: red; text-decoration:
underline;
  line-height: 200%; text-align: center}

name
{ display: block; font: bold small-caps; color: orange; line-height: 3.5}

price_per_unit, unique_characteristics, rname, rank, test_field, js_function
{ display: none}

marketing_blurb
{ display: block;}

ingredient_list
{ display: block; font: italic; text-transform: capitalize; text-decoration:
underline;}

ingredient
{ display: inline;}
```

```
/* Cascading style sheet for use with the jamcracker.xml file */

jamcracker_product_info
{ display: block; font: normal normal normal 12pt Times, serif; color: black
  text-transform: none}

title
{ display: block; font: 600 36pt sans-serif; color: red; text-decoration:
underline;
  line-height: 200%; text-align: center}

name
{ display: block; font: bold small-caps; color: orange; line-height: 3.5;
  text-align: center}

price_per_unit, unique_characteristics, rname, rank, test_field, js_function
{ display: none}

marketing_blurb
{ display: block;}

ingredient_list
{ display: block; font: italic; text-transform: capitalize; text-decoration:
underline;}

ingredient
{ display: inline;}
```

■1 Open or create the style sheet file.

■ See Chapter 8 for more on how to create a style sheet.

■2 Place the cursor where you want to declare your text-align property.

■3 Type **text-align:** and the desired choice.

■ In this example, the title element has a text-align value of center.

■4 Type any other desired text-align properties for other elements.

■ In this example, the name is also centered.

■5 Save the style sheet file.

Extra

CSS-supporting browsers may interpret the `text-align` value justify as "justify left" or "justify right," depending on whether the element's default writing direction is left-to-right or right-to-left, respectively. For example, Internet Explorer 5.5 interprets `justify` as "justify left." CSS-supporting browsers may also choose to stretch justified text (Internet Explorer 5.5 doesn't).

The `text-align` property allows you to specify alignment for inline content of a block. Additional approaches to text alignment include the following:

- Horizontal alignment within a column (used in HTML table cells; for more information, visit www.w3.org/TR/REC-CSS2/tables.html#column-alignment)

- The `letter-spacing` property (see the "Space Letters in Elements" section coming up next)

- The `word-spacing` property (see the Extra section on the next page for more)

6 If you have not already done so, open up the source code for the Web page you are formatting, attach the style sheet, and then close the file.

■ For more information, see Chapter 8.

■ When you open up the Web page in a browser, the page displays the specified `text-align` properties. This example shows both the title and the name centered.

SPACE LETTERS IN ELEMENTS

Occasionally you may want to spread the letters of an element out across the page horizontally. You can use the `letter-spacing` property to control this spacing.

The basic syntax is

elementName {letter-spacing: *value*}

elementName is the name of the element to which you want to apply the `letter spacing` property. The *value* can be defined as:

- `normal`, which leaves the spacing as is.

- A multiplier relative to the parent property, given either as a percentage of the given spacing or in terms of *em* (the width of the letter m in the current font), *ex* (the height of the letter x in the current font), or *px* (the size of a pixel).

- An absolute size value, meaning a number paired with common abbreviations such as cm, in, mm, pc, or pt, such as 2cm for two centimeters.

You can also use negative values with the `letter-spacing` property to decrease the spacing between letters.

The `letter-spacing` property is inherited. This means that if you don't want a child element to adopt spacing properties, you must specify a `letter-spacing` property for the child.

SPACE LETTERS IN ELEMENTS

```
Untitled - Notepad
File  Edit  Search  Help
/* Cascading style sheet for use with the jamcracker.xml file */

jamcracker_product_info
{ display: block; font: normal normal normal 12pt Times, serif; color: black
  text-transform: none}

title
{ display: block; font: 600 36pt sans-serif: color: red: text-decoration: und
  line-height: 200%; text-align: center; letter-spacing: 15px}

name
{ display: block; font: bold small-caps; color: orange; line-height: 3.5;
  text-align: center}

price_per_unit, unique_characteristics, rname, rank, test_field, js_function
{ display: none}

marketing_blurb
{ display: block}

ingredient_list
{ display: block; font: italic; text-transform: capitalize; text-decoration:

ingredient
{ display: inline}

Start    Untitled - Notepad                                    12:00 PM
```

```
Untitled - Notepad
File  Edit  Search  Help
/* Cascading style sheet for use with the jamcracker.xml file */

jamcracker_product_info
{ display: block; font: normal normal normal 12pt Times, serif; color: black
  text-transform: none}

title
{ display: block; font: 600 36pt sans-serif; color: red; text-decoration: und
  line-height: 200%; text-align: center; letter-spacing: 15px}

name
{ display: block; font: bold small-caps; color: orange; line-height: 3.5;
  text-align: center; letter-spacing: 10px}

price_per_unit, unique_characteristics, rname, rank, test_field, js_function
{ display: none}

marketing_blurb
{ display: block}

ingredient_list
{ display: block; font: italic; text-transform: capitalize; text-decoration:

ingredient
{ display: inline}

Start    Untitled - Notepad                                    12:00 PM
```

1 Open or create the style sheet file.

■ See Chapter 8 for more on how to create a style sheet.

2 Place the cursor where you want to place your `letter-spacing` property.

3 Type **letter-spacing:** and the desired choice.

■ This example shows the `title` element given a `letter-spacing` value of `15px`.

4 Type any other desired `letter-spacing` properties for other elements.

■ This example shows `name` given a spacing value of `10px`.

5 Save the style sheet file.

Extra

Letter spacing handles the spacing between individual letters *in* a word; however, if you want to control the spacing *between* words, you can use the `word-spacing` property. The syntax is:

elementName {word-spacing: *value*}

The *value* can be:

■ `normal` (the default), which lets the browser decide the spacing;

■ an absolute value (such as 1mm);

■ or a relative value (such as 3px). See the introduction on the previous page for more about absolute and relative values.

The value can also be either positive or negative. A positive value increases the space between words; a negative value decreases the space between words.

The `word-spacing` property has limited applications. You will usually find the `text-align` property (see "Align Text," earlier in this chapter) to be more practical.

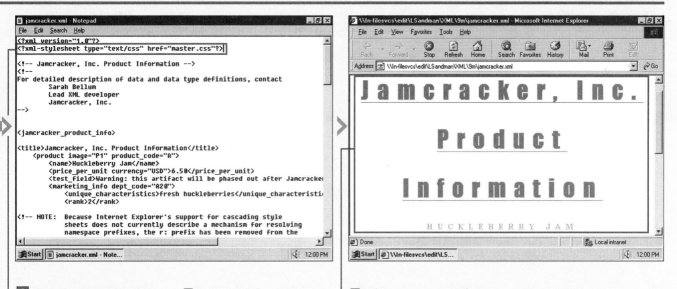

■6 If you have not already done so, open up the source code for the Web page you are formatting, attach the style sheet, and then close the file.

■ For more information, see Chapter 8.

■ When you open up the Web page in a browser, the page displays the specified `letter-spacing` properties. In this example, both the title and the product name have additional spacing between their letters.

INDENT TEXT

Long blocks of text and professional documents often look better when the first line is indented. You can use the `text-indent` property to specify which block-level elements indent the first line, and by how much. The browser simply displays blank space in the indentation area.

Use this basic syntax for the `text-indent` property:

elementName {text-indent:*value*}

elementName is the name of the element to which you want to apply the `text-indent` property. The *value* can be defined as:

- `normal`, which leaves the spacing as is.

- A multiplier relative to the parent property, given either as a percentage of the total width of the element's text or in terms of *em* (the width of the letter m in the current font), *ex* (the height of the letter x in the current font), or *px* (the size of a pixel).

- An absolute size value, meaning a number paired with common abbreviations such as *cm*, *in*, *mm*, *pc*, or *pt*, such as .5in for half an inch.

The `text-indent` property is inherited. This means that if you don't want a child element to adopt the indentation, you must specify a `text-indent` property for the child.

INDENT TEXT

```
/* Cascading style sheet for use with the jamcracker.xml file */

jamcracker_product_info
{ display: block; font: normal normal normal 12pt Times, serif; color: black
  text-transform: none}

title
{ display: block; font: 600 36pt sans-serif; color: red; text-decoration:
underline;
  line-height: 200%; text-align: center; letter-spacing: 15px}

name
{ display: block; font: bold small-caps; color: orange; line-height: 3.5;
  text-align: center; letter-spacing: 10px}

price_per_unit, unique_characteristics, rname, rank, test_field, js_function
{ display: none}

marketing_blurb
{ display: block; text-indent: 3em}

ingredient_list
{ display: block; font: italic; text-transform: capitalize; text-decoration:
underline}

ingredient
{ display: inline}
```

```
/* Cascading style sheet for use with the jamcracker.xml file */

jamcracker_product_info
{ display: block; font: normal normal normal 12pt Times, serif; color: black
  text-transform: none}

title
{ display: block; font: 600 36pt sans-serif; color: red; text-decoration:
underline;
  line-height: 200%; text-align: center; letter-spacing: 15px}

name
{ display: block; font: bold small-caps; color: orange; line-height: 3.5;
  text-align: center; letter-spacing: 10px}

price_per_unit, unique_characteristics, rname, rank, test_field, js_function
{ display: none}

marketing_blurb
{ display: block; text-indent: 3em}

ingredient_list
{ display: block; font: italic; text-transform: capitalize; text-decoration:
underline;
  text-indent: 5em}

ingredient
```

■ 1 Open or create the style sheet file.

■ See Chapter 8 for more on how to create a style sheet.

■ 2 Place the cursor where you want to place your `text-indent` property.

■ 3 Type **text-indent:** and the desired choice.

■ This example shows the `marketing_blurb` element indented by a value of 3em.

■ 4 Type any other desired `text-indent` properties for other elements.

■ This example shows the `ingredient_list` indented by 5em.

■ 5 Save the style sheet file.

Extra

The `text-indent` property only affects the first line of a multi-line paragraph. To indent an entire paragraph, you define a text box, margins, or padding, all of which Chapter 10 discusses. The next section, "Using a Hanging Indent," discusses another option — hanging indents, which indent all the lines of a multi-line paragraph except the first line.

If your application is destined to be displayed on multiple display devices (for example, from tiny hand-held devices to large-screen computers), specifying a relative value for the `text-indent` property is safer than specifying an absolute value.

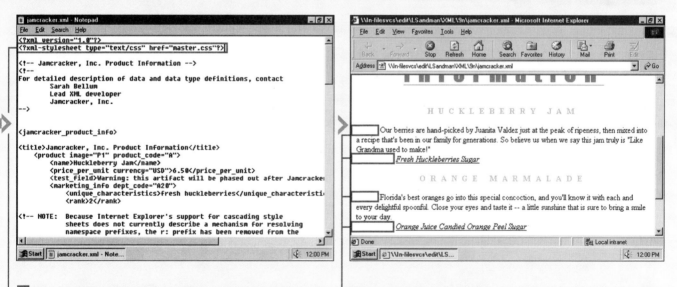

■ **6** If you have not already done so, open up the source code for the Web page you are formatting, attach the style sheet, and then close the file.

■ For more information on attaching style sheets, see Chapter 8.

■ When you open up the Web page in a browser, the page displays the specified `text-indent` properties. This example shows both the marketing blurb and the list of ingredients indented.

USE A HANGING INDENT

You can add a hanging indent to one of your page's elements using the text-indent property.

Putting a hanging indent into your text can sometimes add a dramatic flair to your Web page. For example, if you have margin elements down the left-hand side of the page, a hanging indent can provide additional white space for the margin elements to stand out.

Use the same basic syntax for a hanging indent as with the text-indent property:

elementName {text-indent:*value*}

elementName is the name of the element to which you want to apply the text-indent property. See the previous section, "Indent Text," for information on the acceptable definitions of *value*. The important difference for a hanging indent is that the *value* must be negative; for example, -5em.

Keep in mind when using a hanging indent that if the designated element is at the left margin, applying a negative indent value will cause the text to start off the visible edge of the page. You can, however, use margin, box, and padding properties (described in greater detail in Chapter 10) to give you the space necessary for an effective and visible hanging indent.

USE A HANGING INDENT

```
Untitled - Notepad
File  Edit  Search  Help
/* Cascading style sheet for use with the jamcracker.xml file */

jamcracker_product_info
{ display: block; font: normal normal normal 12pt Times, serif; color: black
  text-transform: none; padding: 4em}
/* Padding has been added to show the negative text-indent property*/

title
{ display: block; font: 600 36pt sans-serif; color: red; text-decoration:
underline;
  line-height: 200%; text-align: center; letter-spacing: 15px}

name
{ display: block; font: bold small-caps; color: orange; line-height: 3.5;
  text-align: center; letter-spacing: 10px}

price_per_unit, unique_characteristics, rname, rank, test_field, js_function
{ display: none}

marketing_blurb
{ display: block; text-indent: }

ingredient_list
{ display: block; font: italic; text-transform: capitalize; text-decoration:
underline}

ingredient

Start   Untitled - Notepad                              12:00 PM
```

```
Untitled - Notepad
File  Edit  Search  Help
jamcracker_product_info
{ display: block; font: normal normal normal 12pt Times, serif; color: black
  text-transform: none; padding: 4em}
/* Padding has been added to show the negative text-indent property*/

title
{ display: block; font: 600 36pt sans-serif; color: red; text-decoration: und
  line-height: 200%; text-align: center; letter-spacing: 15px}

name
{ display: block; font: bold small-caps; color: orange; line-height: 3.5;
  text-align: center; letter-spacing: 10px}

price_per_unit, unique_characteristics, rname, rank, test_field, js_function
{ display: none}

marketing_blurb
{ display: block; text-indent: -3em }

ingredient_list
{ display: block; font: italic; text-transform: capitalize; text-decoration:

ingredient
{ display: inline}

Start   Untitled - Notepad                              12:00 PM
```

1 Open or create the style sheet file.

■ See Chapter 8 for more on how to create a style sheet.

2 Place the cursor where you want to declare your text-indent property.

3 Type **text-indent:**.

4 Type the desired negative text-indent: value.

■ In this example, the marketing_blurb element is indented by a value of -3em.

5 Save the style sheet file.

Extra

Internet Explorer 5.5 allows you to change style properties dynamically at runtime. For example, the following HTML file contains code that

- Creates two indented styles: -2cm (hanging indent) and 3 cm (regular indent).

- Associates these two styles with the JavaScript `onclick` and `ondblclick` event handlers, so that clicking the text changes the display from a hanging indent to a regular indent and double-clicking changes the display back to a hanging indent.

Example:

```
<HTML> <HEAD> <STYLE>
  DIV { text-indent:"-2cm" }
  .click1 { text-indent:"10%" }
  .click2 { text-indent:"" }
</STYLE> </HEAD> <BODY> <BLOCKQUOTE CLASS="body"> <DIV
STYLE="font-size:14"
onclick="this.className='click1'"
ondblclick="this.className='click2'">

<BLOCKQUOTE>This text indent is set by
using the <B>DIV</B> element as an HTML
selector in the embedded style sheet.
Click the text to indent 10 percent
using inline script. Double-click for
original indent.</BLOCKQUOTE>
</DIV> </BLOCKQUOTE> </BODY> </HTML>
```

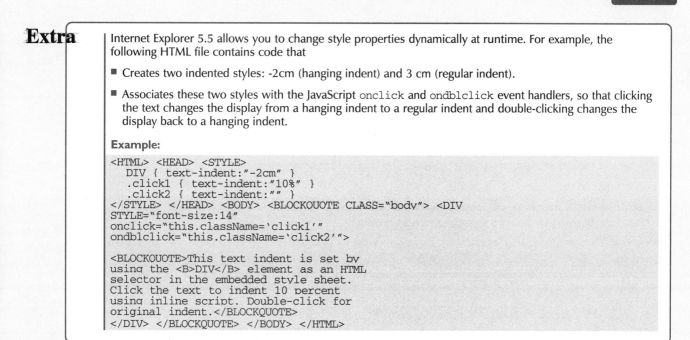

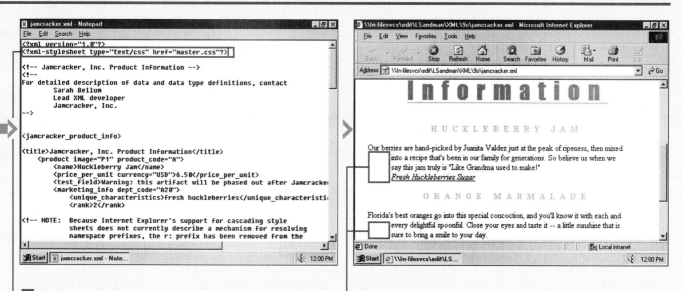

6 If you have not already done so, open up the source code for the Web page you are formatting, attach the style sheet, and then close the file.

■ For more information on attaching style sheets, see Chapter 8.

■ When you open up the Web page in a browser, the page displays the specified `text-indent` properties. This example shows the marketing blurb with a hanging indent.

Note: For display purposes, padding was added to the code of this page as compared to previous examples using this page in this chapter. For more on padding, see Chapter 10.

USE SUPERSCRIPT OR SUBSCRIPT TEXT

You can turn elements into superscript or subscript using the `vertical-align` property.

Most cases of superscript or subscript relate a child element to a parent element. The basic syntax is

elementName{vertical-align:*keyword*}

elementName is the name of the element to which you want to apply the `vertical-align` property. You have a choice of *keyword* values:

- `baseline`, which aligns the baseline of the element's box with the baseline of the parent box.

- `sub`, which turns the element into subscript.

- `super`, which turns the element into superscript.

- `middle`, which aligns the element with the middle of the parent element.

- `text-top`, which aligns the top of the element's text box (see Chapter 10) with the top of the parent's text box.

- `text-bottom`, which aligns the bottom of the two elements' text boxes.

You can also specify a relative percentage value or an absolute numerical value. (See "Indent Text," earlier in this chapter, for more about relative and absolute values in style sheets.) Specifying a positive value raises the child element relative to the parent element, while a negative value lowers the child element.

Because child elements inherit many `font` properties, if you want your subscript or superscript text to differ from its parent element, you should define those `font` properties at the same time you declare the `vertical-align` property.

USE SUPERSCRIPT OR SUBSCRIPT TEXT

```
Untitled - Notepad
File  Edit  Search  Help
jamcracker_product_info
{ display: block; font: normal normal normal 12pt Times, serif; color: black
  text-transform: none; padding: 4em}
/* Padding has been added to show the negative text-indent property*/

title
{ display: block; font: 600 36pt sans-serif; color: red; text-decoration:
underline;
  line-height: 200%; text-align: center; letter-spacing: 15px}

name
{ display: inline; font: bold small-caps; color: orange; line-height: 3.5;
  text-align: center; letter-spacing: 10px}

price_per_unit, unique_characteristics, rname, rank, test_field, js_function
{ display: none}

marketing_blurb
{ display: block; text-indent: -3em}

ingredient_list
{ display: block; font: italic; text-transform: capitalize; text-decoration:
underline}

extra
{ font-size: 75%; color: blue;
```

```
Untitled - Notepad
File  Edit  Search  Help
jamcracker_product_info
{ display: block; font: normal normal normal 12pt Times, serif; color: black
  text-transform: none; padding: 4em}
/* Padding has been added to show the negative text-indent property*/

title
{ display: block; font: 600 36pt sans-serif; color: red; text-decoration:
underline;
  line-height: 200%; text-align: center; letter-spacing: 15px}

name
{ display: inline; font: bold small-caps; color: orange; line-height: 3.5;
  text-align: center; letter-spacing: 10px}

price_per_unit, unique_characteristics, rname, rank, test_field, js_function
{ display: none}

marketing_blurb
{ display: block; text-indent: -3em}

ingredient_list
{ display: block; font: italic; text-transform: capitalize; text-decoration:
underline}

extra
{ font-size: 75%; color: blue; vertical-align: super}
```

1 Open or create the style sheet file.

2 Place the cursor where you want to declare your `vertical-align` property.

■ This example uses the `extra` element.

3 Type { and any font properties that will be different from the parent element.

4 Type **vertical-align:** and the desired keyword.

■ In this example, `extra` is set to be a superscript to its parent element.

5 Save the style sheet file.

Extra

For static superscript and subscript applications targeted to Web browsers, you may find using the HTML ^{...} and _{...} tags easier, which allow you to superscript and subscript text, respectively.

Example:

```
<HTML><BODY>
Here is a <SUP>superscript</SUP>    and here is a <SUB>subscript</SUB>
</BODY></HTML>
```

The vertical-align property is more useful in aligning text dynamically. For example, the following code aligns the text in the left-hand table cell dynamically in response to the onmouseover and onmouseout events.

```
<HTML><BODY><CENTER>
<P>Run your mouse over the left cell to align its contents to the bottom of the
table. (Removing the mouse causes the text to pop up to the top of the table.)</P>
<TABLE BORDER width=100><TR>
<TD onmouseover="this.style.verticalAlign='bottom'"
    onmouseout="this.style.verticalAlign='top'">text to align</TD>
<TD>This text is placed here for contrast, so that the alignment in the cell to the
left is apparent.</TD>
</TR></TABLE></CENTER></BODY></HTML>
```

■6 If you have not already done so, open up the source code for the Web page you are formatting, attach the style sheet, and then close the file.

■ For more information on attaching style sheets, see Chapter 8.

■ When you open up the Web page in a browser, the page displays the specified vertical-align property. In this example, note that "Sugar-Free Available!" appears as a superscript next to the Huckleberry Jam ingredients.

STYLE SHEET TEXT AND DISPLAY ELEMENTS

THE BOX MODEL

The CSS displays all elements using a box model. Understanding the terms used in this box model is critical to properly positioning your Web page elements.

- You can define the *border* width, color, and style using the `border` properties. See "Choose a Border Style," "Specify a Border Width," Choose a Border Color," and Using Border Property Shorthand," later in this chapter.

- The center of the box model is where the element's content resides.

- The *padding* is the area between the content and the border. You control the padding with the `padding` property; see "Set Padding," later in this chapter.

- The *margin* is an invisible area outside the border to the edge of the element. You control the margin with the `margin` property; see "Set Margins," later in this chapter.

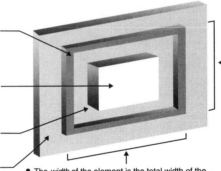

- The *height* of the element is the total height of the element's border, padding, and content. See "Set an Element's Height," later in this chapter.

- The *width* of the element is the total width of the element's border, padding, and content. See "Set an Element's Width," later in this chapter.

INSTRUCTION APPLICATION ORDER

Several properties — particularly the `margin`, `padding`, and `border` properties discussed in this chapter — give you the option of designating one, two, three, or four property styles to the edges of objects. The instructions are processed depending on how many values you designate:

- With one value, the style is applied to all four sides.

- With two values, the first is applied to the top and bottom, the second value to the sides.

- With three values, the first style is applied to the top, the second style to the sides, and the third style to the bottom.

- With four values, the styles are applied to the top, right, bottom, and left, in that order (or clockwise, starting at the top).

ABSOLUTE LENGTH VALUES

Five abbreviations for absolute length values are recognized in cascading style sheets:

- *mm*, for millimeter

- *cm*, for centimeter

- *in*, for inch

- *pc*, for pica

- *pt*, for point

RELATIVE LENGTH VALUES

Three abbreviations for relative length values are recognized in cascading style sheets:

- *em*, for the width of the letter m in the designated font

- *ex*, for the height of the letter x in the designated font

- *px*, for the size of a pixel

COLORS

Common Colors

You can designate colors four different ways in XML: by hexadecimal *RGB* (red, green, blue) value, by decimal RGB value, by percentage RGB value, or by name.

Hexadecimal is a base 16 numbering system (in contrast to the base 10, or *decimal*, numbering system we use every day). What this situation means is that instead of ten digits, from 0 to 9, the hexadecimal system provides 16 digits: 0 to 9 and A to F.

The hexadecimal values described in "Supported Color Names" comprise three separate values: one each for the red, green, and blue contribution to a color. To create your own custom colors, you can increase or decrease any of these three values, from 00 (the lowest hexadecimal number) to FF (the highest). For example, the color aqua has a red value of 00, a green value of FF, and a blue value of FF, giving a complete hexadecimal value of 00FFFF.

Supported Color Names

The following 16 color names are universally supported, meaning that you can designate them just by name.

COLOR NAME	HEXADECIMAL VALUE	COLOR NAME	HEXADECIMAL VALUE
Aqua	#00FFFF	Navy	#000080
Black	#000000	Olive	#808000
Blue	#0000FF	Purple	#800080
Fuchsia	#FF00FF	Red	#FF0000
Gray	#808080	Silver	#C0C0C0
Green	#00FF00	Teal	#008080
Lime	#00FF00	White	#FFFFFF
Maroon	#800000	Yellow	#FFFF00

Other Internet Safe Colors

In addition to the 16 named colors, you should generally have no problems if you use hexadecimal RGB values made up of any three of the following components: 00, 33, 66, 99, CC, and FF.

Internet Explorer-Supported Color Names

Version 4.0 and later versions of Internet Explorer support not only the 16 standard color names, but also the following additional color names. If you are designing an intranet page for a company with 100 percent Internet Explorer implementation, you may want to consider using these additional color names.

ADDITIONAL INTERNET EXPLORER COLOR NAMES

COLOR NAME	HEXADECIMAL VALUE	COLOR NAME	HEXADECIMAL VALUE
AliceBlue	F0F8FF	Burlywood	#DEB887
AntiqueWhite	FAEBD7	CadetBlue	#5F9EA0
Aquamarine	#7FFFD4	Chartreuse	#7FFF00
Azure	#F0FFFF	Chocolate	#D2691E
Beige	#F5F5DC	Coral	#FF7F50
Bisque	#FFE4C4	Cornflower	#6495ED
BlanchedAlmond	#FFEBCD	Cornsilk	#FFF8DC
BlueViolet	#8A2BE2	Crimson	#DC143C
Brown	#A52A2A	Cyan	#00FFFF

STYLE SHEET TEXT AND DISPLAY ELEMENTS (CONTINUED)

COLORS

ADDITIONAL INTERNET EXPLORER COLOR NAMES (CONTINUED)

COLOR NAME	HEXADECIMAL VALUE	COLOR NAME	HEXADECIMAL VALUE
Darkblue	00008B	Goldenrod	DAA520
Darkcyan	008B8B	Greenyellow	ADFF2F
Darkgoldenrod	B8860B	Honeydew	F0FFF0
Darkgray	A9A9A9	Hotpink	FF69B4
Darkgreen	006400	Indianred	CD5C5C
Darkkhaki	BDB76B	Indigo	4B0082
Darkmagenta	8B008B	Ivory	FFFFF0
Darkolivegreen	556B2F	Khaki	F0E68C
Darkorange	FF8C00	Lavender	E6E6FA
Darkorchid	9932CC	Lavenderblush	FFF0F5
Darkred	8B0000	Lawngreen	7CFC00
Darksalmon	E9967A	Lemonchiffon	FFFACD
Darkseagreen	8FBC8F	Lightblue	ADD8E6
Darkslateblue	483D8B	Lightcoral	F08080
Darkslategray	2F4F4F	Lightcyan	E0FFFF
Darkturquoise	00CED1	Lightgoldenrodyellow	FAFAD2
Darkviolet	9400D3	Lightgreen	90EE90
Deeppink	FF1493	Lightgrey	D3D3D3
Deepskyblue	00BFFF	Lightpink	FFB6C1
Dimgray	696969	Lightsalmon	FFA07A
Dodgerblue	1E90FF	Lightseagreen	20B2AA
Firebrick	B22222	Lightskyblue	87CEFA
Floralwhite	FFFAF0	Lightslategray	778899
Forestgreen	228B22	Lightsteelblue	B0C4DE
Gainsboro	DCDCDC	Lightyellow	FFFFE0
Ghostwhite	F8F8FF	Limegreen	32CD32
Gold	FFD700	Linen	FAF0E6

COLORS

ADDITIONAL INTERNET EXPLORER COLOR NAMES (CONTINUED)

COLOR NAME	HEXADECIMAL VALUE	COLOR NAME	HEXADECIMAL VALUE
Magenta	FF00FF	Pink	FFC0CB
Mediumaquamarine	66CDAA	Plum	DDA0DD
Mediumblue	0000CD	Powderblue	B0E0E6
Mediumorchid	BA55D3	Rosybrown	BC8F8F
Mediumpurple	9370DB	Royalblue	4169E1
Mediumseagreen	3CB371	Saddlebrown	8B4513
Mediumslateblue	7B68EE	Salmon	FA8072
Mediumspringgreen	00FA9A	Sandybrown	F4A460
Mediumturquoise	48D1CC	Seagreen	2E8B57
Mediumvioletred	C71585	Seashell	FFF5EE
Midnightblue	191970	Senna	A0522D
Mintcream	F5FFFA	Silver	C0C0C0
Mistyrose	FFE4E1	Skyblue	87CEEB
Moccasin	FFE4B5	Slateblue	6A5ACD
Navajowhite	FFDEAD	Slategray	708090
Oldlace	FDF5E6	Snow	FFFAFA
Olivedrab	6B8E23	Springgreen	00FF7F
Orange	FFA500	Steelblue	4682B4
Orangered	FF4500	Tan	D2B48C
Orchid	DA70D6	Thistle	D8BFD8
Palegoldenrod	EEE8AA	Tomato	FF6347
Palegreen	98FB98	Turquoise	40E0D0
Paleturquoise	AFEEEE	Violet	EE82EE
Palevioletred	DB7093	Wheat	F5DEB3
Papayawhip	FFEFD5	Whitesmoke	F5F5F5
Peachpuff	FFDAB9	Yellowgreen	9ACD32
Peru	CD853F		

APPLY BACKGROUND COLOR

You can consistently apply background colors to elements using the `background-color` property. The basic syntax is

elementName `{background-color:` *value*`}`

elementName is the name of the element for which you want to assign the background color. The *value* can have several different settings:

- `transparent`, the default setting
- One of the 16 defined color names (see "Style Sheet Text and Display Elements," earlier in this chapter)

- A hexadecimal RGB (red, green, and blue) value (for example, #FFFFFF for white)
- A percentage RGB value, such as `rgb(100%,100%,100%)` for white

In general, the safest choice is to use a named color value, because they have the widest support.

The `background-color` property is not inherited, meaning that child elements do not automatically adopt the background of parent elements. However, because `transparent` is the default setting, unless a separate background is defined for a child element, the parent element's background will show through.

APPLY BACKGROUND COLOR

Untitled - Notepad
File Edit Search Help

```
    text-transform: none; padding: 4em}
/* Padding has been added to show the negative text-indent property*/

title
{ display: block; font: 36pt sans-serif; color: red; text-decoration:
underline;
    line-height: 150%; text-align: center; letter-spacing: 15px;
background-color: }

name
{ display: block; font: bold small-caps; color: orange; line-height: 3.5;
    text-align: center; letter-spacing: 10px}

price_per_unit, unique_characteristics, rname, rank, test_field, js_function,
retailers
{ display: none}

marketing_blurb
{ display: block; text-indent: -3em; line-height: 2em}

ingredient_list
{ display: block; font: italic; text-transform: capitalize; text-decoration:
underline}

ingredient
{ display: inline}
```

Start Untitled - Notepad   12:00 PM

Untitled - Notepad
File Edit Search Help

```
    text-transform: none; padding: 4em}
/* Padding has been added to show the negative text-indent property*/

title
{ display: block; font: 36pt sans-serif; color: red; text-decoration:
underline;
    line-height: 150%; text-align: center; letter-spacing: 15px;
background-color: silver}

name
{ display: block; font: bold small-caps; color: orange; line-height: 3.5;
    text-align: center; letter-spacing: 10px}

price_per_unit, unique_characteristics, rname, rank, test_field, js_function,
retailers
{ display: none}

marketing_blurb
{ display: block; text-indent: -3em; line-height: 2em}

ingredient_list
{ display: block; font: italic; text-transform: capitalize; text-decoration:
underline}

ingredient
{ display: inline}
```

Start Untitled - Notepad   12:00 PM

1 Open the style sheet file or create a new style sheet file.

■ See Chapter 8 for more on style sheets.

2 Place the cursor where you want to declare the `background-color`.

3 Type **background-color:**.

■ If necessary, type an opening bracket (`{`).

4 Type the desired `background-color` property.

■ In this example, the named color `silver` is entered.

■ If necessary, type a closing bracket (`}`).

5 Type any other desired `background-color` properties.

6 Save the style sheet file.

Extra

Another approach to creating custom background colors is to use a visual tool — such as the color control panel in Windows 95 (click My Computer, then Control Panel, then Display, then Appearance, then Color, then Other) — and then convert the value from decimal form to hexadecimal. Here's how: Multiply the rightmost digit by 16^0, the second rightmost digit by 16^1, the third rightmost digit by 16^2, and so on. For example,

Hexadecimal value	Decimal Value
327 (base 16) =	$(3 \times 256) + (2 \times 16) + (7 \times 1)$
	= 807 (base 10)

You can use another more limited method to enter RGB color values in a style sheet: a three-digit RGB code, such as #0F0. When you enter a three-digit RGB value, the device converts the three digits into six digits by duplicating each of the digits — so #0F0 becomes #00FF00, the code for lime. The disadvantage, of course, is that this method limits your color selections.

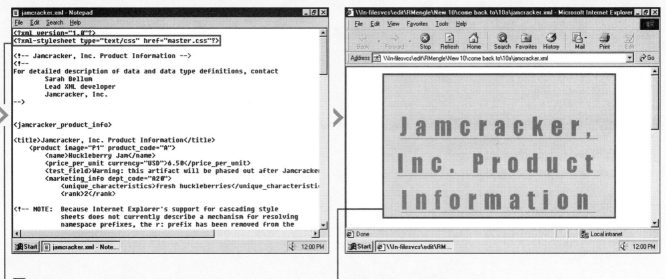

7 If you have not already done so, open up the text file for the Web page, attach the style sheet, and then save the Web page text file.

■ See Chapter 8 for more on attaching style sheets.

■ When the Web page is opened, the backgrounds reflect the designated colors.

INSERT A BACKGROUND IMAGE

Colors are not the only background choices that style sheets offer you. You can also designate an image for use as a background by using the background-image property.

The basic syntax is

elementName {background-image: location}

elementName is the name of the element to which you want to assign the background image. The *location* can have two settings:

- none: This choice is the default, and tells the browser not to bother looking for a background image.

- url(*location*): The *location* is the relative location of the image file, which is put in quotes. For example, url("marmelade.gif") tells the browser to place the marmelade.gif image in the background.

Background images are not inherited. You can, however, display a background image and a background color. In such cases, the image is placed on top of the color, so the color only shows through transparent sections of the image.

INSERT A BACKGROUND IMAGE

```
Untitled - Notepad
File  Edit  Search  Help
/* Cascading style sheet for use with the jamcracker.xml file */

jamcracker_product_info
{ display: block; font: normal normal normal 12pt Times, serif; color: black;
  text-transform: none; padding: 4em; background-image: }
/* Padding has been added to show the negative text-indent property*/

title
{ display: block; font: 36pt sans-serif; color: red; text-decoration:
underline;
  line-height: 150%; text-align: center; letter-spacing: 15px;
background-color: silver}

name
{ display: block; font: bold small-caps; color: orange; line-height: 3.5;
  text-align: center; letter-spacing: 10px}

price_per_unit, unique_characteristics, rname, rank, test_field, js_function,
retailers
{ display: none}

marketing_blurb
{ display: block; text-indent: -3em; line-height: 2em}

ingredient_list
{ display: block; font: italic; text-transform: capitalize; text-decoration:
underline}

Start    Untitled - Notepad                                    12:00 PM
```

```
1006.txt - Notepad
File  Edit  Search  Help
/* Cascading style sheet for use with the jamcracker.xml file */

jamcracker_product_info
{ display: block; font: normal normal normal 12pt Times, serif; color: black;
  text-transform: none; padding: 4em; background-image: url("TEST.jpg")}
/* Padding has been added to show the negative text-indent property*/

title
{ display: block; font: 36pt sans-serif; color: red; text-decoration:
underline;
  line-height: 150%; text-align: center; letter-spacing: 15px;
background-color: silver}

name
{ display: block; font: bold small-caps; color: orange; line-height: 3.5;
  text-align: center; letter-spacing: 10px}

price_per_unit, unique_characteristics, rname, rank, test_field, js_function,
retailers
{ display: none}

marketing_blurb
{ display: block; text-indent: -3em; line-height: 2em}

ingredient_list
{ display: block; font: italic; text-transform: capitalize; text-decoration:
underline}

Start    1006.txt - Notepad                                    12:00 PM
```

1 Open the style sheet file or create a new style sheet file.

■ See Chapter 8 for more on style sheets.

2 Place the cursor where you want to declare the **background image** property.

3 Type **background-image:**.

■ If necessary, type an opening bracket (**{**).

4 Enter the desired location.

■ In this example, the browser is told to look for the **TEST.jpeg** image.

■ If necessary, type a closing bracket (**}**).

5 Type any additional **background-image** properties.

6 Save the style sheet file.

Extra

Selecting a background color that complements foreground text and images can be tricky. For a professional look, stick to backgrounds with subtle shadings. Loud colors and non-Web-safe color combinations can distract readers — and even prevent them from being able to read page content.

In most cases, you want to store the background image you choose in the same directory in which your cascading style sheet code resides. If you're incorporating multiple images, however, you may want to organize all of your image files in a separate subdirectory. To reference a background image in a subdirectory, add the directory specification to the `location` value, like this:

```
url("images/marmelade.gif")
```

You don't always have to use quotes when specifying the image `location` value, but using quotes is the safest way. Some implementations let non-quoted strings pass, but omitting the quotes is not a good programming habit to get into.

To create your own backgrounds by repeating, or tiling, small images, see "Tile Background Images" next in this chapter.

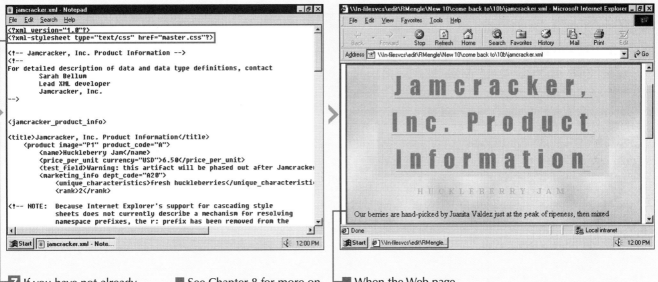

7 If you have not already done so, open up the text file for the Web page, attach the style sheet, and then save the Web page text file.

■ See Chapter 8 for more on attaching style sheets.

■ When the Web page is opened, the specified background images display.

TILE BACKGROUND IMAGES

If you have a background image that you want to repeat on your page, you can use the `background-repeat` property. Furthermore, you can use the property to specify whether the image tiles horizontally, vertically, both, or neither.

The basic syntax for using the `background-repeat` property is

elementName {background-image: *location* background-repeat: *value*}

elementName is the name of the element to which you want to assign the background image. `background-image:` *location* is the name and

location of the background image you want t' repeat. (See "Insert a Background Image," earlier in this chapter.) `background-repeat:` specifies that the image be tiled on-screen according to one of four different *value* settings:

- `repeat-x`: Repeats the image horizontally.
- `repeat-y`: Repeats the image vertically.
- `repeat`: Repeats the image both horizontally and vertically.
- `no-repeat`: Specifies that only one copy of the image displays, which is the default value.

The `background-repeat` property is not inherited.

TILE BACKGROUND IMAGES

```
Untitled - Notepad
File  Edit  Search  Help
/* Cascading style sheet for use with the jamcracker.xml file */

jamcracker_product_info
{ display: block; font: normal normal normal 12pt Times, serif; color: black;
  text-transform: none; padding: 4em; background-image: url("TEST.jpg");
  background-repeat: }
/* Padding has been added to show the negative text-indent property*/

title
{ display: block; font: 36pt sans-serif; color: red; text-decoration:
underline;
  line-height: 150%; text-align: center; letter-spacing: 15px;
background-color: silver}

name
{ display: block; font: bold small-caps; color: orange; line-height: 3.5;
  text-align: center; letter-spacing: 10px}

price_per_unit, unique_characteristics, rname, rank, test_field, js_function,
retailers
{ display: none}

marketing_blurb
{ display: block; text-indent: -3em; line-height: 2em}

ingredient_list
{ display: block; font: italic; text-transform: capitalize; text-decoration:
Start   Untitled - Notepad                                        12:00 PM
```

```
1010.txt - Notepad
File  Edit  Search  Help
/* Cascading style sheet for use with the jamcracker.xml file */

jamcracker_product_info
{ display: block; font: normal normal normal 12pt Times, serif; color: black;
  text-transform: none; padding: 4em; background-image: url("TEST.jpg");
  background-repeat: repeat-x}
/* Padding has been added to show the negative text-indent property*/

title
{ display: block; font: 36pt sans-serif; color: red; text-decoration:
underline;
  line-height: 150%; text-align: center; letter-spacing: 15px;
background-color: silver}

name
{ display: block; font: bold small-caps; color: orange; line-height: 3.5;
  text-align: center; letter-spacing: 10px}

price_per_unit, unique_characteristics, rname, rank, test_field, js_function,
retailers
{ display: none}

marketing_blurb
{ display: block; text-indent: -3em; line-height: 2em}

ingredient_list
{ display: block; font: italic; text-transform: capitalize; text-decoration:
Start   1006.txt - Notepad                                        12:00 PM
```

1 Open the style sheet file or create a new style sheet file.

■ See Chapter 8 for more on style sheets.

2 Place the cursor where you want to declare the `background-repeat` property.

3 Type **background-repeat:** and the desired value.

■ If necessary, type an opening bracket (**{**).

4 Enter the desired location.

■ In this example, the image is instructed to repeat vertically.

■ If necessary, type a closing bracket (**}**).

5 Type any additional `background-repeat` properties.

6 Save the style sheet file.

Extra

Not every image can be tiled to good effect. Keep in mind some simple rules when using background images:

- Make sure when using this feature that the background generated is visually compatible with any foreground text and images.

- Use subtle images. Repeating an image containing intense colors or patterns typically doesn't produce a visually appealing background. The exception may be a limited use as a kind of border, such as a Mayan pattern across the top of a page.

- When the background image and foreground text do clash, sometimes the simplest solution is to move the text. See Chapter 9 for more on how to align or position text.

By default, all background images display at the top-left corner of the element to which they're attached. However, you can change this location using the `background-position` property.

The next section, "Position a Background Image," shows you how to place a background image on a particular section of a page and lock it into place.

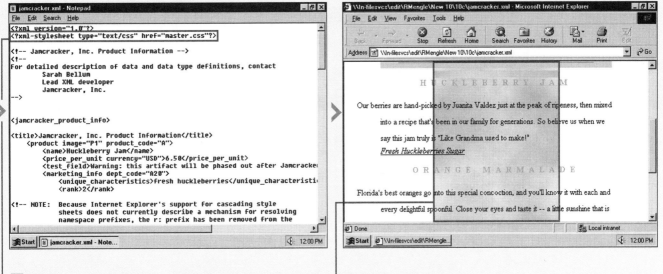

7 If you have not already done so, open up the text file for the Web page, attach the style sheet, and then save the Web page text file.

■ See Chapter 8 for more on attaching style sheets.

■ When the Web page is opened, the background images repeat as directed.

POSITION A BACKGROUND IMAGE

I f you want to change the location of a background image, you can use the `background-position` property.

To position a background image, you simply add:

`background-position:` *location*

somewhere in your background image code. When you specify the *location*, you can select from three different kinds of values:

- Percentages of the parent element's width and height: These percentage values are given as first an x coordinate (the left-right positioning) and then a y coordinate (the top-bottom positioning). The values

range from 0% (left edge for the x value, top edge for the y value) to 100% (right edge for the x value, bottom edge for the y value). A value of `background-position: 50% 40%` puts the image right in the center horizontally and just above center vertically.

- Keyword combinations: You can use two of six specified keywords — `left`, `center`, and `right` for x values, and `top`, `center`, and `bottom` for y values. For example, `top center` puts the image at the middle of the top of the page.

- Absolute values: See "Style Sheet Text and Display Elements," earlier in this chapter, for more on acceptable values.

POSITION A BACKGROUND IMAGE

1 Open the style sheet file or create a new style sheet file.

■ See Chapter 8 for more on style sheets.

2 Place the cursor where you want to declare the `background-position` property.

3 Type **background-position:**.

■ If necessary, type an opening bracket (**{**).

4 Enter the desired location.

■ In this example, `top center` is entered.

■ If necessary, type a closing bracket (**}**).

5 Type any additional `background-position` properties.

6 Save the style sheet file.

Extra

Using relative values to position your image is a good idea — especially if your application has multiple target display devices.

For example, positioning an image absolutely may look great on a small layout, but totally inappropriate on a large screen. Using relative values to position your background won't make your image display identical on both platforms, but it will help ensure consistency.

Whether you choose relative or absolute coordinates, add a comment that describes the effect you're trying to achieve (and, if appropriate, the reasoning behind your choice). Thoroughly commenting on your code is always good practice, but the lack of standard implementation and documentation for style sheets makes doing so essential when constructing a style sheet application.

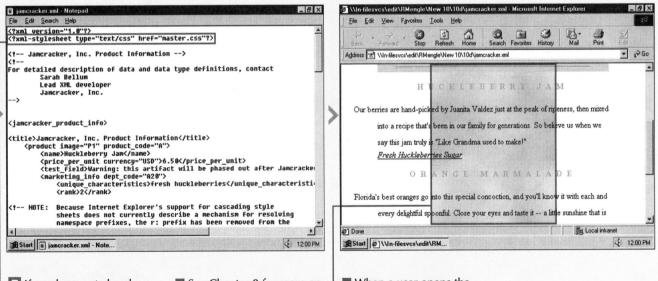

7 If you have not already done so, open up the text file for the Web page, attach the style sheet, and then save the Web page text file.

■ See Chapter 8 for more on attaching style sheets.

■ When a user opens the Web page, the background image appears in the specified location.

ATTACH A BACKGROUND IMAGE

Background images are attached to elements. Consequently, when that element scrolls off the screen, by default the background image scrolls off, too. However, you can use the `background-attachment` property to keep a background image fixed on the screen, even as the user scrolls around the page.

This property has many uses in the business world. For example, if you're designing a business Web page with the logo of the company as the background image, you may well want to keep the company's logo prominently displayed, no matter where the user navigates.

To attach a background image, you simply add

```
background-attachment: type
```

somewhere in your background image code. You can choose from two *type* values:

- `fixed`, which keeps the image in the same location in the viewing window, regardless of how the user navigates

- `scroll`, the default value, which keeps the image attached to the document

The `background-attachment` property is not inherited and, unfortunately, is not yet supported by all browsers.

ATTACH A BACKGROUND IMAGE

```
Untitled - Notepad                                      _ & X
File  Edit  Search  Help
/* Cascading style sheet for use with the jamcracker.xml file */

jamcracker_product_info
{ display: block; font: normal normal normal 12pt Times, serif; color: black;
  text-transform: none; padding: 4em; background-image: url("TEST.jpg");
  background-repeat: repeat-y; background-position: top center;
  background-attachment: }
/* Padding has been added to show the negative text-indent property*/

title
{ display: block; font: 36pt sans-serif; color: red; text-decoration:
underline;
  line-height: 150%; text-align: center; letter-spacing: 15px;
background-color: silver}

name
{ display: block; font: bold small-caps; color: orange; line-height: 3.5;
  text-align: center; letter-spacing: 10px}

price_per_unit, unique_characteristics, rname, rank, test_field, js_function,
retailers
{ display: none}

marketing_blurb
{ display: block; text-indent: -3em; line-height: 2em}

ingredient_list

Start | Untitled - Notepad                            12:00 PM
```

```
Untitled - Notepad                                      _ & X
File  Edit  Search  Help
/* Cascading style sheet for use with the jamcracker.xml file */

jamcracker_product_info
{ display: block; font: normal normal normal 12pt Times, serif; color: black;
  text-transform: none; padding: 4em; background-image: url("TEST.jpg");
  background-repeat: repeat-y; background-position: top center;
  background-attachment: fixed}
/* Padding has been added to show the negative text-indent property*/

title
{ display: block; font: 36pt sans-serif; color: red; text-decoration:
underline;
  line-height: 150%; text-align: center; letter-spacing: 15px;
background-color: silver}

name
{ display: block; font: bold small-caps; color: orange; line-height: 3.5;
  text-align: center; letter-spacing: 10px}

price_per_unit, unique_characteristics, rname, rank, test_field, js_function,
retailers
{ display: none}

marketing_blurb
{ display: block; text-indent: -3em; line-height: 2em}

ingredient_list

Start | Untitled - Notepad                            12:00 PM
```

■1 Open the style sheet file or create a new style sheet file.

■ See Chapter 8 for more on style sheets.

■2 Place the cursor where you want to declare the `background-attachment` property.

■3 Type **background-attachment:**.

■ If necessary, type an opening bracket (**{**).

■4 Type the desired value.

■ In this example, the image is set to be `fixed` to the background.

■ If necessary, type a closing bracket (**}**).

■5 Type any additional desired `background-attachment` properties.

■6 Save the style sheet file.

Extra

The biggest challenge involved in using cascading style sheets is the lack of standard implementation. The World Wide Web Consortium (www.w3c.org) proposes standards, but providing consistent support is up to vendors such as Microsoft and Netscape.

Although products (the W3 calls them "user agents") claiming support for the various CSS standards, including CSS1 and CSS2, must provide a certain level of baseline support, they're free to introduce new, non-standard elements. Microsoft, for example, calls these add-on elements "proposed" elements.

`background-position-x` and `background-position-y` are two add-on, or "proposed," properties that Internet Explorer 5.5 supports — but that have not yet been formally adopted into the W3C's specification.

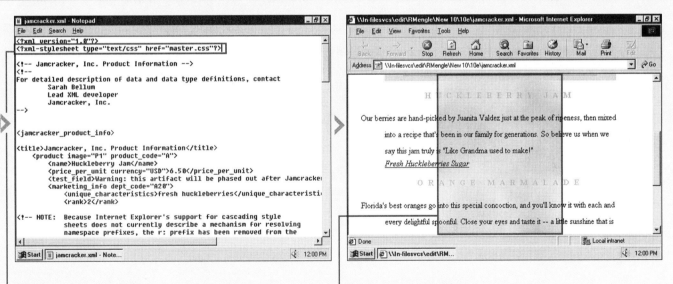

7 If you have not already done so, open up the text file for the Web page, attach the style sheet, and then save the Web page text file.

■ See Chapter 8 for more on attaching style sheets.

■ When the Web page is re-opened, the background image either stays fixed or scrolls, as designated.

USING BACKGROUND PROPERTY SHORTHAND

If you want to shorten the amount of code that you type in for background properties, you can use background property shorthand. The basic syntax is:

```
elementName {background:-image color
repeat attachment position}
```

elementName is the name of the element to which you want to assign the background. After the background: keyword, the order of the other five elements is optional. The five elements are as follows:

- image(location) represents the background-image property. (See the "Insert a Background Image" section earlier in this chapter for code values.)

- color represents the background-color property. (See "Apply Background Color" earlier in this chapter for code values.)

- repeat represents the background-repeat property. (See "Tile Background Images" earlier in this chapter for code values.)

- attachment stands for the background-attachment property. (See "Attach a Background Image" earlier in this chapter for code values.)

- *position* stands for the background-position property. (See "Position a Background Image" earlier in this chapter for code values.)

The background property shorthand is not inherited by child elements.

USING BACKGROUND PROPERTY SHORTHAND

1 Open the style sheet file or create a new style sheet file.

■ See Chapter 8 for more on style sheets.

2 Place the cursor where you want to declare the background property.

3 Type **background:**.

■ If necessary, type an opening bracket ({).

4 Type the desired values.

■ If necessary, type a closing bracket (}).

5 Type any additional desired background properties.

6 Save the style sheet file.

Extra

In general, spelling out your wishes explicitly is better than implying them using shorthand notation, such as the `background` property demonstrated in this section. Saving a line or two of code doesn't affect runtime performance materially, and because an estimated 90 percent of the cost of software is associated with maintenance, making your code as easy to understand as possible is well worth the time and trouble.

However, many programmers appreciate the simplicity and brevity of the shorthand approach. If you do decide to use shorthand notation, make sure you include frequent comments in your code.

For large applications that demand a similar look and feel across the interface, you want to create the desired shorthand notation once, store it, and replicate it for all your CSS documents. (Or use one of the CSS tools on the market, many of which generate code automatically.)

7 If you have not already done so, open up the text file for the Web page, attach the style sheet, and then save the Web page text file.

■ See Chapter 8 for more on attaching style sheets.

■ When the Web page is opened, the background displays as specified.

CHOOSE A BORDER STYLE

Most elements on your Web pages have invisible borders. However, if you want to add a border, you can designate what kind of border with the border-style property. The basic syntax is

elementName {border-style: *type*}

elementName is the name of the element to which you want to assign the border. The default value of *type* is none, but you can choose from eight other values:

- dotted
- dashed
- solid

- double
- groove
- ridge
- inset, which makes the border look as though it is embedded in the canvas
- outset, which is the opposite of inset

The border-style property is not inherited by child elements.

You can specify between one and four values for the border-style property. (See "Style Sheet Text and Display Elements," earlier in this chapter, for more information on the instruction application order.)

CHOOSE A BORDER STYLE

```
Untitled - Notepad                                      _ 8 X
File  Edit  Search  Help
jamcracker_product_info
{ display: block; font: normal normal normal 12pt Times, serif; color: black;
  text-transform: none; padding: 4em; background: url("TEST.jpg") repeat-y
  top center fixed}
/* Padding has been added to show the negative text-indent property*/

title
{ display: block; font: 36pt sans-serif; color: red; text-decoration:
underline;
  line-height: 150%; text-align: center; letter-spacing: 15px; background:
silver}

name
{ display: block; font: bold small-caps; color: orange; line-height: 3.5;
  text-align: center; letter-spacing: 10px}

price_per_unit, unique_characteristics, rname, rank, test_field, js_function,
retailers
{ display: none}

marketing_blurb
{ display: block; text-indent: -3em; line-height: 2em}

ingredient_list
{ display: block; font: italic; text-transform: capitalize; text-decoration:
underline;
  border-style: }
Start   Untitled - Notepad                              12:00 PM
```

```
Untitled - Notepad                                      _ 8 X
File  Edit  Search  Help
jamcracker_product_info
{ display: block; font: normal normal normal 12pt Times, serif; color: black;
  text-transform: none; padding: 4em; background: url("TEST.jpg") repeat-y
  top center fixed}
/* Padding has been added to show the negative text-indent property*/

title
{ display: block; font: 36pt sans-serif; color: red; text-decoration:
underline;
  line-height: 150%; text-align: center; letter-spacing: 15px; background:
silver}

name
{ display: block; font: bold small-caps; color: orange; line-height: 3.5;
  text-align: center; letter-spacing: 10px}

price_per_unit, unique_characteristics, rname, rank, test_field, js_function,
retailers
{ display: none}

marketing_blurb
{ display: block; text-indent: -3em; line-height: 2em}

ingredient_list
{ display: block; font: italic; text-transform: capitalize; text-decoration:
underline;
  border-style: solid}
Start   Untitled - Notepad                              12:00 PM
```

■1 Open the style sheet file or create a new style sheet file.

■ See Chapter 8 for more on style sheets.

■2 Place the cursor where you want to declare the border-style property.

■3 Type **border-style:**.

■ If necessary, type an opening bracket ({).

■4 Type the desired style.

■ In this example, a solid border is specified.

■ If necessary, type a closing bracket (}).

■5 Type any additional desired border-style properties.

■6 Save the style sheet file.

Apply It

Changing the value for the `border-width` property dynamically — for example, when a user moves a mouse over an image — can be very effective in alerting users that an image is clickable. The following code displays an image with a solid border, and then dynamically changes the border to "grooved" in response to a `mouseover`.

Example:

```
<HTML>
<BODY onload="oImg.style.borderWidth='0.5cm'; oImg.style.borderStyle='SOLID'"
TOPMARGIN=0 LEFTMARGIN=0 BGPROPERTIES="FIXED" BGCOLOR="#FFFFFF" LINK="#000000"
VLINK="#808080" ALINK="#000000">
<BLOCKQUOTE CLASS="body">
<P>The image is loaded in a table with <B>borderStyle</B> of <B>SOLID</B>.
Roll your cursor over the image to change style to <B>GROOVE</B>. <P>
<CENTER><TABLE BORDER><TR>
<TD ID="oImg" onmouseover="this.style.borderWidth='0.5cm';
this.style.borderStyle='GROOVE'"
onmouseout="this.style.borderWidth='0.5cm'; this.style.borderStyle='SOLID'"
ALIGN=center VALIGN=middle>
<IMG src="surprised.gif" height="80" width="80" border="0"></TD>
</TR></TABLE></CENTER>
</BLOCKQUOTE>
</BODY>
</HTML>
```

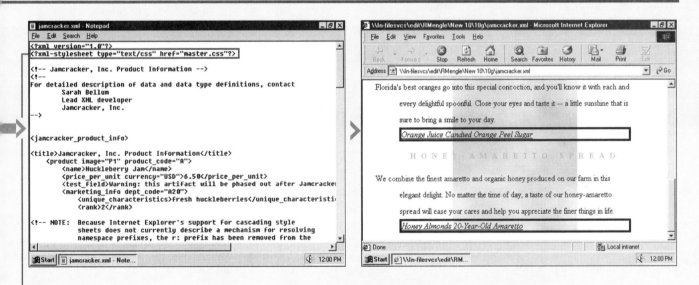

7 If you have not already done so, open up the text file for the Web page, attach the style sheet, and then save the Web page text file.

■ See Chapter 8 for more on attaching style sheets.

■ Until a border width is specified (see "Specify a Border Width," coming up next), the border is displayed with the default width.

SPECIFY A BORDER WIDTH

Once you have specified a border style, you can specify a width using the `border-width` property.

You can approach the `border-width` syntax one of two ways. The simplest approach is to use `border-width` property shorthand:

elementName {border-width: *width*}

You can designate up to four values for the *width*; see "Style Sheet Text and Display Elements," earlier in this chapter, for more information on the instruction application order.

If you desire more specific control or do not want to put a border on every side, you can use this syntax:

elementName {border-top-width: *width*; border-right-width: *width*; border-bottom-width: *width*; border-left-width: *width*}

You can omit the code for any border you do not want to specify.

The *width* values can fall into three categories:

- The keywords `thin`, `medium`, and `thick`.
- Relative values, such as `2em`. (See "Style Sheet Text and Display Elements," earlier in this chapter, for more information.)
- Absolute values, such as `9mm`. (See "Style Sheet Text and Display Elements," earlier in this chapter.)

The `border-width` property is not inherited.

SPECIFY A BORDER WIDTH

Untitled - Notepad
File Edit Search Help

```
jamcracker_product_info
{ display: block; font: normal normal normal 12pt Times, serif; color: black;
  text-transform: none; padding: 4em; background: url("TEST.jpg") repeat-y
  top center fixed}
/* Padding has been added to show the negative text-indent property*/

title
{ display: block; font: 36pt sans-serif; color: red; text-decoration:
underline;
  line-height: 150%; text-align: center; letter-spacing: 15px; background:
silver}

name
{ display: block; font: bold small-caps; color: orange; line-height: 3.5;
  text-align: center; letter-spacing: 10px}

price_per_unit, unique_characteristics, rname, rank, test_field, js_function,
retailers
{ display: none}

marketing_blurb
{ display: block; text-indent: -3em; line-height: 2em}

ingredient_list
{ display: block; font: italic; text-transform: capitalize; text-decoration:
underline;
  border-style: solid; border-width: }
```

Start | Untitled - Notepad   12:00 PM

Untitled - Notepad
File Edit Search Help

```
jamcracker_product_info
{ display: block; font: normal normal normal 12pt Times, serif; color: black;
  text-transform: none; padding: 4em; background: url("TEST.jpg") repeat-y
  top center fixed}
/* Padding has been added to show the negative text-indent property*/

title
{ display: block; font: 36pt sans-serif; color: red; text-decoration:
underline;
  line-height: 150%; text-align: center; letter-spacing: 15px; background:
silver}

name
{ display: block; font: bold small-caps; color: orange; line-height: 3.5;
  text-align: center; letter-spacing: 10px}

price_per_unit, unique_characteristics, rname, rank, test_field, js_function,
retailers
{ display: none}

marketing_blurb
{ display: block; text-indent: -3em; line-height: 2em}

ingredient_list
{ display: block; font: italic; text-transform: capitalize; text-decoration:
underline;
  border-style: solid; border-width: medium}
```

Start | Untitled - Notepad   12:00 PM

1 Open the style sheet file or create a new style sheet file.

■ See Chapter 8 for more on style sheets.

2 Place the cursor where you want to declare the `border-width` property.

3 Type **border-width:**.

■ If necessary, type an opening bracket ({).

4 Type the desired width.

■ In this example, a width of medium is specified.

■ If necessary, type a closing bracket (}).

5 Type any additional desired `border-width` properties.

6 Save the style sheet file.

Extra

Given the wide variety of display devices on the market today, consider using keyword values when specifying a `border-width` property. Using a keyword lets the device interpret just how thick to make the border.

Letting, say, a handheld computer decide what `thick` is promises easier readability than a one-inch border on the same device. Further, the W3C mandates that the keyword values be interpreted consistently throughout a document, so what `thick` is on the home page will be the same as on page seven.

The `border-width` and `border-style` properties are related; they work together to describe how, if at all, a border appears around an image. If the `border-style` property is set to `none` (see the previous section, "Choose a Border Style," for details), the border will not be rendered, and all values associated with the `border-width` property will be ignored.

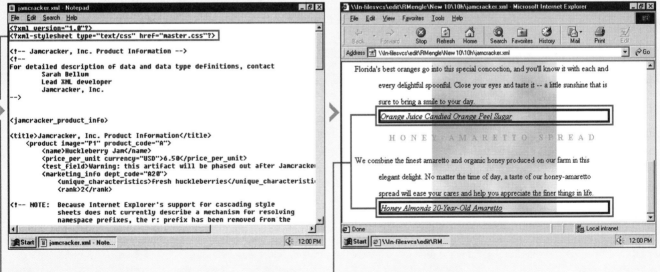

7 If you have not already done so, open up the text file for the Web page, attach the style sheet, and then save the Web page text file.

■ See Chapter 8 for more on attaching style sheets.

■ When the Web page is opened, the border appears in the width and style specified.

CHOOSE A BORDER COLOR

Borders, as with many other Web page elements, can be a variety of colors. You can designate the colors for your elements' borders by using the border-color property.

You can specify the border color by using the following basic syntax:

elementName {border-color: *color*}

elementName is the name of the element to which you want to assign the border color. Up to four different *color* values can be specified. See "Choose a Border Style," earlier in this chapter, for the order in which the *color* values are applied.

The *color* value can be from four different categories:

- transparent, the default setting
- One of the 16 defined color names
- A hexadecimal RGB value (for example, #FFFFFF for white)
- A percentage RGB value, such as rgb(100%,100%,100%) for white

See the "Style Sheet Text and Display Elements" section earlier in this chapter, for more information on RGB values and color names.

CHOOSE A BORDER COLOR

```
Untitled - Notepad
File   Edit   Search   Help
jamcracker_product_info
{ display: block; font: normal normal normal 12pt Times, serif; color: black;
  text-transform: none; padding: 4em; background: url("TEST.jpg") repeat-y
  top center fixed}
/* Padding has been added to show the negative text-indent property*/

title
{ display: block; font: 36pt sans-serif; color: red; text-decoration:
underline;
  line-height: 150%; text-align: center; letter-spacing: 15px; background:
silver}

name
{ display: block; font: bold small-caps; color: orange; line-height: 3.5;
  text-align: center; letter-spacing: 10px}

price_per_unit, unique_characteristics, rname, rank, test_field, js_function,
retailers
{ display: none}

marketing_blurb
{ display: block; text-indent: -3em; line-height: 2em}

ingredient_list
{ display: block; font: italic; text-transform: capitalize; text-decoration:
underline;
  border-style: solid; border-width: medium; border-color: }

Start    Untitled - Notepad                                    12:00 PM
```

```
Untitled - Notepad
File   Edit   Search   Help
ng style sheet for use with the jamcracker.xml file */

_product_info
  block; font: normal normal normal 12pt Times, serif; color: black;
nsform: none; padding: 4em; background: url("TEST.jpg") repeat-y
er fixed}
  has been added to show the negative text-indent property*/

  block; font: 36pt sans-serif; color: red; text-decoration: underline;
ght: 150%; text-align: center; letter-spacing: 15px; background: silver}

  block; font: bold small-caps; color: orange; line-height: 3.5;
gn: center; letter-spacing: 10px}

unit, unique_characteristics, rname, rank, test_field, js_function, retailers
  none}

blurb
  block; text-indent: -3em; line-height: 2em}

_list
  block; font: italic; text-transform: capitalize; text-decoration: underline;
tyle: solid; border-width: medium; border-color: red}

Start    Untitled - Notepad                                    12:00 PM
```

1 Open the style sheet file or create a new style sheet file.

■ See Chapter 8 for more on style sheets.

2 Place the cursor where you want to declare the border-color property.

3 Type **border-color:**.

■ If necessary, type an opening bracket ({).

4 Type the desired color.

■ In this example, the chosen color is red.

■ If necessary, type a closing bracket (}).

5 Type any additional desired border-color properties.

6 Save the style sheet file.

Extra

Internet Explorer 5.5 supports the border-left-color and border-right-color properties, which allow you to specify different colors for different portions of a displayed border. For details, visit http://msdn.microsoft.com/workshop/author/dhtml/reference/properties/borderLeftColor.asp#borderLeftColor and http://msdn.microsoft.com/workshop/author/dhtml/reference/properties/borderRightColor.asp#borderRightColor, respectively.

The following code displays a red border that changes to blue dynamically, in response to a `mouseover`:

Example:

```
<HTML><HEAD><STYLE>
TD { border-color: "red"; border-width: "0.5cm"} .blue { border-color: "blue" }
</STYLE></HEAD>
<BODY TOPMARGIN=0 LEFTMARGIN=0 BGPROPERTIES="FIXED" BGCOLOR="#FFFFFF" LINK="#000000"
VLINK="#808080" ALINK="#000000">
<BLOCKQUOTE CLASS="body"><CENTER>
<P>Mouse over the image to see the border color change from blue to red.</P>
<P><TABLE BORDER><TR>
<TD onmouseover="this.className='blue'" onmouseout="this.className=''">
<IMG src="surprised.gif" height="80" width="80" border=0 ></TD>
</TR></TABLE></CENTER></BLOCKQUOTE></BODY></HTML>
```

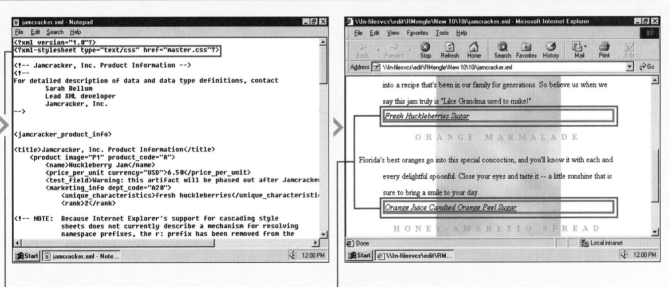

7 If you have not already done so, open up the text file for the Web page, attach the style sheet, and then save the Web page text file.

■ See Chapter 8 for more on attaching style sheets.

■ When the Web page is opened, your chosen border colors appear.

USING BORDER PROPERTY SHORTHAND

The border property has a shorthand style that you can use to define your border size, style, and color quickly. The basic syntax is

`elementName {border: size style color}`

elementName is the name of the element to which you want to assign the border. Regarding the other three entries:

- *size* refers to the border width. See "Specify a Border Width," earlier in this chapter.
- *style* refers to the border style. See "Choose a Border Style," earlier in this chapter.
- *color* refers to the border color. See "Choose a Border Color," earlier in this chapter.

The order of the three values is not critical. You can omit any of the values, but omitted values may inherit the specifications of a parent element.

One disadvantage to using border-property shorthand is that you cannot designate different values on the four borders. However, you can use a variant of the border-property shorthand for a specific border. The syntax is

`elementName {border-which: size style color}`

which refers to the border in question — top, right, bottom, or left.

USING BORDER PROPERTY SHORTHAND

```
Untitled - Notepad                                      _ 8 X
File  Edit  Search  Help
jamcracker_product_info
{ display: block; font: normal normal normal 12pt Times, serif; color: black;
  text-transform: none; padding: 4em; background: url("TEST.jpg") repeat-y
  top center fixed}
/* Padding has been added to show the negative text-indent property*/

title
{ display: block; font: 36pt sans-serif; color: red; text-decoration:
underline;
  line-height: 150%; text-align: center; letter-spacing: 15px; background:
silver}

name
{ display: block; font: bold small-caps; color: orange; line-height: 3.5;
  text-align: center; letter-spacing: 10px}

price_per_unit, unique_characteristics, rname, rank, test_field, js_function,
retailers
{ display: none}

marketing_blurb
{ display: block; text-indent: -3em; line-height: 2em}

ingredient_list
{ display: block; font: italic; text-transform: capitalize; text-decoration:
underline;
  border: }
Start   Untitled - Notepad                              12:00 PM
```

```
Untitled - Notepad                                      _ 8 X
File  Edit  Search  Help
jamcracker_product_info
{ display: block; font: normal normal normal 12pt Times, serif; color: black;
  text-transform: none; padding: 4em; background: url("TEST.jpg") repeat-y
  top center fixed}
/* Padding has been added to show the negative text-indent property*/

title
{ display: block; font: 36pt sans-serif; color: red; text-decoration:
underline;
  line-height: 150%; text-align: center; letter-spacing: 15px; background:
silver}

name
{ display: block; font: bold small-caps; color: orange; line-height: 3.5;
  text-align: center; letter-spacing: 10px}

price_per_unit, unique_characteristics, rname, rank, test_field, js_function,
retailers
{ display: none}

marketing_blurb
{ display: block; text-indent: -3em; line-height: 2em}

ingredient_list
{ display: block; font: italic; text-transform: capitalize; text-decoration:
underline;
  border: solid medium red}
Start   Untitled - Notepad                              12:00 PM
```

1 Open the style sheet file or create a new style sheet file.

■ See Chapter 8 for more on style sheets.

2 Place the cursor where you want to declare the border property.

3 Type **border:**.

■ If necessary, type opening bracket ({).

4 Type the desired values.

■ In this example, a solid, medium red border is specified.

■ If necessary, type a closing bracket (}).

5 Type any additional desired border properties.

6 Save the style sheet file.

Extra

You must specify a style when specifying a width or color; otherwise, the border will not render. All individual border properties not set by the shorthand `border` property are set to their default values. For example, the default value for a border's width is `medium`.

Setting a border to zero (or omitting the attribute) causes no border to be displayed. Supplying the `border` attribute without a value defaults to a single border. If a border color is not specified, the text color is used.

The following code shows how to use the `border` shorthand notation both to create a border and to remove it dynamically:

Example:

```
<HTML><HEAD><STYLE>.applyBorder {Border:"0.2cm GROOVE ORANGE"}
.removeBorder {Border:""}</STYLE></HEAD>
<BODY TOPMARGIN=0 LEFTMARGIN=0 BGPROPERTIES="FIXED" BGCOLOR="#FFFFFF" LINK="#000000"
VLINK="#808080" ALINK="#000000">
<BLOCKQUOTE CLASS="body">
<CENTER><P>This example uses the border shorthand notation both to apply and to
remove a border. (Mouse over the image to apply the border.)</P>
<TABLE BORDER><TR><TD onmouseover="this.className='applyBorder'"
onmouseout="this.className='removeBorder'" ALIGN="middle" VALIGN="center">
<IMG src="surprised.gif" height="80" width="80"></TD></TR></TABLE>
</BLOCKQUOTE>
</BODY></HTML>
```

7 If you have not already done so, open up the text file for the Web page, attach the style sheet, and then save the Web page text file.

■ See Chapter 8 for more on attaching style sheets.

■ When the Web page is opened, the border appears as specified.

SET PADDING

Utilizing the `padding` property, you can define just how much space you want between the element's content and the border.

You can define padding two ways. One way is to define specific padding values, such as

elementName {padding-*which*: *size*}

elementName is the name of the element to which you want to assign the padding. *which* is the particular piece of padding you want to define — top, bottom, left, or right.

The other way to define padding is to use `padding` property shorthand:

elementName {padding: *size* ...}

You can define up to four *size* values. The *size* values can be of two different kinds:

- An absolute value, such as 2cm
- A relative value, such as 2em

See "Style Sheet Text and Display Elements," earlier in this chapter, for the order in which instructions are applied and for more on absolute and relative values.

SET PADDING

```
top center fixed}
/* Padding has been added to show the negative text-indent property*/

title
{ display: block; font: 36pt sans-serif; color: red; text-decoration:
underline;
  line-height: 150%; text-align: center; letter-spacing: 15px; background:
silver}

name
{ display: block; font: bold small-caps; color: orange; line-height: 3.5;
  text-align: center; letter-spacing: 10px}

price_per_unit, unique_characteristics, rname, rank, test_field, js_function,
retailers
{ display: none}

marketing_blurb
{ display: block; text-indent: -3em; line-height: 2em}

ingredient_list
{ display: block; font: italic; text-transform: capitalize; text-decoration:
underline;
  border: solid medium red; padding: }

ingredient_list
{display: block}
```

```
top center fixed}
/* Padding has been added to show the negative text-indent property*/

title
{ display: block; font: 36pt sans-serif; color: red; text-decoration:
underline;
  line-height: 150%; text-align: center; letter-spacing: 15px; background:
silver}

name
{ display: block; font: bold small-caps; color: orange; line-height: 3.5;
  text-align: center; letter-spacing: 10px}

price_per_unit, unique_characteristics, rname, rank, test_field, js_function,
retailers
{ display: none}

marketing_blurb
{ display: block; text-indent: -3em; line-height: 2em}

ingredient_list
{ display: block; font: italic; text-transform: capitalize; text-decoration:
underline;
  border: solid medium red; padding: 2em}

ingredient_list
{display: block}
```

1 Open the style sheet file or create a new style sheet file.

■ See Chapter 8 for more on style sheets.

2 Place the cursor where you want to declare the `padding` property.

3 Type an opening bracket ({), if necessary, and the `padding` property command.

■ In this example, the `padding` shorthand property command is used.

4 Type the desired values.

■ In this example, a uniform padding of 2em is specified.

■ If necessary, type a closing bracket (}).

5 Type any additional desired `padding` properties.

6 Save the style sheet file.

Extra

Because padding only exists in relation to a border, the `padding` property only comes into play when you specify a border for an image. (See the "Using Border Property Shorthand" section earlier in this chapter for details on specifying borders.)

While you can't assign color to the padding around an image, you can create a similar effect by creating a colored border with no padding. (See "Choose a Border Color" for instructions on creating colored borders.)

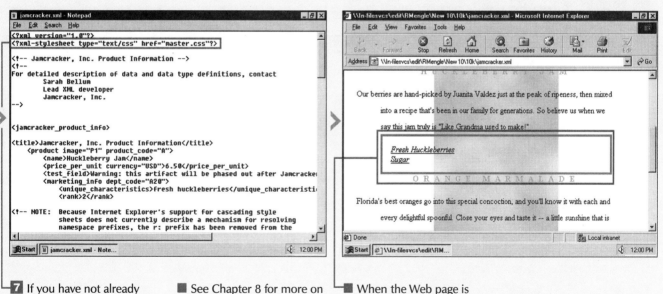

7 If you have not already done so, open up the text file for the Web page, attach the style sheet, and then save the Web page text file.

■ See Chapter 8 for more on attaching style sheets.

■ When the Web page is opened, the border and the element content are separated by the specified amount of padding.

SET MARGINS

You can set the margins — the area between the border and the edge of the element — in a style sheet by using the `margin` property.

As with padding (see the "Set Padding" section in this chapter), you can define margins in two ways:

- With a command or commands specifying a margin for a specific edge @ `top`, `right`, `bottom`, `left`. The basic code syntax for this method is:

`elementName {margin-edge: size}`

`edge` is the name of the edge in question.

- With `padding` property shorthand:

`elementName {padding: size ...}`

You can define up to four values for `size` using the shorthand method.

The `size` values can be either

- An absolute value, such as 2cm
- A relative value, such as 2em

See "Style Sheet Text and Display Elements," earlier in this chapter, for the order in which instructions are applied and for more on absolute and relative values.

SET MARGINS

```
top center fixed}
/* Padding has been added to show the negative text-indent property*/

title
{ display: block; font: 36pt sans-serif; color: red; text-decoration:
underline;
  line-height: 150%; text-align: center; letter-spacing: 15px; background:
silver}

name
{ display: block; font: bold small-caps; color: orange; line-height: 3.5;
  text-align: center; letter-spacing: 10px}

price_per_unit, unique_characteristics, rname, rank, test_field, js_function,
retailers
{ display: none}

marketing_blurb
{ display: block; text-indent: -3em; line-height: 2em}

ingredient_list
{ display: block; font: italic; text-transform: capitalize; text-decoration:
underline;
  border: solid medium red; padding: 1em; margin: 1em 1em 1.5em}

ingredient
{display: block}
```

```
top center fixed}
/* Padding has been added to show the negative text-indent property*/

title
{ display: block; font: 36pt sans-serif; color: red; text-decoration:
underline;
  line-height: 150%; text-align: center; letter-spacing: 15px; background:
silver}

name
{ display: block; font: bold small-caps; color: orange; line-height: 3.5;
  text-align: center; letter-spacing: 10px; margin-top: .5em}

price_per_unit, unique_characteristics, rname, rank, test_field, js_function,
retailers
{ display: none}

marketing_blurb
{ display: block; text-indent: -3em; line-height: 2em}

ingredient_list
{ display: block; font: italic; text-transform: capitalize; text-decoration:
underline;
  border: solid medium red; padding: 1em; margin: 1em 1em 1.5em}

ingredient
{display: block}
```

1 Open the style sheet file or create a new style sheet file.

2 Place the cursor where you want to declare the `margin` property.

3 Type **margin:** and the desired values.

■ If necessary, type opening and closing brackets ({ and }).

■ Here, margins are added to `ingredient_list`.

4 Type any additional `margin` values.

■ A margin is added to the `name` element in this example.

5 Save the style sheet file.

Apply It

The ability to define margins can be useful when embedding elements inside HTML table cells. You can even change margin width dynamically in response to user interaction, using Internet Explorer's scriptable style sheet elements.

For example, the following code displays several images using an initial margin width of zero. When a user moves a mouse over the center image, the margins between all the images are expanded dynamically.

Example:

```
<HTML>
<BODY TOPMARGIN=0 LEFTMARGIN=0 BGPROPERTIES="FIXED" BGCOLOR="#FFFFFF" >
<BLOCKQUOTE CLASS="body">
<CENTER>
<P><B>Drag your mouse over the center image</B> to expand the margins dynamically;
mouseout to return to default margins.
</P>
<IMG src="surprised.gif" height="80" width="80" border="0"><BR>
<IMG src="surprised.gif" height="80" width="80" border="0">
<IMG src="surprised.gif" onmouseover="this.style.margin='5mm 5mm 5mm 5mm'"
onmouseout="this.style.margin=''">
<IMG src="surprised.gif" height="80" width="80" border="0" ><BR>
<IMG src="surprised.gif" height="80" width="80" border="0">
</CENTER>
</BLOCKQUOTE>
</BODY>
</HTML>
```

---

6 If you have not already done so, open up the text file for the Web page, attach the style sheet, and then save the Web page text file.

■ See Chapter 8 for more on attaching style sheets.

■ The Web page now reflects the new margin settings.

SET AN ELEMENT'S WIDTH

You can define exactly how much width you want to give an element's content, padding, and border area by using the `width` property.

The basic syntax is

```
elementName {width: value}
```

`elementName` is the name of the element whose `width` you want to set. The `value` options include

- `auto`, the default value, which allows the browser to automatically figure the value.

- Absolute values, such as `5cm` or `4pt`. See "Style Sheet Text and Display Elements," earlier in the chapter, for more on absolute values.

- Relative values, such as `2em` or `1ex`. See the text and display elements page for more information.

- Relative percentages. For example, `50%` tells the browser to size the element half the width of the parent element.

The `width` property is not inherited. Also, you cannot specify a negative width for an element.

SET AN ELEMENT'S WIDTH

```
top center fixed}
/* Padding has been added to show the negative text-indent property*/

title
{ display: block; font: 36pt sans-serif; color: red; text-decoration:
underline;
  line-height: 150%; text-align: center; letter-spacing: 15px; background:
silver}

name
{ display: block; font: bold small-caps; color: orange; line-height: 3.5;
  text-align: center; letter-spacing: 10px; margin-top: .5em}

price_per_unit, unique_characteristics, rname, rank, test_field, js_function,
retailers
{ display: none}

marketing_blurb
{ display: block; text-indent: -3em; line-height: 2em}

ingredient_list
{ display: block; font: italic; text-transform: capitalize; text-decoration:
underline;
  border: solid medium red; padding: 1em; margin: 1em 1em 1.5em; width: }

ingredient
{display: block}
```

```
top center fixed}
/* Padding has been added to show the negative text-indent property*/

title
{ display: block; font: 36pt sans-serif; color: red; text-decoration:
underline;
  line-height: 150%; text-align: center; letter-spacing: 15px; background:
silver}

name
{ display: block; font: bold small-caps; color: orange; line-height: 3.5;
  text-align: center; letter-spacing: 10px; margin-top: .5em}

price_per_unit, unique_characteristics, rname, rank, test_field, js_function,
retailers
{ display: none}

marketing_blurb
{ display: block; text-indent: -3em; line-height: 2em}

ingredient_list
{ display: block; font: italic; text-transform: capitalize; text-decoration:
underline;
  border: solid medium red; padding: 1em; margin: 1em 1em 1.5em; width: 2in}

ingredient
{display: block}
```

1 Open the style sheet file or create a new style sheet file.

■ See Chapter 8 for more on style sheets.

2 Place the cursor where you want to declare the `width` property.

3 Type **width:**.

■ If necessary, type the opening bracket ({).

4 Type the desired `width` value.

■ Here, a width of `2in` is specified for the `ingredient_list`.

■ If necessary, type a closing bracket (}).

5 Type any additional `margin` values.

6 Save the style sheet file.

Apply It

The `width` property defines how large an image will be displayed on the screen. You can "squeeze" images down using the `width` and `height` properties. (The `height` property is described in the next section, "Set an Element's Height.")

In the following code, the image's width is reduced to 1 centimeter in response to a mouse click; a double-click restores the original dimensions.

Example:

```
<HTML>
<BODY TOPMARGIN=0 LEFTMARGIN=0 BGPROPERTIES="FIXED" BGCOLOR="#FFFFFF" LINK="#000000"
VLINK="#808080" ALINK="#000000">
<BLOCKQUOTE CLASS="body">
<BLOCKQUOTE>Click on the image to shrink its width to 1cm. Double-click on the
image to return its width to the initial size.
<P>
<IMG src="surprised.gif" onclick="this.style.width='1cm'" HEIGHT="80"
ondblclick="this.style.width=''"></P>
</BLOCKQUOTE>
</BODY>
</HTML>
```

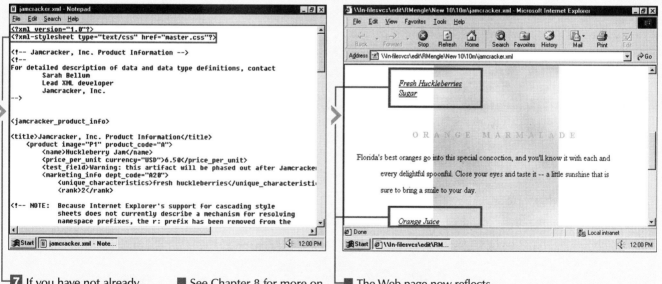

7 If you have not already done so, open up the text file for the Web page, attach the style sheet, and then save the Web page text file.

■ See Chapter 8 for more on attaching style sheets.

■ The Web page now reflects the specified width. In this example, the ingredients list box is now 2 inches wide.

SET AN ELEMENT'S HEIGHT

You can use the height property to define how much vertical space you want to give to all of an element's content, padding, and border area.

The basic syntax for the height property is

elementName {height: value}

elementName is the element for which you want to set a height. As with the width property (see "Set an Element's Width," earlier in this chapter), the value options include

- auto, the default value, which allows the browser to automatically figure the value.

- Absolute values, such as 7mm or .5in. See "Style Sheet Text and Display Elements," earlier in the chapter, for more on absolute values.

- Relative values, such as 2px or 3em. See the text and display elements page for more information.

- Relative percentages. For example, 75% tells the browser to size the element three-quarters the height of the parent element.

The height property is not inherited, and negative height values will not work.

SET AN ELEMENT'S HEIGHT

```
/* Padding has been added to show the negative text-indent property*/

title
{ display: block; font: 36pt sans-serif; color: red; text-decoration:
underline;
  line-height: 150%; text-align: center; letter-spacing: 15px; background:
silver}

name
{ display: block; font: bold small-caps; color: orange; line-height: 3.5;
  text-align: center; letter-spacing: 10px; margin-top: .5em}

price_per_unit, unique_characteristics, rname, rank, test_field, js_function,
retailers
{ display: none}

marketing_blurb
{ display: block; text-indent: -3em; line-height: 2em}

ingredient_list
{ display: block; font: italic; text-transform: capitalize; text-decoration:
underline;
  border: solid medium red; padding: 1em; margin: 1em 1em 1.5em; width: 2in;
height: }

ingredient
{display: block}
```

```
/* Padding has been added to show the negative text-indent property*/

title
{ display: block; font: 36pt sans-serif; color: red; text-decoration:
underline;
  line-height: 150%; text-align: center; letter-spacing: 15px; background:
silver}

name
{ display: block; font: bold small-caps; color: orange; line-height: 3.5;
  text-align: center; letter-spacing: 10px; margin-top: .5em}

price_per_unit, unique_characteristics, rname, rank, test_field, js_function,
retailers
{ display: none}

marketing_blurb
{ display: block; text-indent: -3em; line-height: 2em}

ingredient_list
{ display: block; font: italic; text-transform: capitalize; text-decoration:
underline;
  border: solid medium red; padding: 1em; margin: 1em 1em 1.5em; width: 2in;
height: 1em}

ingredient
{display: block}
```

■1 Open the style sheet file or create a new style sheet file.

■ See Chapter 8 for more on style sheets.

■2 Place the cursor where you want to declare the height property.

■3 Type **height:**.

■ If necessary, type the opening bracket ({).

■4 Type the desired height value.

■ Here, the height of ingredient_list is set to 1em.

■ If necessary, type the closing bracket (}).

■5 Type any additional height values.

■6 Save the style sheet file.

Apply It

The height property defines how tall an image will be displayed on the screen. You can "squeeze" images down using the `width` and `height` properties, as shown in the following code. (For more on the `width` property, see the previous section, "Set an Element's Width.")

In the following code, the image's height is reduced to 1 centimeter in response to a mouse click; a double-click restores the image to its original dimensions.

Example:

```
<HTML>
<BODY TOPMARGIN=0 LEFTMARGIN=0 BGPROPERTIES="FIXED" BGCOLOR="#FFFFFF" LINK="#000000"
VLINK="#808080" ALINK="#000000">
<BLOCKQUOTE CLASS="body">
<BLOCKQUOTE>Click on the image to shrink its height to 1cm. Double-click on the
image to return its height to the original size.
<P><IMG src="surprised.gif" onclick="this.style.height='1cm'" WIDTH="104"
ondblclick="this.style.height=''"></P>
</BLOCKQUOTE>
</BODY>
</HTML>
```

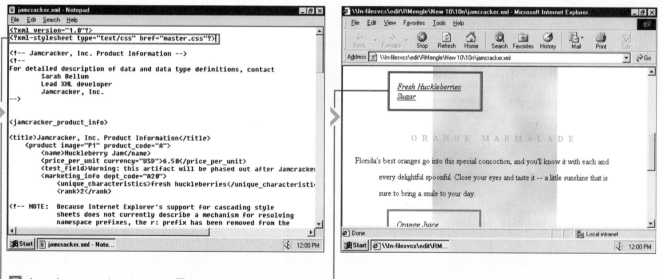

7 If you have not already done so, open up the text file for the Web page, attach the style sheet, and then save the Web page text file.

■ See Chapter 8 for more on attaching style sheets.

■ The new height is reflected on the Web page.

USING THE FLOAT PROPERTY

Elements generally display in order horizontally on the Web page. However, if you want an element to display to the left or right of the element that follows it, you can do so using the float property.

The most common use of the float property is to place images next to text. However, you can use the float property with any element. The basic syntax is

elementName {float: *direction*}

elementName is the name of the element in question. The *direction* can be one of three options:

- A value of none, the default value, prevents a float and places the elements in order horizontally.

- A value of left puts the element on the left side of the box and subsequent element(s) on the right.

- A value of right puts the element on the right side and subsequent element(s) on the left.

The float property is not inherited.

USING THE FLOAT PROPERTY

```
title
{ display: block; font: 36pt sans-serif; color: red; text-decoration:
underline;
  line-height: 150%; text-align: center; letter-spacing: 15px; background:
silver}

name
{ display: block; font: bold small-caps; color: orange; line-height: 3.5;
  text-align: center; letter-spacing: 10px; margin-top: .5em}

price_per_unit, unique_characteristics, rname, rank, test_field, js_function,
retailers
{ display: none}

marketing_blurb
{ display: block; text-indent: -3em; line-height: 2em}

ingredient_list
{ display: block; font: italic; text-transform: capitalize; text-decoration:
underline;
  border: solid medium red; padding: 1em; margin: 1em 1em 1.5em; width: 2in;
height: 1em;
  float }

ingredient
{display: block}
```

```
title
{ display: block; font: 36pt sans-serif; color: red; text-decoration:
underline;
  line-height: 150%; text-align: center; letter-spacing: 15px; background:
silver}

name
{ display: block; font: bold small-caps; color: orange; line-height: 3.5;
  text-align: center; letter-spacing: 10px; margin-top: .5em}

price_per_unit, unique_characteristics, rname, rank, test_field, js_function,
retailers
{ display: none}

marketing_blurb
{ display: block; text-indent: -3em; line-height: 2em}

ingredient_list
{ display: block; font: italic; text-transform: capitalize; text-decoration:
underline;
  border: solid medium red; padding: 1em; margin: 1em 1em 1.5em; width: 2in;
height: 1em;
  float: right}

ingredient
{display: block}
```

1 Open the style sheet file or create a new style sheet file.

■ See Chapter 8 for more on style sheets.

2 Place the cursor where you want to declare the float property.

3 Type **float:**.

■ If necessary, type the opening bracket ({).

4 Type the desired float value.

■ Here, the ingredient_list is set to float to the right.

5 Type any additional float values.

■ If necessary, type the closing bracket (}).

5 Type any additional float values.

6 Save the style sheet file.

Apply It

A floating object is moved left or right until it reaches the border, padding, or margin of another block-level object.

In the following example code, two images — one specified as floating left, the other as floating right — float to the left and right of a text paragraph, all the way to the edges of the display area.

Example:

```
<HTML>
<BODY TOPMARGIN=0 LEFTMARGIN=0 BGPROPERTIES="FIXED" BGCOLOR="#FFFFFF"
LINK="#000000" VLINK="#808080" ALINK="#000000">
<BLOCKQUOTE CLASS="body">
<IMG src="surprised.gif" height="80" width="80" border="0" style="float:left">
<IMG src="neutral.gif" height="80" width="80" style="float:right">
<P>This is an example of how you can position images to "float" to the edges of
text. In this example, one image is positioned to float left; the other, to float
right. Note that the images are aligned to the top of the text by default.</P>
</BLOCKQUOTE>
</BODY>
</HTML>
```

7 If you have not already done so, open up the text file for the Web page, attach the style sheet, and then save the Web page text file.

■ See Chapter 8 for more on attaching style sheets.

■ When the Web page is opened, the element floats in the designated manner.

Note: You can sometimes use the clear *property to resolve display issues created by the* float *property. See "Using the Clear Property," next in this chapter.*

USING THE CLEAR PROPERTY

You may not want certain elements on your Web page to align next to floating elements. For example, you may want to ensure that text is bounded by a certain amount of space, even if the text is aligned next to an image. In such cases, you can use the clear property.

The basic syntax is

elementName {clear: *direction*}

elementName is the name of the element in question. The *direction* can be one of four options, which basically define which sides of an element's box cannot be next to a floating element's box:

- A value of none, the default value, has no effect on floating elements.

- A value of left forbids the element from having floating elements on the left.

- A value of right forbids the element from having floating elements on the right.

- A value of both forbids the element from having floating elements on either side.

The clear property is not inherited.

USING THE CLEAR PROPERTY

```
🗏 Untitled - Notepad                                          _ 🗗 ✕
File  Edit  Search  Help
/* Cascading style sheet for use with the jamcracker.xml file */

jamcracker_product_info
{ display: block; font: normal normal normal 12pt Times, serif; color: black;
  text-transform: none; padding: 4em; background: url("TEST.jpg") repeat-y
  top center fixed}
/* Padding has been added to show the negative text-indent property*/

title
{ display: block; font: 36pt sans-serif; color: red; text-decoration:
underline;
  line-height: 150%; text-align: center; letter-spacing: 15px; background:
silver}

name
{ display: block; font: bold small-caps; color: orange; line-height: 3.5;
  text-align: center; letter-spacing: 10px; margin-top: .5em; clear: }

price_per_unit, unique_characteristics, rname, rank, test_field, js_function,
retailers
{ display: none}

marketing_blurb
{ display: block; text-indent: -3em; line-height: 2em}

ingredient_list
{ display: block; font: italic; text-transform: capitalize; text-decoration: ▾

🏁Start  🗏 Untitled - Notepad                                 ⌛ 12:00 PM
```

```
🗏 Untitled - Notepad                                          _ 🗗 ✕
File  Edit  Search  Help
/* Cascading style sheet for use with the jamcracker.xml file */

jamcracker_product_info
{ display: block; font: normal normal normal 12pt Times, serif; color: black;
  text-transform: none; padding: 4em; background: url("TEST.jpg") repeat-y
  top center fixed}
/* Padding has been added to show the negative text-indent property*/

title
{ display: block; font: 36pt sans-serif; color: red; text-decoration:
underline;
  line-height: 150%; text-align: center; letter-spacing: 15px; background:
silver}

name
{ display: block; font: bold small-caps; color: orange; line-height: 3.5;
  text-align: center; letter-spacing: 10px; margin-top: .5em; clear: both}

price_per_unit, unique_characteristics, rname, rank, test_field, js_function,
retailers
{ display: none}

marketing_blurb
{ display: block; text-indent: -3em; line-height: 2em}

ingredient_list
{ display: block; font: italic; text-transform: capitalize; text-decoration: ▾

🏁Start  🗏 Untitled - Notepad                                 ⌛ 12:00 PM
```

■1 Open the style sheet file or create a new style sheet file.

■ See Chapter 8 for more on style sheets.

■2 Place the cursor where you want to declare the clear property.

■3 Type **clear:**.

■ If necessary, type the opening bracket ({).

■4 Type the desired clear value.

■ Here, the name is set to be clear to both sides.

■5 Type any additional clear commands.

■6 Save the style sheet file.

■ If necessary, type the closing bracket (}).

Extra

Besides clear, the three main properties that affect box generation and layout are the display, position, and float properties. These properties are interrelated; in other words, specifying a value for one may affect the behavior for the others. For example:

- If the display property is associated with a value of none, browsers will ignore position and float. Otherwise, position has the value absolute or fixed, display is set to block, and float is set to none. The position of the element is determined by the top, right, bottom, and left properties of the element's containing block.

- If float has a value other than none, display is set to block and the element is floated. Otherwise, the remaining display properties apply as specified.

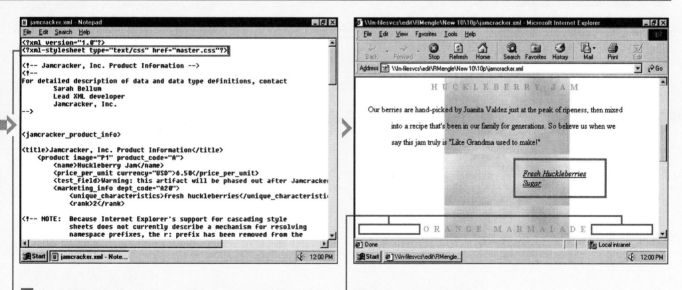

7 If you have not already done so, open up the text file for the Web page, attach the style sheet, and then save the Web page text file.

■ See Chapter 8 for more on attaching style sheets.

■ When the Web page is opened, the clear property command controls nearby floating elements. In this case, the name is clear of adjacent floating elements on both sides.

CREATE A SIMPLE XSL STYLE SHEET

You can create a simple XML style sheet (XSS) using the Extensible Style Language (XSL) to load XML data into a client-side object model, manipulate that data, format, and display it.

Here is the syntax:

```
<?xml:stylesheet
xmlns:xsl="http://www.w3.org/tR/WD-xsl">
</xsl:stylesheet>
```

You can create cascading style sheets to format and display XML data, as shown in Chapter 8. However, XSS offers several advantages over CSS:

- XSS enables you to "plug" XML data into a display template, much as you "plug" addresses into a form letter. Using CSS, you can only display information declared in the XML document.

- XSS enables you to format and display XML attributes and elements. CSS enables you to format and display XML elements only.

- XSS enables you to manipulate, reorder, and display data dynamically. CSS enables you to display static XML data only.

Because scant support for this emerging standard is currently available, XSS is currently appropriate for prototyping efforts only.

CREATE A SIMPLE XSL STYLE SHEET

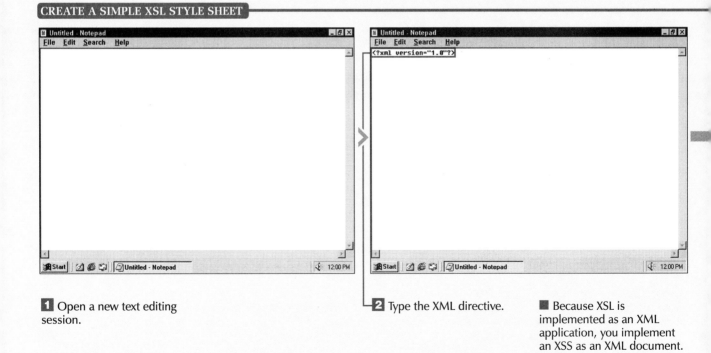

1 Open a new text editing session.

2 Type the XML directive.

■ Because XSL is implemented as an XML application, you implement an XSS as an XML document.

Extra

The World Wide Web Consortium's working draft divides XSL into two separate pieces:

- **A transformation language for XML documents.** This transformation language enables you to transfer an XML document into another SGML-conforming document format. For example, using XSL you can transform an XML document into an HTML document populated with XML data, as shown in this chapter.

- **An XML vocabulary for formatting semantics.** When completed, this vocabulary will define sophisticated formatting rules you can apply to XML data. Some examples include the ability to control footnotes, layout of multiple columns, and spacing around objects.

Currently, Internet Explorer 5 supports only a subset of the preceding bullet.

For current information on the XSL working draft, visit the World Wide Web Consortium at www.w3.org/TR/xsl/.

For details on XSL support in Internet Explorer, visit the XSL Developers Guide at http://msdn. microsoft.com/isapi/msdnlib.idc?theURL=/library/psdk/xmlsdk/xslp8tlx.htm.

☰ Untitled - Notepad
File Edit Search Help

```
<?xml version="1.0"?>
<xsl:stylesheet xmlns:xsl="http://www.w3.org/TR/WD-xsl">
```

☰Start ☐Untitled - Notepad ⏰ 12:00 PM

☰ Untitled - Notepad
File Edit Search Help

```
<?xml version="1.0"?>
<xsl:stylesheet xmlns:xsl="http://www.w3.org/TR/WD-xsl">

</xsl:stylesheet>
```

☰Start ☐Untitled - Notepad ⏰ 12:00 PM

3 Type the opening tag for the XSL directive.

■ Required by the MSXML parser, this directive associates the xsl: prefix with the required *stylesheet* namespace.

4 Type the closing tag for the XSL directive.

■ Although technically an XSS filename need not contain the `.xsl` extension, including it is good programming practice.

5 Save the file.

ADD A COMMENT

You can add a comment to an XML style sheet (XSS) to aid in code debugging and maintenance.

Here is the syntax:

```
<!-- comment -->
```

Although the length of a style sheet varies according to its complexity, an XSS for a typical XML application is quite lengthy.

As with any application development effort, thorough and appropriate documentation is crucial. Documenting your style sheets enables you to describe display rules so that human readers can easily understand the intent and purpose of each rule — including browser-specific workarounds. Because XSS are implemented as XML files, you document an XSS using an XML comment line.

ADD A COMMENT

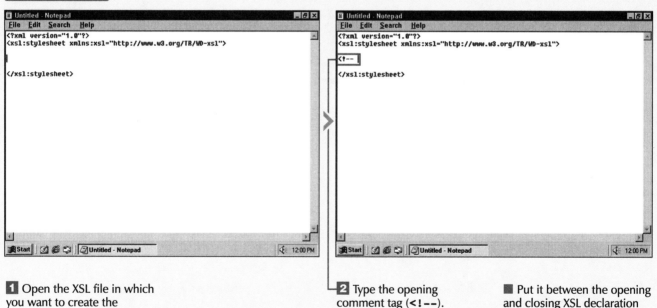

1 Open the XSL file in which you want to create the comment.

2 Type the opening comment tag (`<!--`).

■ Put it between the opening and closing XSL declaration statements.

Extra

Tool support for XSS is maturing apace with the XSS and XML specifications. At the time of this writing, however, support for XML style sheets is extremely immature. In addition, XSS syntax is fairly complex, incorporating elements from

- XML
- Microsoft's style sheet vocabulary
- HTML
- JavaScript
- The client-side object model

Because the syntax for XSS is non-intuitive, and because gaps in Microsoft's implementation may require elaborate workarounds in the near future, commenting your XSS documents thoroughly is very important.

You implement an XSS as an XML document, so XSS comments follow the standard XML comment guidelines:

- Comments can appear anywhere in a style sheet except before the XML declaration. For example, the following generates a parse error:

```
<!-- XML style sheet for Jamcracker, Inc.
product data -->
<?xml version="1.0"?>
```

You also may *not* use comments inside tags. For example, the following generates a parse error:

```
<?xml <!-- Jamcracker, Inc. product
information --> version="1.0"?>
```

- The string "– –" cannot appear in an XSS comment. For example, the following is illegal and causes a parse error:

```
<!-- comment 1 <!-- comment 2 --> -->
```

- Comments can span lines.

3 Type the comment line.

4 Type the closing comment tag (**-->**).

5 Save the file.

FORMAT AND DISPLAY ELEMENT DATA

You can create rules in an XML style sheet to transform and display each XML element.

Here is the syntax:

```
<xsl:directive>
rule syntax
</xsl:directive>
```

XSL transforms XML into HTML, so every XSS typically contains a mix of well-formed

- **HTML statements.** Using HTML tags, you define an HTML document and any layout structures — for example, tables — you want to hold your formatted XML data.

- **XSS syntax.** Using the XML elements and attributes implemented by Microsoft as an XSL vocabulary, you define the elements you want to display and where in the document you want them to appear.

FORMAT AND DISPLAY ELEMENT DATA

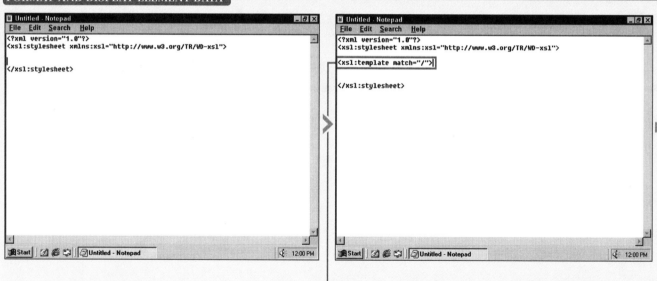

■ Open the XSL file in which you want to create the XSL rules.

② Type the beginning XSL directive for the XSL rule you want to create.

■ In this example, the beginning XSL directive is `<xsl:template match="/">`, which defines an output template spanning the entire XML document.

Extra

You declare a *template* element to define how you want to transform/display the XML data *nodes*, or elements, specified by the template's match attribute.

In the example in this section, the following template defines how all the XML nodes will display at runtime, beginning with the root node.

```
<xsl:template match="/">
...
</xsl:template>
```

You declare a for-each element to traverse the elements specified by the for-each element's select attribute. In the example in this section, the following directs the XML parser to loop through all the item elements contained by the jamcracker_product_information element:

```
<xsl:for-each select="jamcracker_product_info/item">
...
</xsl:for-each>
```

You declare a *value-of* element to display the value of the element specified by the value-of element's select attribute. For example, the following single-line tag displays the value of the price_per_unit element:

```
<xsl:value-of select="price_per_unit"/>
```

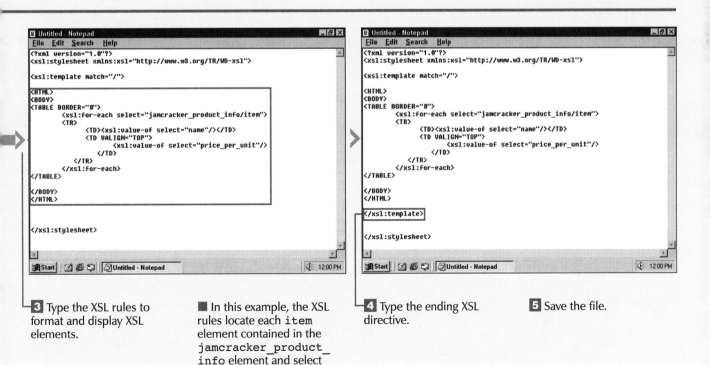

3 Type the XSL rules to format and display XSL elements.

■ In this example, the XSL rules locate each item element contained in the jamcracker_product_info element and select both the value of the name element and the value of the price_per_unit element.

4 Type the ending XSL directive.

5 Save the file.

FORMAT/DISPLAY ATTRIBUTE DATA

You can create rules in an XML style sheet to transform XML attributes and display them in a Web browser.

Here is the syntax:

`<xsl:value-of select="pattern"/>`

pattern is a valid XSS data-matching pattern.

One of the limitations of the cascading style sheet support currently available for XML is that you cannot display XML attribute data using a cascading style sheet. (You *can* display XML *element* data using a cascading style sheet, however.) If you need to format and display XML attributes, you can do so using XML style sheets. (You can also write custom processing code to extract and display XML attribute data; you see an example of this approach in Chapters 12 and 13.)

FORMAT/DISPLAY ATTRIBUTE DATA

1 Open the XSL file in which you want to create the XSS attribute display rule.

2 Type the XSL directives necessary to identify an XML element.

■ In this example, the XML element being identified is the `item` element contained in the `jamcracker_product_info` element.

Apply It

XSL elements such as `value-of` typically operate within a *context*, or scope. You define a context by the order in which you specify XSL elements. Defining a context enables you to pinpoint a specific element or attribute nested within one or more containing elements.

In the following example, Internet Explorer searches for the attribute named `product_code` associated only with instances of the *name* element.

Example:

```
<TD>
            <xsl:value-of
select="name"/>
            <xsl:value-of
select="@product_code"/>
    </TD>
```

The "@" (attribute) symbol is just one of the many operators and special characters you use to construct data-matching *patterns* in an XSS. For details on pattern construction as well as all the special characters Internet Explorer 5 supports, visit http://msdn.microsoft.com/isapi/msdnlib.idc?theURL=/library/psdk/xmlsdk/xslr8ko5.htm and click XSL Pattern Syntax.

Note: Many of the operators Internet Explorer 5 supports have not been accepted by the World Wide Web Consortium's working XSL draft.

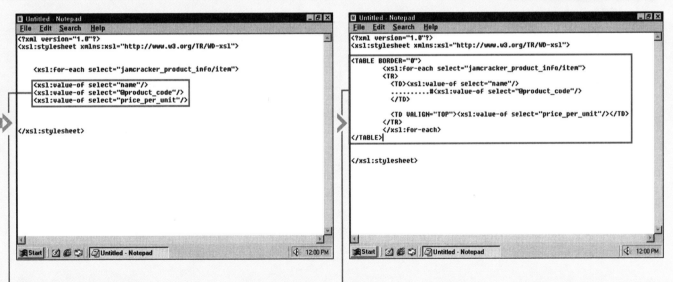

3 Type the XSL directives necessary to identify an XML attribute associated with that XML element.

■ This example shows the `product_code` attribute.

4 Type the XSL directives necessary to format and display the attribute data.

■ This example shows HTML `<TABLE>` tags used to display repeating `product_code` attribute data.

5 Save the file.

DISPLAY NON-XML DATA

You can add non-XML data to a formatted XML document at runtime using XSL rules.

One of the limitations of using cascading style sheets to format and display XML data is that you cannot add descriptive information using a cascading style sheet; you can only format and display those elements declared in the XML document. In some cases, discovering the need for additional information at display time means that you need to restructure the XML document itself; for descriptive presentation-related data however, a better strategy is to add the data at runtime using an XML style sheet.

For example, using an XML style sheet, you can add any of the following at runtime without modifying the underlying XML document:

- Titles
- Column headings
- Explanations
- Data keys

DISPLAY NON-XML DATA

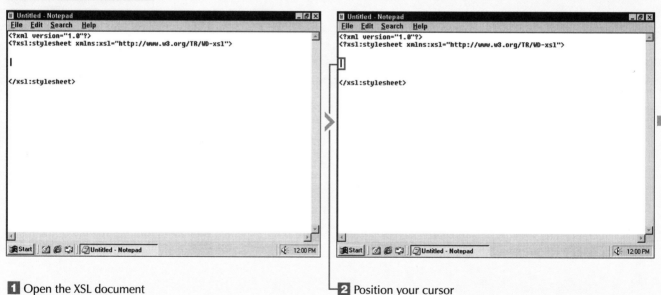

1 Open the XSL document to which you want to add rules to display non-XML data.

2 Position your cursor between the XSL opening and closing directive tags.

Apply It

Because XML parsers are more stringent than most HTML interpreters in requiring well-formed syntax, non-well-formed HTML code may display correctly in a Web browser but generate an error if embedded in an XSS.

Follow these rules to ensure that your HTML is well-formed:

- Close all tags in order.

  Invalid: `<B>XML: Your Visual Blueprint by <I>IDG Books Worldwide</B></I>`

  Valid: `<B>XML: Your Visual Blueprint by </B><I><B>IDG Books Worldwide</B></I>`

- Use consistent tag case.

  Invalid: `<B>XML: Your Visual Blueprints</b>`

  Valid: `<B>XML: Your Visual Blueprints</B>`

- Surround all attributes with quotes.

  Invalid: `<IMG SRC="aFile.jpg" HEIGHT=200 WIDTH=200>`

  Valid: `<IMG SRC="aFile.jpg" HEIGHT="200" WIDTH="200">`

- Embed all scripts in a CDATA section.

  Invalid:
  ```
  <SCRIPT LANGUAGE="JavaScript>
  // This script sorts product data based
  on user-defined criteria
  function sort() {
      /* JavaScript code goes here */
  }
  </SCRIPT>
  ```

  Valid:
  ```
  <SCRIPT LANGUAGE="JavaScript><![CDATA[
  // Sort description function sort() {
      /* JavaScript code goes here */
  }
  ]]></SCRIPT>
  ```

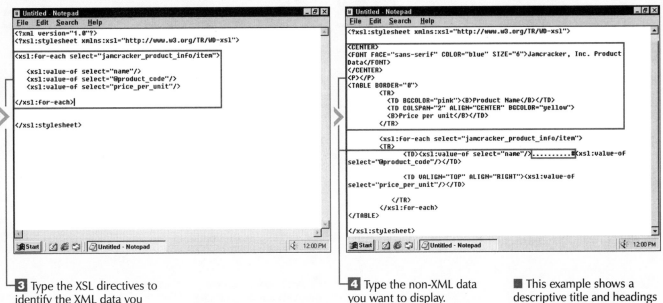

3 Type the XSL directives to identify the XML data you want to display.

4 Type the non-XML data you want to display.

■ This example shows a descriptive title and headings added to the XML data to create a formatted report.

5 Save the document.

SORT ELEMENT DATA

You can sort XML data elements on the fly at runtime using XSL.

Here is the syntax:

```
<xsl:for-each select="element1" order-
by="element2">
</xsl:for-each>
```

element1 is the name of a container XML element and *element2* is the name of the contained XML element on which you want to sort the data.

One of the limitations of using cascading style sheets to format and display XML data is that you cannot change the order in which XML data elements appear using a cascading style sheet.

To change the order in which XML data elements display, you must do one of the following:

- Reorder the data element declarations in the XML document.
- Create an XML style sheet to sort the elements on the fly.
- Develop a custom XML processor to reorder the elements on the fly.

Of these, the second method is by far the easiest. It is also the option you see described in this section.

SORT ELEMENT DATA

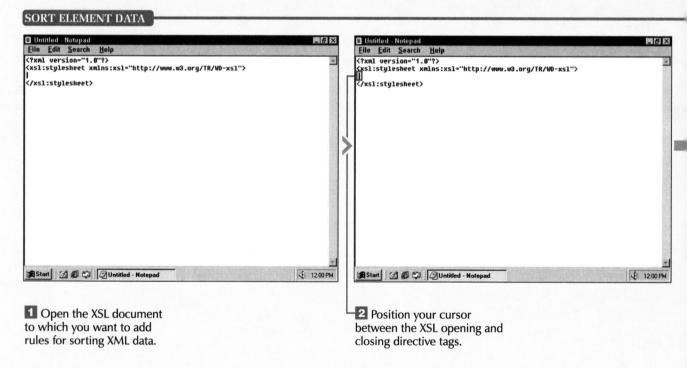

1 Open the XSL document to which you want to add rules for sorting XML data.

2 Position your cursor between the XSL opening and closing directive tags.

Extra

You can specify any of the following for the `order-by` attribute of the `for-each` element:

- A single element name. The default sort order is ascending based on the first character in each name string traversed.

  `xsl:for-each select="jamcracker_product_info/item"` **order-by="name"**

- A semicolon-separated list of element names. The default sort order is ascending based on the first character of each name string traversed, from the first name in the list to the last.

  `xsl:for-each select="jamcracker_product_info/item"` **order-by="name; price_per_unit"**

- A plus (+) or minus (-). A (+) symbol specifies ascending order; a (–) denotes descending order. Each name in a list may be prefaced with a (+) or (–). If you supply neither a (+) nor a (–), the default sorting order applied will be ascending.

  `xsl:for-each select="jamcracker_product_info/item"` **order-by="-name; +price_per_unit"**

For detailed syntax notes on the `order-by` attribute and the `for-each` element, visit http://msdn. microsoft.com/isapi/msdnlib.idc?theURL=/library/psdk/xmlsdk/xslr2bxw.htm.

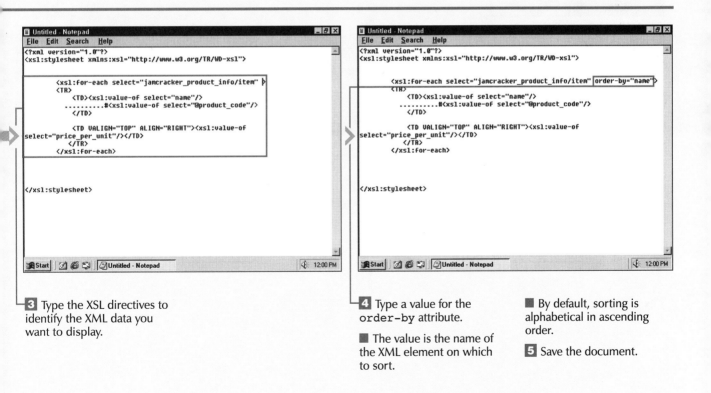

3 Type the XSL directives to identify the XML data you want to display.

4 Type a value for the `order-by` attribute.

■ The value is the name of the XML element on which to sort.

■ By default, sorting is alphabetical in ascending order.

5 Save the document.

MODIFY AND FILTERING DATA

You can use simple and complex conditional statements to identify and modify the display of specific XML data elements at runtime.

Here is the syntax for the `if` element:

```
<xsl:if
expr="script-expression"
language="language-name"
test="pattern" >
```

`expr` is an optional script expression that evaluates to a boolean value. If a value for `script-expression` exists, returns true, and the `test` `pattern` (described

later) succeeds, the contents of `xsl:if` are placed in the output. If no value for this attribute exists, the contents of `xsl:if` are placed in the output by default.

`language` specifies the scripting language you want Internet Explorer to use when evaluating `expr`. Possible values `for` `language-name` include JScript, JavaScript, and VBScript. If no value for this attribute exists, JScript is assumed.

`test` specifies the condition, or *pattern*, to test.

MODIFY AND FILTERING DATA

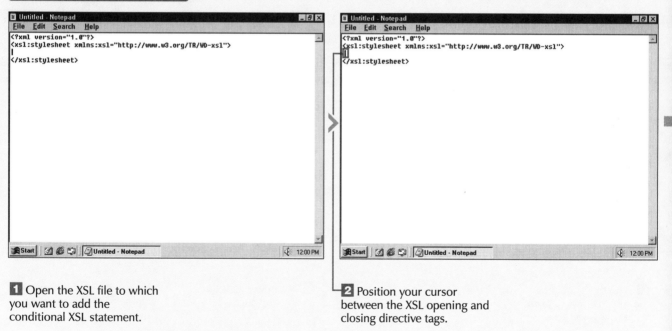

1 Open the XSL file to which you want to add the conditional XSL statement.

2 Position your cursor between the XSL opening and closing directive tags.

Extra

Using an XML style sheet, you can test XML data values at runtime and determine how you want to display them; you can also decide at runtime whether you want to display certain XML data values at all.

Internet Explorer's XSL support provides two conditional elements:

- **`if`**: This simple conditional enables you to specify an action if a condition (typically a pattern match) is met. This is the conditional element described in this section. `else` is not currently supported; for either/or processing, use `choose-when-otherwise`.

- **`choose-when-otherwise`**: Like the more traditional `if`/`then`, this complex conditional enables you to specify an action both when a condition is met and when it is not.

Defining a pattern for a conditional is a fairly complex process, involving operators (boolean, comparison, set expression); special characters; collections; and much more. For help with pattern-matching, visit http://msdn.microsoft.com/isapi/msdnlib.idc?theURL=/library/psdk/xmlsdk/xslr73nc.htm.

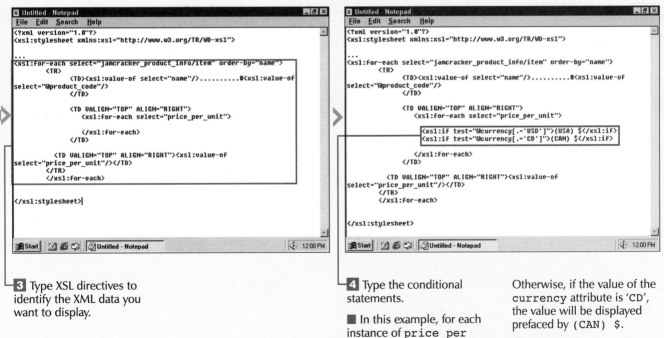

3 Type XSL directives to identify the XML data you want to display.

4 Type the conditional statements.

■ In this example, for each instance of `price_per_unit`, if the value of the `currency` attribute is 'USD', the value will be displayed prefaced by (USA) $.

Otherwise, if the value of the `currency` attribute is 'CD', the value will be displayed prefaced by (CAN) $.

5 Save the file.

IDENTIFY CHILD ELEMENTS

Y ou can identify the child elements associated with a given parent element, if any; iterate over them one by one; and display them as you want.

Elements that are contained inside other elements are called contained, or *child*, elements. Elements that contain other elements are called container, or *parent*, elements. This parent/child structure, which you define by the structure of your XML document, can be traversed at runtime using a combination of:

- Conditional elements. You use the XSL `if` element to identify a specific parent element.

- Context-sensitive patterns. Using the built-in `context()` method, you can loop through all the child elements associated with a specified parent element.

Here is the syntax:

```
<xsl:for-each select="elementName">
<xsl:value-of />
<xsl:if test="context()[not(end())]">
</xsl:for-each>
```

Where `elementName` is the name of the parent element over which you want to iterate.

IDENTIFY CHILD ELEMENTS

```
Untitled - Notepad                                    _ 8 X
File  Edit  Search  Help
<?xml version="1.0"?>
<xsl:stylesheet xmlns:xsl="http://www.w3.org/TR/WD-xsl">



</xsl:stylesheet>



Start   🖉 🎯 🖎  🖉 Untitled - Notepad          🔆 12:00 PM
```

```
Untitled - Notepad                                    _ 8 X
File  Edit  Search  Help
<?xml version="1.0"?>
<xsl:stylesheet xmlns:xsl="http://www.w3.org/TR/WD-xsl">



</xsl:stylesheet>



Start   🖉 🎯 🖎  🖉 Untitled - Notepad          🔆 12:00 PM
```

1 Open the XSL file to which you want to add the iterative XSL statement.

2 Position your cursor between the XSL opening and closing directive tags.

Apply It

You can combine non-XML data with the identification of child elements to create formatted lists.

Example:

```
*   <xsl:for-each select="jamcracker_product_info/item"
                                 order-by="name">
            ...
*        <xsl:for-each select="ingredient_list/ingredient" >
*            <xsl:value-of /><xsl:if test="context()[not(end())]">, </xsl:if>
                </xsl:for-each>
```

In the preceding code, for each *item* declared in the XML document whose root element is *jamcracker_product_info* (the first example), and for each `ingredient` inside each `ingredient_list` associated with that `item` (second example), check (third example) to see whether the `ingredient` found is the last one for this *ingredient_list*. If it is the last one, do nothing; if not, display a comma and a space.

Internet Explorer's XSL parser supports dozens of pattern methods and operators, including the ones used above:

- `context()`: A method that returns the first element in the previously defined context.

- `end()`: A method that returns true for the last element in a collection and false for all other elements.

- `not()`: The negation operator.

- `[ ]`: An operator that applies a filter pattern; translates to "where."

3 Type XSL directives to identify the XML element over which you want to iterate.

4 Type XSL directives to iterate over contained elements.

■ In this example, you see how to loop through each `ingredient` element contained in the `ingredient_list` element.

5 Save the file.

ADD DYNAMIC REDISPLAY WITH A SCRIPT

Y ou can sort and display XML data dynamically, based on user-selected criteria, using XSL.

You do this by

- Defining XSL templates. XSL templates enable you to organize your display into static and dynamic portions. At runtime, you can specify that only the dynamic subset of your display be re-rendered, rather than the entire display.

- Creating a script. Using a scripting language such as JavaScript or JScript, you can access the in-memory document object model, or DOM, that Internet Explorer automatically populates with your XSL and XML elements. After you access the DOM, you can modify and redisplay the data it contains.

ADD DYNAMIC REDISPLAY WITH A SCRIPT

```
Untitled - Notepad
File  Edit  Search  Help
<?xml version="1.0"?>
<xsl:stylesheet xmlns:xsl="http://www.w3.org/TR/WD-xsl">
|

</xsl:stylesheet>
```

```
Untitled - Notepad
File  Edit  Search  Help
<?xml version="1.0"?>
<xsl:stylesheet xmlns:xsl="http://www.w3.org/TR/WD-xsl">
|

</xsl:stylesheet>
```

1 Open the XSL file to which you want to add the script.

2 Position your cursor between the XSL opening and closing directive tags.

Extra

Sorting XML data dynamically requires:

- An XSL template. You define an XSL template to describe how you want a subset of your XML document to display.

- A script. Implemented as part of the XSL document, the script — which can be implemented in JavaScript — defines a sort function. For example, a link titled "Sort by price" might invoke the sort() function with the XML element value "price_per_unit". A link titled "Sort by name" might invoke the sort() function with the XML element value "name".

The sort() function accesses Internet Explorer's document object model to

- Locate the XSL code responsible for sorting product data

- Replace the old sort criteria with the new sort criteria

- Redisplay the product data based on the new sort criteria

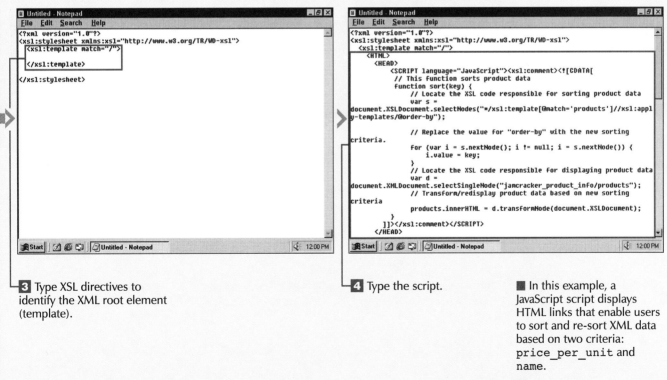

3 Type XSL directives to identify the XML root element (template).

4 Type the script.

■ In this example, a JavaScript script displays HTML links that enable users to sort and re-sort XML data based on two criteria: price_per_unit and name.

5 Save the file.

ATTACH AN XSL STYLE SHEET

You can separate XSL style rules from XML data and combine them at runtime.

Here is the syntax:

```
<?xml-stylesheet
type="stylesheetType"
href="stylesheetFile"?>
```

stylesheetType is the MIME type of the style sheet you want to attach to an XML document. MIME, which stands for Multipurpose Internet Mail Extensions, is a specification for formatting non-text messages for transfer over the Internet. Valid MIME type values for the *stylesheetType* attribute include

- `text/xsl`: Specifies an XML style sheet
- `text/css`: Specifies a cascading style sheet

Note: You see how to create and attach a cascading style sheet in Chapter 8.

stylesheetFile is the name of the external XSL file you want to attach to the XML document. If you do not qualify the value for this attribute with a path, such as */xsl/stylesheet/task9.css*, Internet Explorer searches for the XSL file in the same directory where the XML document is located.

ATTACH AN XSL STYLE SHEET

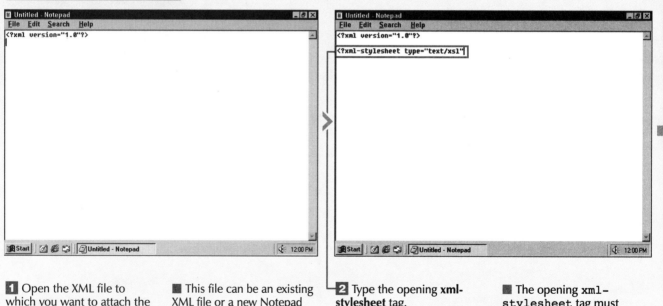

1 Open the XML file to which you want to attach the XSL reference.

■ This file can be an existing XML file or a new Notepad file.

2 Type the opening **xml-stylesheet** tag.

■ The opening **xml-stylesheet** tag must follow the XML directive.

Extra

Specifying display rules separately from your data allows you much greater flexibility in presenting your data than combining rules and data in the same document.

HTML files are a good example of documents that contain both data and display rules. XML syntax, on the other hand, enables you to store data and rules separately in the form of XML documents (data) and style sheets (display rules).

To apply a style sheet to an XML document, all you need to do is enter a single processing instruction to your XML document that references the name of the style sheet you want to apply.

3 Type values for the `type` and `href` attributes.

■ In this example, the value for the `type` attribute is `text/xsl` and the value for the `href` attribute is `some.xsl`.

■ `text/xsl` specifies an XSL stylesheet, as opposed to a cascading or other stylesheet.

■ `some.xsl` specifies the name of the XML stylesheet file to attach to this XML document.

4 Enter the closing **xml-stylesheet** tag.

5 Save the file.

DEBUG YOUR XSL STYLE SHEET

At the time of this writing, you can validate an XML style sheet three different ways:

- You can load it into Internet Explorer. This approach enables you to debug syntax errors within the XSS, but does not take the attached XML data into consideration.

- You can load the XML document that references your XSS into Internet Explorer. This approach, discussed in this section, enables you to test XSS behavior.

- You can load the XML and attached XSS into a debugging utility and step through the XSS. There is currently only one such utility widely available. This utility, Microsoft's XSL Debugger, is currently available in beta form only, and should only be relied on for prototype efforts.

Note: By the time you read this, the XSL Debugger may appear or behave slightly differently than described here.

DEBUG YOUR XSL STYLE SHEET

1 Run Internet Explorer.

2 Load an XML file that contains a reference to an XSS.

■ This example shows the task9.xml file (which contains a reference to the task9.xsl XSS) loaded into the browser window.

Extra

The Microsoft XSL Debugger enables you to set breakpoints and step through an XML/XSS application to aid in the debugging process. You can access this online utility at http://msdn. microsoft.com/downloads/ samples/internet/xml/xsl_debugger/default.asp.

As of the time of this writing, the XSL Debugger is not yet stable enough to provide solid debugging information for non-trivial XSL documents. In addition, unless your monitor is configured for high resolution, you may not be able to view the entire debug interface. By stepping through the default XML document and attached style sheet, however, you can use this tool to learn how Internet Explorer processes simple style sheets. An updated, more robust version of the XSL Debugger may be available by the time you read this.

To debug your own documents, type the name of your style sheet and XML documents into the XSL Stylesheet and XML Source fields, respectively, and click the Reload button next to each.

Note: The files you specify must reside on a Web server; the XSL Debugger generates an error if you specify the name of a file on your local machine.

3 Note the initial display.

4 Exercise and debug the application.

CREATE A SKELETON HTML FILE

You can access XML data from within an HTML by embedding an XML document inside an HTML file using Microsoft's <XML> tag, similar to the way you embed an image inside an HTML file using the <IMG> tag. An embedded XML document is called a *data island*. The sections in this chapter show you how to create, populate, and access a data island using HTML and JavaScript syntax. *Note:* Only Internet Explorer 5 currently supports data islands.

Here is the syntax required to create an HTML file:

```
<HTML>
html_code
</HTML>
```

html_code can contain either an XML data island or a script that accesses XML data.

CREATE A SKELETON HTML FILE

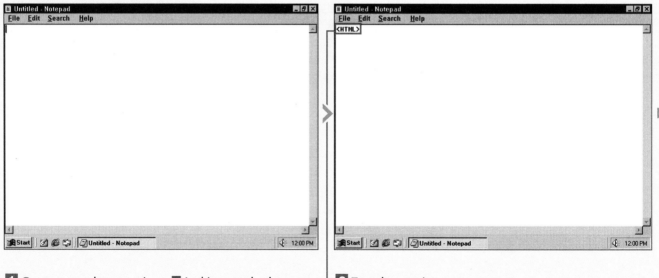

1 Create a new document in a text editor.

■ In this example, the Notepad text editor is shown.

2 Type the opening **<HTML>** tag.

Extra

You can create HTML files

■ Using a text editor, as shown in this section. A text editor is appropriate if you want to create a small, simple HTML file.

■ Using a graphical HTML editor. HTML editors are optimized for building HTML documents. They include such features as WYSIWYG interfaces, built-in templates, and color coding. The companion CD includes trial versions of two popular HTML editors — Sausage Software's HotDog and Allaire's HomeSite.

The following resources are useful in discovering how to implement and test HTML documents:

■ CNET.com offers a comprehensive HTML authoring site containing articles, reference materials, and down-loadable HTML editors at http://home.cnet.com/category/0,10000,0-7259,00.html.

■ The World Wide Web Consortium's HTML validation service validates HTML files residing on an HTTP server for conformance with the HTML standard. Go to http://validator.w3.org/.

■ Microsoft's HTML authoring site contains basic as well as advanced HTML instruction, optimized for Internet Explorer; go to http://msdn. microsoft.com/workshop/author/default.asp.

An alternative to using data islands is to load an XML document inside an HTML file using a scripting language — such as JScript, JavaScript, or VBScript — and the XML document object model methods. The sections in Chapter 13 show you how to load, access, and manipulate XML data using a combination of JavaScript and the XML document object model.

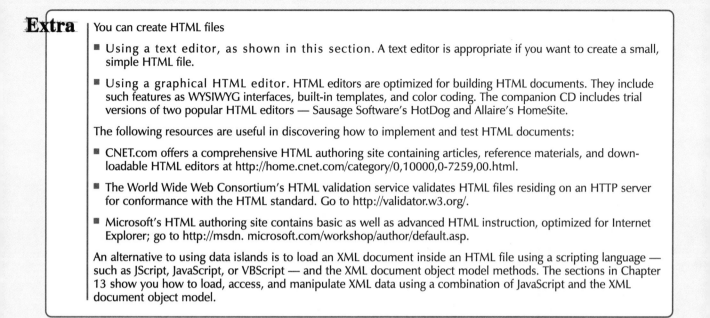

3 Type the closing </HTML> tag.

4 Save the file using either an .htm or .html extension.

■ In this example, the filename used is some.htm.

CREATE A DATA ISLAND

You can use the <XML> tag supported in Internet Explorer 5 to embed an XML *data island* into an HTML file. Data islands enable you to work with XML data inside an HTML file.

Here is the syntax required to create a data island:

```
<XML
        ID="xmlID"
        SRC="xmlSource">
</XML>
```

xmlID is a name you assign the data island. You reference this name, which must begin with a letter or underscore and contain only letters, underscores, and

numbers, to access individual elements contained in the data island.

xmlSource is the name of the XML document you want to load into the data island. The value for *xmlSource* can be qualified or unqualified; if it is unqualified, Internet Explorer searches for the XML document in the same directory where the HTML file resides.

After you declare and load a data island using the <XML> tag, you can access, manipulate, and display the contents of that data island using a script implemented in JScript, JavaScript, or VBScript.

CREATE A DATA ISLAND

1 Open the HTML file in which you want to create a data island.

2 Position your cursor at the section in the HTML file in which you want to embed the data island.

■ In this example, the data island is being embedded in the HTML body section.

3 Type the beginning and ending **<XML>** tags.

Apply It

You can declare a data island inline, rather than using the SRC attribute described previously. The following syntax declares a data island inline.

Example:

```
<HTML>
<BODY>
<XML ID="myXMLFile">
    <jamcracker_product_info>
        <product image="P1"
product_code="A">
            <name>Huckleberry Jam</name>
            <price_per_unit
currency="USD">6.50</price_per_unit>
            ...
    </jamcracker_product_info>
</XML>
</BODY>
</HTML>
```

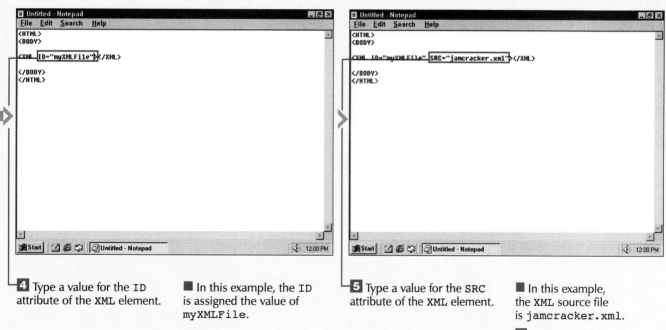

Type a value for the ID attribute of the XML element.

■ In this example, the ID is assigned the value of myXMLFile.

Type a value for the SRC attribute of the XML element.

■ In this example, the XML source file is jamcracker.xml.

Save the file.

ACCESS A DATA ISLAND

Y ou access XML elements contained in a data island using the XML document object model's *documentElement* property.

The documentElement property represents the XML document root element and all the elements contained in that root element. By accessing the documentElement property, you can access all the data contained in the data island.

Here is the syntax:

```
<SCRIPT>
scriptStatements
</SCRIPT>
```

scriptStatements reference a predefined data island and the documentElement object.

The XML document object model, or DOM, is defined by the World Wide Web Consortium in their DOM Level 1 Specification. You can view it at www.w3.org/ TR/REC-DOM-Level-1/. However, Microsoft's DOM support, which this section demonstrates, differs somewhat from the consortium's recommendation. For details, visit http://msdn.microsoft.com/isapi/ msdnlib. idc?theURL=/library/psdk/xmlsdk/xmld2rl1.htm.

ACCESS A DATA ISLAND

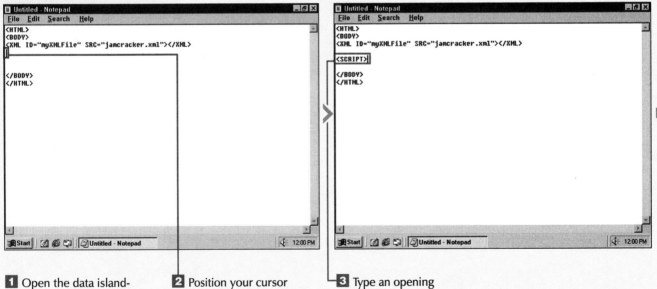

1 Open the data island-containing HTML file from which you want to access XML data.

2 Position your cursor below the embedded data island.

3 Type an opening **<SCRIPT>** tag.

Extra

The document object model, or DOM, defines all the objects, properties, and methods that comprise a Web page. The XML DOM defines the objects, properties, and methods that comprise an XML document.

The code shown in this example, which you see again next, dumps the entire contents of the data island to the screen.

```
document.write(myXMLFile.documentElement
.text);
```

Microsoft's XML DOM reference contains syntax and examples for each of the properties, methods, and objects Internet Explorer supports; go to http:// msdn.microsoft.com/isapi/msdnlib.idc?theURL=/library/psdk/ xmlsdk/xmld2rl1.htm.

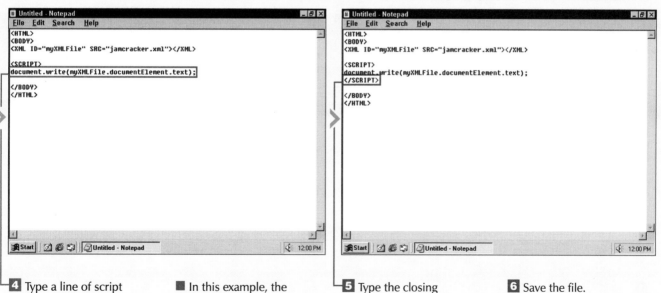

4 Type a line of script that accesses and/or manipulates XML data by referencing the data island's `documentElement` object.

■ In this example, the `document.write()` method is passed the text of the `documentElement` object, which results in the contents of `myXMLFile` displaying on the Web page at runtime.

5 Type the closing `</SCRIPT>` tag.

6 Save the file.

APPLY STYLE SHEET TO A DATA ISLAND

Y ou can apply an XML style sheet to an XML document represented as a data island.

When you load an XML document into Internet Explorer, Microsoft's XSL parser automatically applies any attached style sheet rules and displays the document appropriately.

If you want the additional flexibility of loading an XML document into a data island and manipulating it with

the XML DOM, however, you must apply your style sheet programmatically.

To do this, you load both the XML document and the style sheet into separate data islands, and create an `onload` event handler that uses the `transformNode()` method to apply the style sheet to the XML document and uses the `outerHTML` property to display the formatted data.

APPLY STYLE SHEET TO A DATA ISLAND

| Untitled - Notepad |
| File   Edit   Search   Help |
| `<HTML>` |
| `<BODY>` |
| |
| `</BODY>` |
| `</HTML>` |

| Untitled - Notepad |
| File   Edit   Search   Help |
| `<HTML>` |
| `<BODY>` |
| |
| `<XML ID="xmlDoc" SRC="task4.xml"> </XML>` |
| `<XML ID="styleDoc" SRC="task4.xsl"></XML>` |
| |
| `</BODY>` |
| `</HTML>` |

1 Open the HTML document in which you want to apply a style sheet to a data island.

2 Type **<XML>** tags to load both the style sheet and the data island.

■ In this example, the name of the style sheet is `styleDoc` and the name of the XML document being embedded as a data island is `xmlDoc`.

Extra

Microsoft's document object model defines and implements the following:

- The `outerHTML` property of the named HTML component (`output.outerHTML`)

- The `transformNode()` method of the embedded data island (`xmlDoc.transformNode()`)

- The `documentElement` property of the embedded stylesheet (`styleDoc.documentElement`)

For more options on applying style sheets to data islands, visit Microsoft's DOM reference at http://msdn.microsoft.com/workshop/author/dhtml/reference/dhtmlrefs.asp.

```
Untitled - Notepad
File  Edit  Search  Help
<HTML>
<BODY>

<XML ID="xmlDoc" SRC="task4.xml"> </XML>
<XML ID="styleDoc" SRC="task4.xsl"></XML>

<DIV ID="output"></DIV>

</BODY>
</HTML>
```

```
Untitled - Notepad
File  Edit  Search  Help
<HTML>
<BODY>

<HEAD><SCRIPT>

Function window.onload() {
    output.outerHTML =
        xmlDoc.transformNode(styleDoc.documentElement);
}

</SCRIPT></HEAD>

<XML ID="xmlDoc" SRC="task4.xml"> </XML>
<XML ID="styleDoc" SRC="task4.xsl"></XML>

<DIV ID="output"></DIV>

</BODY>
</HTML>
```

3 Create a named HTML component through which to display the formatted XML data.

■ In this example, the `<DIV>` tag is used to create a component named `output`.

4 Type a script to apply the embedded stylesheet to the embedded data island, specifying the named component through which to display the result.

■ In this example, the named component is `output`. The `transformNode()` method applies the embedded stylesheet (`styleDoc`) to the data island (`xmlDoc`).

5 Save the file.

ACCESS AND DISPLAY DOCUMENT ELEMENTS

You can access individual XML elements within a data island and display them individually.

Because virtually all XML documents contain nested elements, as an XML developer you must have a way to identify individual elements contained within the root.

The XML DOM provides the *childNodes* property for this purpose. The childNodes property holds a list of all the child elements, or *nodes*, a given XML element contains.

The previous section demonstrates how to locate the first element in an XML document stored as a data island, using the documentElement property.

The XML DOM provides hundreds of properties and methods you can use to pinpoint specific XML elements and attributes stored in a data island. For details, visit Microsoft's XML DOM reference site at http://msdn. microsoft.com/isapi/msdnlib.idc?theURL=/library/psdk/ xmlsdk/xmld2rl1.htm.

ACCESS AND DISPLAY DOCUMENT ELEMENTS

1 Open the HTML document in which you want to isolate an individual element of a data island.

2 Position your cursor beneath the embedded data island (beneath the beginning and ending <XML> tags).

3 Type the opening **<SCRIPT>** tag.

The `childNodes` property is just one of the properties you can use to access XML elements. More options include:

- `firstChild`: The first child element (node) associated with a `documentElement`.
- `lastChild`: The last child element (node) associated with a `documentElement`.
- `nodeValue`: The text associated with an element.
- `parentNode`: The parent node (for nodes that can have parents).
- `nextSibling`: The next element in a list of elements.
- `previousSibling`: The previous element in a list of elements.

All the properties and methods you can use to access XML elements are implemented as part of Microsoft's document object model. To keep up with the latest additions and modifications to the DOM, visit http://msdn.microsoft.com/xml/reference/scriptref/ XMLDOMElement_object.asp.

4 Type in a line of script that accesses the `childNodes` property.

■ In this example, the first child element of the data island called `myXMLFile` is identified and displayed on the screen at runtime.

5 Type the closing **</SCRIPT>** tag.

6 Save the file.

LOOP THROUGH NESTED DATA

You can loop, or *iterate*, through nested elements. This ability enables you to examine, modify, and display each child element appropriately.

You access the XML data contained in a data island by creating scripts that access the XML DOM. To iterate through data, then, you need to use a combination of

- The iteration support built into the script language you choose. Most scripting languages support the for, while, and do while iteration statements, for example.

- The XML DOM methods and properties. The XML DOM provides a wealth of methods and properties that enable you to identify the number name, and contents of all the elements contained in another.

In this section you see how to use the length property to determine the number of item elements contained in the jamcracker_product_info element; then you see how to use that number to loop through and display each item.

LOOP THROUGH NESTED DATA

1 Open the HTML document in which you want to iterate through XML elements.

2 Position your cursor below the data island declaration (the <XML> tags).

3 Type the beginning <SCRIPT> tag.

Extra

Other logical constructs useful for looping through elements (besides the `for` loop) are the `while` loop and the `do while` loop, both of which virtually every scripting language implements.

Example:

```
while (some condition is true) {
  perform some action, such as examining
an element in a list
  change the condition
}
do (some action; change the condition)
{
} while a condition is true
```

The `while` loop enables you to examine an element before performing any action; the `do while` loop enables you to examine an element only after performing an action one time.

When looping through elements, be aware that the value of all list lengths is always one less than the actual number of elements. For example, if `childNodes` refers to a list of 10 elements, the value for the `length` property is 9; if `childNodes` refers to a list of 3, length is 2. This seeming contradiction is due to the common programming convention that all lists begin at 0, not 1.

Untitled - Notepad
File Edit Search Help

```
<HTML>

<BODY>

<XML ID="xmlDoc" SRC="task6.xml"> </XML>

<SCRIPT>
document.writeln("Jamcracker, Inc. Product Data".fontcolor("blue"));
document.writeln("<PRE>");

var numElements = xmlDoc.XMLDocument.documentElement.childNodes.length;

For (var i=0; i<numElements; i++) {
    document.write("Product #" + (i+1) + ": ");

document.writeln(xmlDoc.XMLDocument.documentElement.childNodes.item(i).text);
}

document.writeln("</PRE>");

</BODY>
</HTML>
```

Start | Untitled - Notepad | 12:00 PM

Untitled - Notepad
File Edit Search Help

```
<HTML>

<BODY>

<XML ID="xmlDoc" SRC="task6.xml"> </XML>

<SCRIPT>
document.writeln("Jamcracker, Inc. Product Data".fontcolor("blue"));
document.writeln("<PRE>");

var numElements = xmlDoc.XMLDocument.documentElement.childNodes.length;

For (var i=0; i<numElements; i++) {
    document.write("Product #" + (i+1) + ": ");

document.writeln(xmlDoc.XMLDocument.documentElement.childNodes.item(i).text);
}

document.writeln("</PRE>");
</SCRIPT>

</BODY>
</HTML>
```

Start | Untitled - Notepad | 12:00 PM

■4 Type a script that uses a looping construct and the properties associated with the `childNodes` object to identify and display nested XML elements appropriately.

■ In this example, each of the XML elements in the `xmlDoc` data island begin with the string "Product #" and the number in which they were defined in the XML data file.

■5 Type the closing `</SCRIPT>` tag.

■6 Save the file.

BIND XML DATA WITH A DATA SOURCE OBJECT

Y ou can bind XML data to an HTML table using Microsoft's HTML extensions.

Internet Explorer enables you to bind a data source, such as an XML document, directly to HTML elements. Called *data binding*, this capability enables HTML elements to refer to generic data elements rather than specific data values, so that HTML code need not be rewritten to accommodate data changes. Because both data binding and XML applications were designed to

separate data from presentation, these two technologies are fairly easy to integrate.

Data binding requires

- A pluggable data source object. An XML document implemented as a data island can act as a data source object.
- HTML extensions. Several HTML elements, including tables and input fields, can be "hooked up" to receive data from a data source.

BIND XML DATA WITH A DATA SOURCE OBJECT

```
Untitled - Notepad
File  Edit  Search  Help
<HTML>

<BODY>
<XML ID="xmlDoc" SRC="task7.xml"></XML>


</BODY>

</HTML>
```

```
Untitled - Notepad
File  Edit  Search  Help
<HTML>

<BODY>
<XML ID="xmlDoc" SRC="task7.xml"></XML>

<CENTER>
<H1>Jamcracker, Inc. Product Data</H1><H2>by sales channel</H2>

</CENTER>

</BODY>

</HTML>
```

■1 Open the HTML document in which you want to bind a data island to an HTML extension.

■2 Position your cxursor beneath the data island declaration (the <XML> tags).

■3 Type in HTML code to create a descriptive heading.

■ In this example, the centered heading displayed at runtime is "**Jamcracker, Inc. Product Data by sales channel**".

Extra

Two attributes bind a data source to an HTML element:

- `DATASRC` binds an element to a data source, such as a data island.

- `DATAFLD` binds an element to a specific data field within that data source.

In the example in this section, all the contained elements associated with a single container are bound to an HTML table and organized by a single attribute. Then the process is repeated, so that two levels of contained elements display in the HTML table. As the data defined in the XML data source repeats, Internet Explorer's binding utility generates multiple tables, rows, and cells automatically.

For more information on Internet Explorer's support for data binding, visit http://msdn.microsoft. com/ workshop/author/databind/data_binding.asp.

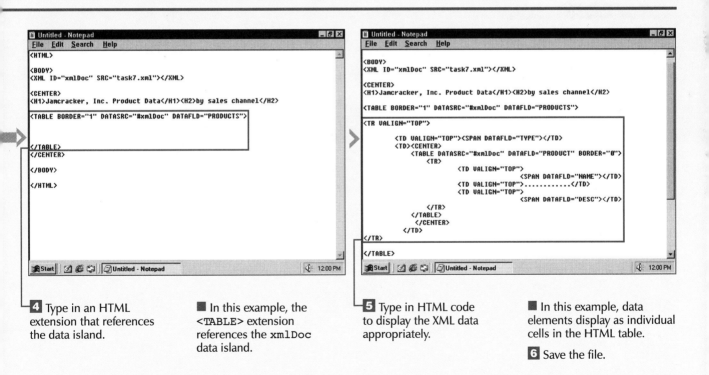

4 Type in an HTML extension that references the data island.

■ In this example, the `<TABLE>` extension references the `xmlDoc` data island.

5 Type in HTML code to display the XML data appropriately.

■ In this example, data elements display as individual cells in the HTML table.

6 Save the file.

CREATE A SCRIPT SKELETON

You can access XML data from inside an HTML file by interacting with the XML document object model through a script. This section shows you how to create a simple HTML file and script skeleton using a text editor. (The remaining sections in this chapter show you how to build on this file to create an XML processor that accesses the XML document object model.)

You can access XML data through the XML DOM two ways:

- Using C, C++, or Visual Basic. To access XML data through one of these languages, you must download and install special header files and libraries. For details, visit http://msdn.microsoft.com/ xml/reference/cvbref/ XMLDOM_Interfaces.asp.

- Using HTML and a scripting language. You can load an XML document inside an HTML file using a scripting language — such as JScript, JavaScript, or VBScript — and then access and manipulate that document using the XML document object model objects, properties, and methods. The sections in this chapter demonstrate this approach.

You can also embed an XML document inside an HTML file using Microsoft's <XML> tag, similar to the way you embed an image inside an HTML file using the <IMG> tag. An embedded XML document is called a *data island*. The sections in Chapter 12 demonstrate how to create a data island.

CREATE A SCRIPT SKELETON

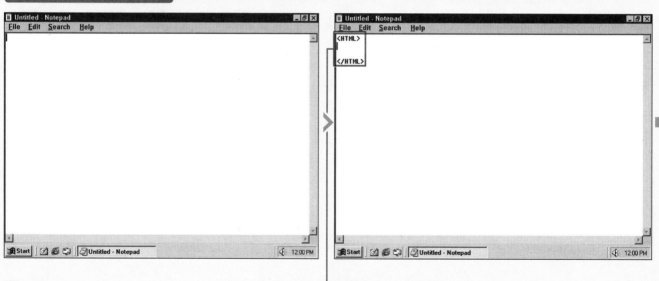

1 Create a new document in a text editor.

■ This example shows Notepad.

2 Type the beginning and ending **<HTML>** tags.

Extra

You can create HTML files

- Using a text editor, as shown in this section. A text editor is appropriate if you want to create a small, simple HTML file.

- Using a graphical HTML editor. HTML editors are optimized for building HTML documents and include such features as WYSIWYG interfaces, built-in templates, and color coding. The companion CD includes trial versions of two popular HTML editors, Sausage Software's HotDog and Allaire's HomeSite. The following resources are useful in learning to create and test HTML documents:

  - CNET.com offers a comprehensive HTML authoring site containing articles, reference materials, and downloadable HTML editors at http://home.cnet.com/category/0,10000,0-7259,00.html.

  - The World Wide Web Consortium's HTML validation service validates HTML files residing on an HTTP server for conformance with the HTML standard. Go to http://validator.w3.org/.

  - Microsoft's HTML authoring site contains basic as well as advanced HTML instruction, optimized for Internet Explorer. Go to http://msdn.microsoft.com/workshop/author/default.asp.

Left screen (Untitled - Notepad):

```
<HTML>
<HEAD>

<SCRIPT>
function loadXML() {

}
</SCRIPT>

</HEAD>


</HTML>
```

Right screen (Untitled - Notepad):

```
<HTML>
<HEAD>

<SCRIPT>
function loadXML() {

}
</SCRIPT>

</HEAD>

<BODY>
<H2>Enter the name of an XML document:</H2>
<INPUT TYPE="TEXT" SIZE="50" ID="URL">
<P>
<INPUT TYPE="BUTTON" VALUE="Load XML document"
        onclick="javascript:loadXML()">
</P>
<DIV ID=RESULTS STYLE="color:red; font-weight:bold;">
</DIV>
</BODY>

</HTML>
```

3 Type the beginning and ending **<HEAD>** tags to create a document head containing a script placeholder.

■ In this example, the name of the (empty) script defined in the HTML document head is loadXML().

4 Type the beginning and ending **<BODY>** tags to create a document body.

■ In this example, an HTML push button is connected to the empty loadXML() function via the onClick event handler.

■ A results component is defined that eventually displays the results of this XML processor to the screen.

5 Save the file, with an .htm or .html extension.

INSTANTIATE AN XML DOCUMENT OBJECT

In order to load an XML document into memory and access the data it contains, you must first create an instance of an ActiveX object of type *XMLDOMDocument*. You create this in-memory object, which represents an empty XML document, using the *new* operator supported in a scripting language such as JavaScript/JScript. After you create this object, you can then use the objects, properties, methods, and events provided by the XML DOM to

- Load the in-memory document with the XML elements and attributes declared in a specific XML document on disk.

- Query the in-memory document to locate and display specific XML elements and attributes, or loop through them sequentially.

- Manipulate the in-memory document by adding, modifying, or deleting XML elements or attributes.

- Copy the in-memory document, or save it to disk.

Here is the syntax:

```
ActiveXObject("Microsoft.XMLDOM")
```

INSTANTIATE AN XML DOCUMENT OBJECT

1 Open the HTML file in which you want to instantiate an empty XML document object.

2 Type a variable declaration to hold the empty XML document.

■ In this JavaScript example, the variable is called `xmlDoc`.

Apply It

Microsoft provides two threading models you can use to create instances of XMLDOMDocument. Although the behavior of the two models is identical, the first provides better performance in cases where multithreading is not necessary.

- **Rental threading model.** To create a document using this model, pass the string "Microsoft.XMLDOM" to the ActiveXObject() method, as shown here:

```
new ActiveXObject("Microsoft.XMLDOM");
```

- **Free-threading model.** To create a document using this model, pass the string "Microsoft.FreeThreaded.XMLDOM" to the ActiveXObject() method:

```
new ActiveXObject("Microsoft.FreeThreaded.XMLDOM");
```

As you see in some of the other sections in this chapter, you can copy one XML document to another; you can also graft nodes, or subsets, of one XML document to another. In order to do this, however, both the target and the source XML documents must be declared using the same model.

You instantiate an empty XML document object in VBScript much as you do in JavaScript/JScript, with two exceptions:

- The *Set* operator replaces *var*

- The CreateObject() method replaces both the new operator and the ActiveXObject() method.

Here is an example of instantiating an empty XML document object in VBScript.

Example:

```
Set xmlDoc =
CreateObject("Microsoft.XMLDOM")
Set xmlDoc = CreateObject("Microsoft.
FreeThreadedXMLDOM")
```

For detailed information on the XMLDOMDocument object, visit http://msdn.microsoft.com/xml/reference/scriptref/xmldomdocument_object.asp.

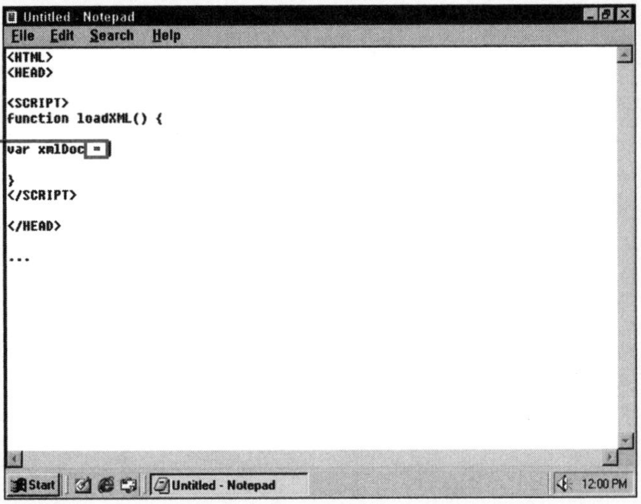

Untitled - Notepad

File Edit Search Help

```
<HTML>
<HEAD>

<SCRIPT>
function loadXML() {

var xmlDoc = |

}
</SCRIPT>

</HEAD>

...
```

Start | Untitled - Notepad | 12:00 PM

3 Type an equal operator (=).

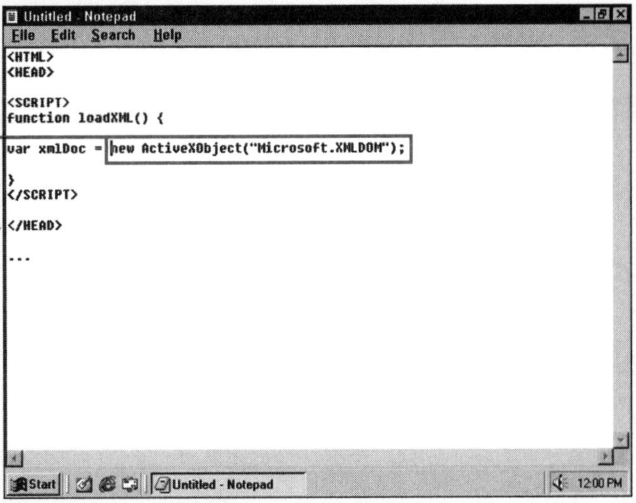

Untitled - Notepad

File Edit Search Help

```
<HTML>
<HEAD>

<SCRIPT>
function loadXML() {

var xmlDoc = new ActiveXObject("Microsoft.XMLDOM");

}
</SCRIPT>

</HEAD>

...
```

Start | Untitled - Notepad | 12:00 PM

4 Type a call to create a new instance of the **ActiveXObject** object.

LOAD AN XML DOCUMENT

Before you can access an external XML document located on disk, you must load it into memory. You do this in two steps:

First, create an empty XML document in memory. "Instantiate a Document Object" earlier in this chapter shows you how to do this.

Next, load the contents of an XML file from disk to the in-memory representation. You do so using the load() method associated with the XMLDOMDocument object, as shown in this section.

Here is the syntax required to load an XML file:

```
boolean = anXMLDOMDocument.load(url)
```

boolean is a return code indicating success or failure of the load process. If load() succeeds, it returns *true*; if it fails, it returns *false*.

anXMLDOMDocument is an instance of type XMLDOMDocument.

url is a string representing the XML document to load.

LOAD AN XML DOCUMENT

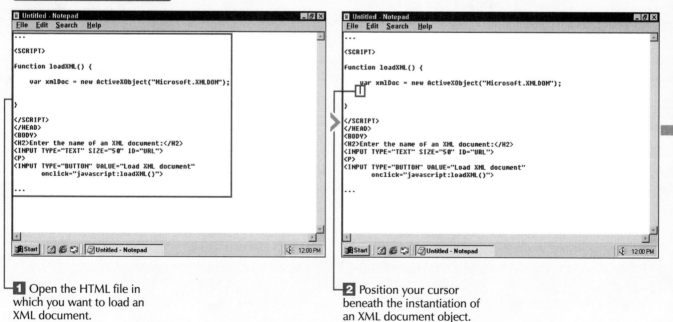

1 Open the HTML file in which you want to load an XML document.

2 Position your cursor beneath the instantiation of an XML document object.

Apply It

When you load an XML file into memory, you are parsing that XML file and using the contents to create a named document *tree* structure. This tree structure comprises multiple *nodes*, and you access XML data by traversing those nodes. A node is any discrete component of an XML document, such as

- An element
- An attribute
- A cdata section
- An entity
- A processing instruction
- A comment

To determine whether the XML document load process succeeded or failed, you can capture the return code of the `load()` method and examine it.

Example:

```
// declare a variable
var returnCode = 0;
 // assign the return value of load() to
this variable
returnCode = xmlDoc.load("aFile.xml");
if (returnCode == false) {
    // the load process failed, so
enerate an error
}
else {
    // the load process succeeded
}
```

The load() method is a Microsoft extension of the World Wide Web Consortium's XML DOM specification. For detailed information on the XMLDOMDocument's load() method, visit http://msdn.microsoft.com/xml/reference/scriptref/XMLDOMDocument_load.asp.

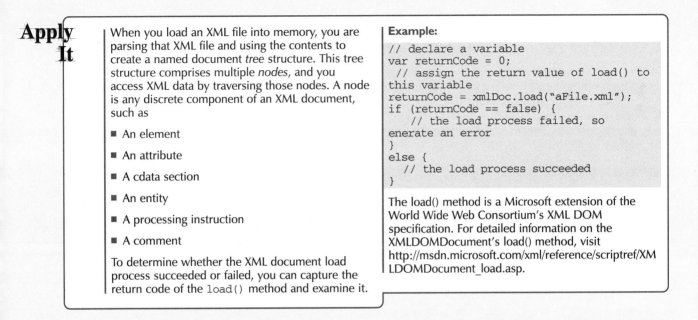

3 Type a call to the `load()` method.

■ The `load()` method is being called on the XML document object named `xmlDoc`.

4 Type a parameter for the `load()` method.

■ In this example, `URL.value` is being passed to the `load()` method. At runtime, `URL.value` (which is defined as an HTML text input field) contains the name of an XML document file.

5 Save the file.

HANDLE LOAD ERRORS GRACEFULLY

By examining the parseError property, you can detect whether an XML load process succeeds, and — if the process fails — how to gather helpful diagnostic information to help you determine the cause of the failure.

Here is the syntax:

anXMLDOMDocument.parseError

anXMLDOMDocument is an instance of type XMLDOMDocument.

parseError itself contains the following diagnostic properties:

- **errorCode:** The error code of the last parse error.
- **filepos:** The absolute file position where the error occurred.
- **line:** The line number that contains the error.
- **linepos:** The character position within the line where the error occurred.
- **reason:** The reason for the error.
- **srcText:** The full text of the line containing the error.
- **url:** The URL of the XML document containing the last error.

HANDLE LOAD ERRORS GRACEFULLY

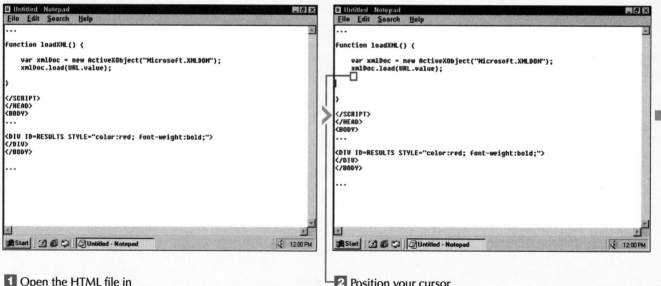

1 Open the HTML file in which you want to handle XML load errors.

2 Position your cursor beneath the XML load statement.

Apply It

You cannot change any of the properties associated with an XML parse error; all of these properties are read-only. The following code displays all the properties associated with an XML parse error (assuming that RESULTS is defined as the ID of the HTML <DIV> tag, as shown in this section).

Example:
```
if (xmlDoc.parseError != 0) {
        RESULTS.innerHTML = xmlDoc.parseError.reason + "<BR>"
        RESULTS.innerHTML += xmlDoc.parseError.url + "<BR>"
        RESULTS.innerHTML += xmlDoc.parseError.errorCode + "<BR>"
        RESULTS.innerHTML += xmlDoc.parseError.filepos + "<BR>"
        RESULTS.innerHTML += xmlDoc.parseError.line + "<BR>"
        RESULTS.innerHTML += xmlDoc.parseError.linepos + "<BR>"
    }
    else {
        RESULTS.innerHTML = "XML document loaded successfully" + "<BR>"
    }
```

The XMLDOMParseError object is a Microsoft extension to the World Wide Web Consortium's XML DOM specification. For detailed information on the XMLDOMParseError object and its properties, http://msdn.microsoft.com/xml/reference/scriptref/XMLDOMParseError_object.asp.

3 Type a logical if statement that determines whether the XML document object load failed.

■ In this example, if the XML document object load fails, the reason for the failure displays on the screen at runtime.

4 Type a logical else statement that specifies an action to take if the XML document object load succeeds.

■ In this example, if the XML document object load succeeds, a success message displays on the screen at runtime.

ACCESS XML ELEMENTS

You can access individual XML elements programmatically using XML DOM objects, properties, and methods.

The XMLDOMDocument object contains dozens of objects, properties, and methods you can use to access XML elements in memory. The most basic of these are demonstrated in this section:

- documentElement: Property of XMLDOMDocument; represents the root XML element

- childNodes: Property of XMLDOMDocument.documentElement;

represents the list of elements contained within the root XML element

- nextNode(): Method of XMLDOMDocument.documentElement.childNodes; represents the next element in a list, beginning with the first element

- text: Property of XMLDOMNode; represents the text content of the element and all of its child elements, if any

Because an XMLDOMDocument object is structured as a tree of nodes, or elements — much like a directory is structured as a tree of files — you must begin at the top and traverse the structure downward.

ACCESS XML ELEMENTS

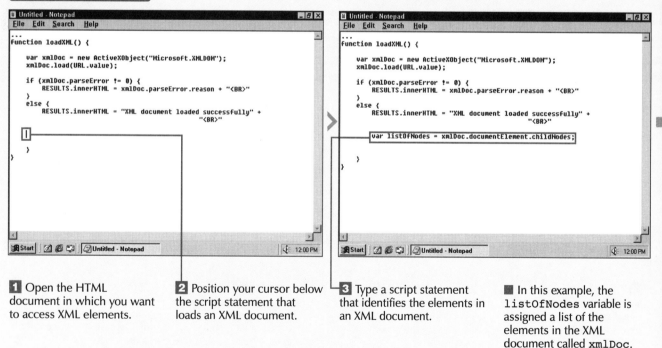

1 Open the HTML document in which you want to access XML elements.

2 Position your cursor below the script statement that loads an XML document.

3 Type a script statement that identifies the elements in an XML document.

■ In this example, the listOfNodes variable is assigned a list of the elements in the XML document called xmlDoc.

Accessing XML elements programmatically requires a thorough understanding of Microsoft's implementation of the XML DOM. If you choose to access the XML DOM through a scripting language, however, you also need to understand

- HTML. You need to understand how to incorporate scripts into HTML documents and how to attach them to automatic or user-initiated events. In this example, the `loadXML()` function is attached to the `onClick` event handler associated with an HTML push button.

- Internet Explorer's document object model. You need to understand how the DOM provides programmatic access to HTML elements, which is similar to the way the XML DOM provides access to XML elements. For example, the code in this section calls the `write()` method on the document object.

- JavaScript, JScript, or VBScript. You need to understand the syntax and built-in constructs of the scripting language (or other programming language, such as C/C++, for that matter) that you choose. For example, the JavaScript code in this section includes the common `while` loop.

Because the documentElement property of the XMLDOMDocument objects represents the root element, it provides access to all the other elements declared in an XML document. For detailed information on this property, visit http://msdn.microsoft.com/xml/reference/scriptref/XMLDOMDocument_documentElement.asp.

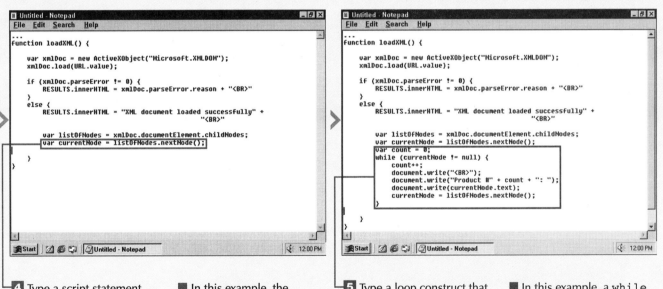

4 Type a script statement that accesses the first element in the document.

■ In this example, the `currentNode` variable is assigned the first element in the XML document.

5 Type a loop construct that traverses all the elements in the document.

■ In this example, a `while` loop traverses the elements in the `xmlDoc` document and writes the text they contain to the screen at runtime.

6 Save the file.

ACCESS XML ATTRIBUTES

I n XML, elements represent data; attributes represent descriptive *metadata,* or data about data. XML developers choose whether to define any particular piece of data as an element or as an attribute. Conceptually, the difference is one of organization and modeling: Data that is integral to an application is often defined as individual elements, and ancillary descriptive data is often defined as attributes. Practically, XML elements and attributes are accessed in different ways, using different methods. Tool support for accessing and displaying XML attributes is currently less sophisticated than it is for accessing and displaying XML elements.

This section shows you how to access the value of attributes declared in an XML document.

The XML DOM provides special properties and methods you can use to identify, access, and modify the values of XML attributes. The most common of these is the *attributes* property, which you see demonstrated in this section.

ACCESS XML ATTRIBUTES

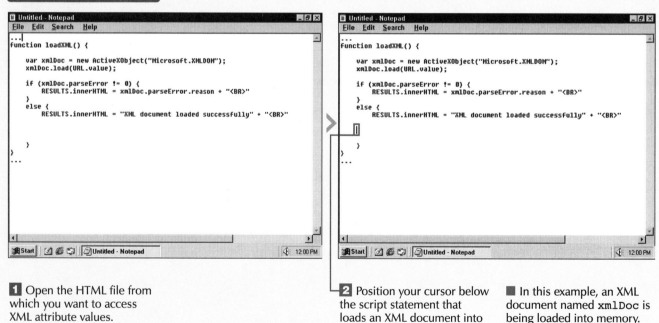

1 Open the HTML file from which you want to access XML attribute values.

2 Position your cursor below the script statement that loads an XML document into memory.

■ In this example, an XML document named xmlDoc is being loaded into memory.

Extra

The `attributes` property represents a list of attributes. This list is implemented as an object of type `XMLDOMNamedNodeMap`. The `XMLDOMNamedNodeMap` method demonstrated in this example is `getNamedItem()`, but several more methods and properties are available. For example,

- `removeNamedItem()` enables you to delete an attribute value.

- `setNamedItem()` enables you to add an attribute value at runtime.

For a complete description of the `attributes` property, visit http://msdn.microsoft.com/library/psdk/xmlsdk/xmld5fzn.htm.

For a complete description of the properties and methods associated with XMLDOMNamedNodeMap, see http://msdn.microsoft.com/library/psdk/xmlsdk/ xmld7j1s.htm.

```
Untitled - Notepad
File  Edit  Search  Help
...
function loadXML() {

    var xmlDoc = new ActiveXObject("Microsoft.XMLDOM");
    xmlDoc.load(URL.value);

    if (xmlDoc.parseError != 0) {
        RESULTS.innerHTML = xmlDoc.parseError.reason + "<BR>"
    }
    else {
        RESULTS.innerHTML = "XML document loaded successfully" + "<BR>"

        var numElements =
            xmlDoc.documentElement.childNodes.length;

    }
}
...
```
```
Start    Untitled - Notepad                          12:00 PM
```

3 Type a script statement to determine the number of elements contained in the XML document.

```
Untitled - Notepad
File  Edit  Search  Help
...
function loadXML() {

    var xmlDoc = new ActiveXObject("Microsoft.XMLDOM");
    xmlDoc.load(URL.value);

    if (xmlDoc.parseError != 0) {
        RESULTS.innerHTML = xmlDoc.parseError.reason + "<BR>"
    }
    else {
        RESULTS.innerHTML = "XML document loaded successfully" + "<BR>"

        var numElements =
                xmlDoc.documentElement.childNodes.length;

        for (var i=0; i<numElements; i++) {
            document.write("Product code #");
document.write(xmlDoc.documentElement.childNodes.item(i).attributes.getNamedItem("product_code").text);
            document.write("</BR>");
        }

    }
}
...
```
```
Start    Untitled - Notepad                          12:00 PM
```

4 Type the script statements that are necessary to identify one or more XML attributes.

■ In this example, the value for the attribute named **product code** displays on the screen at runtime using the `attributes` property of the `element` object.

5 Save the file.

SET XML ELEMENTS

After you load an XML document into memory, you can add elements to that in-memory copy, modify existing elements' values, and delete elements. Changing the in-memory representation of the XML document does not alter the XML file on disk.

Adding an element requires three steps:

- First, create the new element using a creation method such as `createNode()` or `createElement()`.

- Then, type the new element to the in-memory tree structure using a method such as the `insertBefore()`, `replaceChild()`, or `appendChild()` methods.

- Next, set the value of the new element.

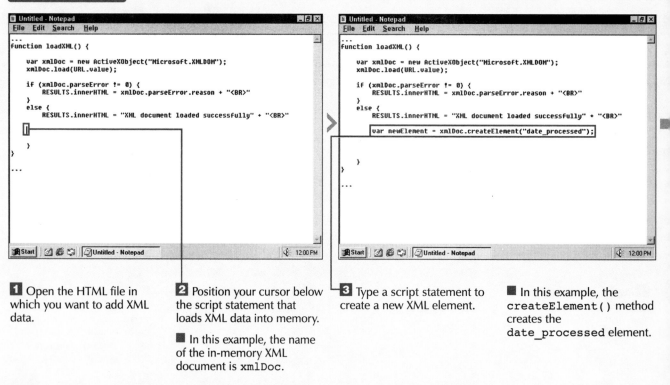

1 Open the HTML file in which you want to add XML data.

2 Position your cursor below the script statement that loads XML data into memory.

■ In this example, the name of the in-memory XML document is xmlDoc.

3 Type a script statement to create a new XML element.

■ In this example, the `createElement()` method creates the `date_processed` element.

Extra

In addition to elements, you can add, modify, and delete any of the other components that make up an XML file (see below). However, keep in mind that the same restrictions currently apply: Changing the in-memory representation of any of the following does not alter the XML file on disk.

- Attributes
- cdata sections
- Comments
- Entities
- Notations
- Processing instructions

Note: You can find detailed instructions for creating all these types of XML components, as well as XML elements, at http://msdn.microsoft.com/library/psdk/xmlsdk/xmld5d5x.htm.

To verify that you have added an element correctly, you can traverse the in-memory tree structure and display its contents.

```
Untitled - Notepad
File   Edit   Search   Help
...
function loadXML() {

    var xmlDoc = new ActiveXObject("Microsoft.XMLDOM");
    xmlDoc.load(URL.value);

    if (xmlDoc.parseError != 0) {
        RESULTS.innerHTML = xmlDoc.parseError.reason + "<BR>"
    }
    else {
        RESULTS.innerHTML = "XML document loaded successfully" + "<BR>"

        var newElement = xmlDoc.createElement("date_processed");
xmlDoc.documentElement.childNodes.item(2).appendChild(newElementTwo);


    }
}
...
```

```
Untitled - Notepad
File   Edit   Search   Help
...
function loadXML() {

    var xmlDoc = new ActiveXObject("Microsoft.XMLDOM");
    xmlDoc.load(URL.value);

    if (xmlDoc.parseError != 0) {
        RESULTS.innerHTML = xmlDoc.parseError.reason + "<BR>"
    }
    else {
        RESULTS.innerHTML = "XML document loaded successfully" + "<BR>"

        var newElement = xmlDoc.createElement("date_processed");
xmlDoc.documentElement.childNodes.item(2).appendChild(newElementTwo);
        today = new Date();
        xmlDoc.documentElement.childNodes.item(2).lastChild.text=today;


    }
}
...
```

■ **4** Type a statement that appends the new element to the in-memory XML data tree.

■ In this example, the `appendChild()` method appends the new element to the in-memory XML data tree.

■ **5** Type one or more statements to set the value of the new XML element.

■ In this example, the value for the `date_processed` element is set to the current date.

■ **6** Save the file.

MODIFY AND DELETE XML ELEMENTS

After you load an XML document into memory, you can modify existing elements' values and delete elements. Changing the in-memory representation of the XML document does not alter the XML file on disk.

Modifying or deleting an element requires that you identify the element you want to modify or delete, and then modify or delete that element.

MODIFY AND DELETE XML ELEMENTS

```
Untitled - Notepad                                          _ 8 X
File  Edit  Search  Help
...
function loadXML() {

    var xmlDoc = new ActiveXObject("Microsoft.XMLDOM");
    xmlDoc.load(URL.value);

    if (xmlDoc.parseError != 0) {
        RESULTS.innerHTML = xmlDoc.parseError.reason + "<BR>"
    }
    else {
        RESULTS.innerHTML = "XML document loaded successfully" + "<BR>"


    }
}

...
```

```
Untitled - Notepad                                          _ 8 X
File  Edit  Search  Help
...
function loadXML() {

    var xmlDoc = new ActiveXObject("Microsoft.XMLDOM");
    xmlDoc.load(URL.value);

    if (xmlDoc.parseError != 0) {
        RESULTS.innerHTML = xmlDoc.parseError.reason + "<BR>"
    }
    else {
        RESULTS.innerHTML = "XML document loaded successfully" + "<BR>"

        // Obtain the first product element
        var firstElement =
            xmlDoc.documentElement.childNodes.item(0);

        // Delete the first element contained in the product element
        firstElement.removeChild(firstElement.childNodes.item(0));
    }
}

...
```

1 Open the HTML file in which you want to modify or delete an XML element.

2 Position your cursor beneath the script statement that loads an XML document into memory.

3 Type a script statement that identifies an XML element to delete.

■ In this example, the first element in the XML file is identified.

4 Type a script statement that deletes the identified XML element.

Apply It

To verify your modifications and deletions, you can traverse the in-memory tree structure and display its contents. To do so, add the following to the code demonstrated in this example:

```
var listOfNodes = xmlDoc.documentElement.childNodes;
    var currentNode = listOfNodes.nextNode();
    while (currentNode != null) {
      // If this element contains child elements
      if (currentNode.childNodes.length > 1) {
        var childList = currentNode.childNodes;
        var innerCurrentNode = childList.nextNode();
        ///////////// children of product element
        while (innerCurrentNode != null) {
            if (innerCurrentNode.childNodes.length > 1) {
                var childList2 = innerCurrentNode.childNodes;
                var innerCurrentNode2 = childList2.nextNode();
                document.write("<UL>")
                ///////////// children of ingredient_list element
                while (innerCurrentNode2 != null) {document.write("<LI>" +
                    innerCurrentNode2.text);innerCurrentNode2 = childList2.nextNode();}
                document.write("</UL>");}
            else {document.write(innerCurrentNode.nodeName + ":  ");
                document.write(innerCurrentNode.text + "<BR>");}
            innerCurrentNode = childList.nextNode();
        }
      }
      currentNode = listOfNodes.nextNode();
    }
```

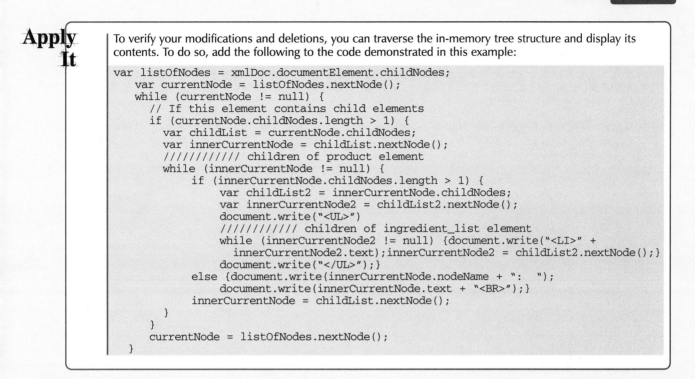

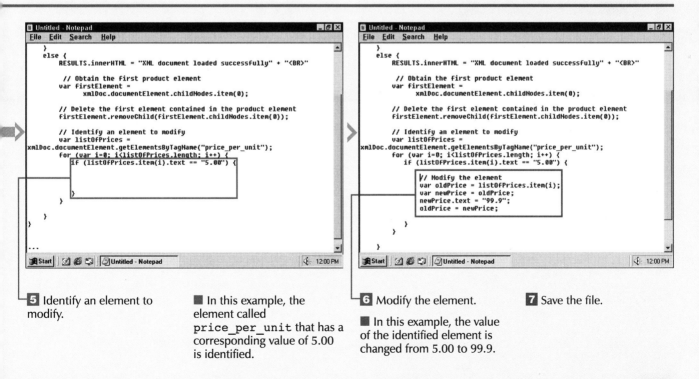

5 Identify an element to modify.

■ In this example, the element called `price_per_unit` that has a corresponding value of 5.00 is identified.

6 Modify the element.

■ In this example, the value of the identified element is changed from 5.00 to 99.9.

7 Save the file.

LOOP THROUGH STRUCTURED DATA

This section shows you how to loop, or *iterate*, through contained XML elements.

The XML DOM exposes an XML document as a structured tree comprising multiple *nodes*. The top, or *root*, node is always the root XML element.

In order to iterate through a list of contained elements, you first obtain the container element, which is

represented in the XML DOM as an object of type XMLDOMNodeList; then you traverse the list.

The XML DOM provides many different methods you can use to iterate through XML data. The method demonstrated in this section is the nextNode() method.

LOOP THROUGH STRUCTURED DATA

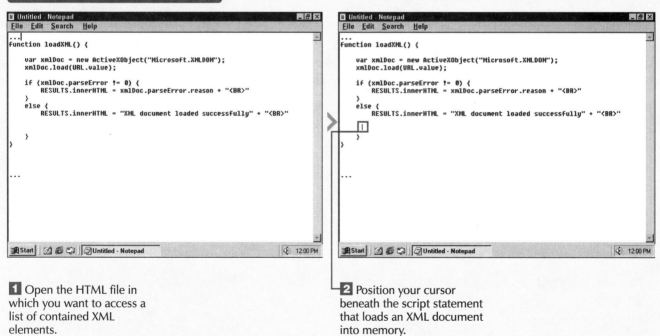

1 Open the HTML file in which you want to access a list of contained XML elements.

2 Position your cursor beneath the script statement that loads an XML document into memory.

Extra

Depending on your application and programming style, you may want to use an alternative method for looping through element lists than the one demonstrated in this section. One alternative you can use to step through multiple child nodes is to determine the number of child elements in a list and query the list exactly that many times.

Example:

```
// Determine the length of the list
var numElements = xmlDoc.documentElement.childNodes.length;
// Beginning with 0, iterate over the list exactly the number of times as
// the list contains elements
for (var i=0; i<numElements; i++) {
    document.write("Product code #");

// xmlDoc.documentElement.childNodes.item(i) takes the
        // place of nextNode(). Both return the next node, or element,
        // in a list.
document.write(xmlDoc.documentElement.childNodes.item(i).attributes.getNamedItem
("product_code").text);
        document.write(".........");
        document.write(xmlDoc.documentElement.childNodes.item(i).text);
        document.write("</BR>");
```

For details on the XMLDOMNodeList, see http://msdn.microsoft.com/library/psdk/xmlsdk/xmld4kvo.htm. Collections of attributes are represented as objects of type XMLDOMNamedNodeMap; for more information on the XMLDOMNamedNodeMap, see http://msdn.microsoft.com/library/psdk/xmlsdk/xmld7j1s.htm.

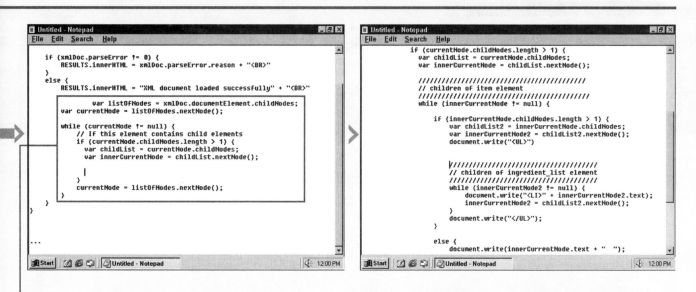

```
if (xmlDoc.parseError != 0) {
    RESULTS.innerHTML = xmlDoc.parseError.reason + "<BR>"
}
else {
    RESULTS.innerHTML = "XML document loaded successfully" + "<BR>"

            var listOfNodes = xmlDoc.documentElement.childNodes;
    var currentNode = listOfNodes.nextNode();

    while (currentNode != null) {
        // If this element contains child elements
        if (currentNode.childNodes.length > 1) {
            var childList = currentNode.childNodes;
            var innerCurrentNode = childList.nextNode();

        }
        currentNode = listOfNodes.nextNode();
    }
}
}
...
```

```
if (currentNode.childNodes.length > 1) {
    var childList = currentNode.childNodes;
    var innerCurrentNode = childList.nextNode();

///////////////////////////////////////////
// children of item element
///////////////////////////////////////////
while (innerCurrentNode != null) {

    if (innerCurrentNode.childNodes.length > 1) {
        var childList2 = innerCurrentNode.childNodes;
        var innerCurrentNode2 = childList2.nextNode();
        document.write("<UL>")

        ///////////////////////////////////////////
        // children of ingredient_list element
        ///////////////////////////////////////////
        while (innerCurrentNode2 != null) {
            document.write("<LI>" + innerCurrentNode2.text);
            innerCurrentNode2 = childList2.nextNode();
        }
        document.write("</UL>");
    }

    else {
        document.write(innerCurrentNode.text + "  ");
```

3 Type a looping construct to iterate through a contained list of elements.

■ In this example, `childList` represents a list of elements contained in the root element of the XML document.

4 Type additional looping constructs to iterate through any nested container levels, as appropriate.

■ In this example, two additional looping constructs iterate through two additional contained element lists.

5 Save the file.

VALIDATE PROGRAMMATICALLY

You can perform custom validations on XML data programmatically using JavaScript and the XML DOM. You do this by accessing and examining XML values at runtime and taking action when a data exception is encountered. This approach gives you the most control over data validation; however, it also exacts the largest price in terms of complexity and custom code.

These alternative ways to validate XML data may be more appropriate than the one demonstrated in this section, depending on your application:

- Construct a Document Type Definition, or DTD. DTDs are similar to table definitions in relational database applications: they constrain both data structure and individual data values. While fairly well supported as this book goes to press, DTDs currently lack sophisticated data validation, such as the ability to ensure that an element contains data in a custom date format. Chapters 3, 4, and 5 demonstrate this approach.

- Construct a schema. Like DTDs, schemas constrain both data structure and individual data values; they also provide for sophisticated data type validation. However, they are currently not well supported. Chapters 6 and 7 demonstrate this approach.

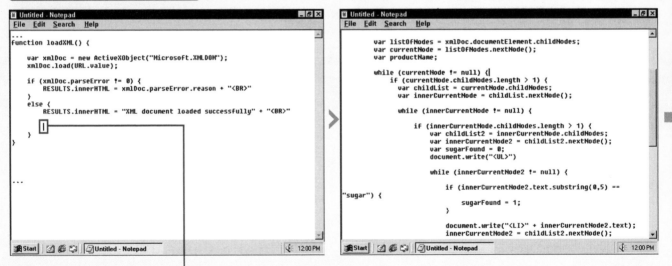

VALIDATE PROGRAMMATICALLY

1 Open the HTML file in which you want to perform a custom XML data validation routine.

2 Position your cursor beneath the script statement that loads an XML document into memory.

3 Type the script statements necessary to access an XML data value.

■ In this example, each element in a container is accessed, and a flag is set (`sugarFound`) if the value of any element contains the string `sugar`.

Extra

When validating XML data programmatically, you can

- Validate individual attributes or elements

- Check for existence, specific values, or patterns, as shown in this section

- Validate the relationships between data

In simple cases — testing the existence of individual elements, for example, or testing straightforward data structures — DTDs are the best way to approach data validation. In cases where you need sophisticated data type support, such as numeric or date/time fields, schemas are the best approach, especially as schema support in products such as Internet Explorer matures. For other, more complex validation needs, however, custom validation routines provide the most flexibility and power.

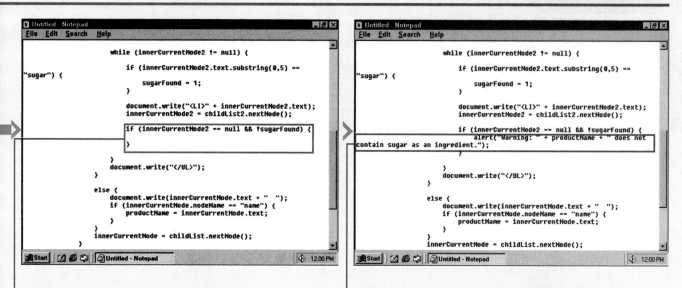

4 Type a script statement to evaluate the XML data value.

■ In this example, the script statement checks to see whether we are at the end of the contained elements and the `sugarFound` flag has not been set.

5 Type a script statement to take action when a data exception occurs.

■ In this example, if the condition is true an error message displays on the screen at runtime when a data exception is encountered.

6 Save the file.

PERSISTING XML DATA

You can save, or *persist*, an XML document to disk using the XML DOM `save()` method.

Microsoft's XML support provides three ways to persist XML data:

- You can save an XML document directly to a file. This approach is currently available only for server-side applications and is not presented in this book.

- You can save an XML document to a new XML document in memory. Technically, this is not persistence at all. However, because the

`save()` method as implemented in Microsoft's Internet Explorer supports this approach, this section demonstrates it. Saving an XML document in memory is the same as performing an in-memory copy.

- You can save an XML document via a COM (Component Object Model) object. Any COM object that supports QueryInterface for IStream, IPersistStream, or IPersistStreamInit can accept and persist XML data. This book does not present this approach.

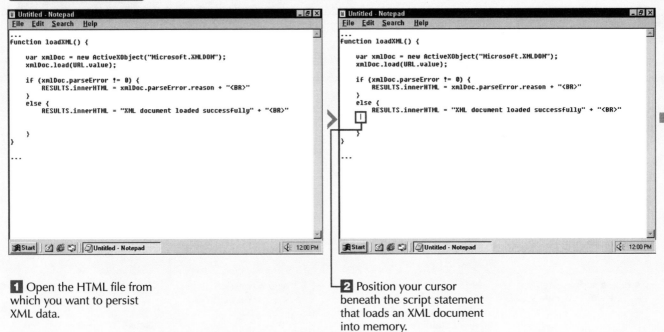

1 Open the HTML file from which you want to persist XML data.

2 Position your cursor beneath the script statement that loads an XML document into memory.

Apply It

Because the `save()` method attempts to parse an XML document before copying it to another in-memory document, using the `save()` method in client-side applications is useful for ensuring that any additions, modifications, or deletions you make to an XML document programmatically do not result in an ill-formed document. If you attempt to save an ill-formed document, `save()` generates an error.

While XML data persistence is not supported in Internet Explorer due to client security restrictions, the following is valid for server-side XML applications.

Example:

```
var xmlDoc = new ActiveXObject("Microsoft.XMLDOM");
    xmlDoc.load(URL.value);
    if (xmlDoc.parseError != 0) {
        RESULTS.innerHTML = xmlDoc.parseError.reason + "<BR>"
    }
    else {
        RESULTS.innerHTML = "XML document loaded successfully" + "<BR>"
        // Save the XML document to disk
        xmlDoc.save("g:\newFile.xml");
    }
```

For details on the `save()` method, which is a Microsoft extension to the World Wide Web Consortium's XML specification, visit http://msdn.microsoft.com/library/psdk/xmlsdk/xmld0z1h.htm.

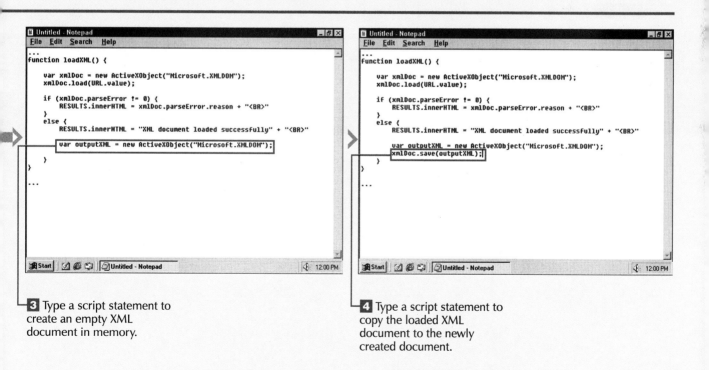

3 Type a script statement to create an empty XML document in memory.

4 Type a script statement to copy the loaded XML document to the newly created document.

CREATE SIMPLE XLINKS

XML links allow you to associate XML documents with each other in much the same way that HTML hyperlinks allow you to associate HTML documents with each other. When fully implemented, XML links are expected to be much more sophisticated than HTML links. For example, XML links will eventually allow developers to dynamically target specific locations in either XML or HTML documents and to create bidirectional links.

You define a simple XML link using a *linking element*. Here is the syntax for a linking element:

```
<linkName xlink:type="linkType"
xlink:href="documentToLinkTo">
linkText
</linkName>
```

linkName is the name you want to associate with the simple link.

linkType is one of *simple*, *extended*, *locator*, *arc*, *resource*, *title*, or *none*.

documentToLinkTo specifies the relative or absolute URI of the target document.

linkText is the text you want to associate with the simple link.

Note: The XLink specification is still in draft form at the time of this writing, and no commercially available software fully supports the syntax described in this section. For this reason, XML links are currently practical only for prototyping efforts.

CREATE SIMPLE XLINKS

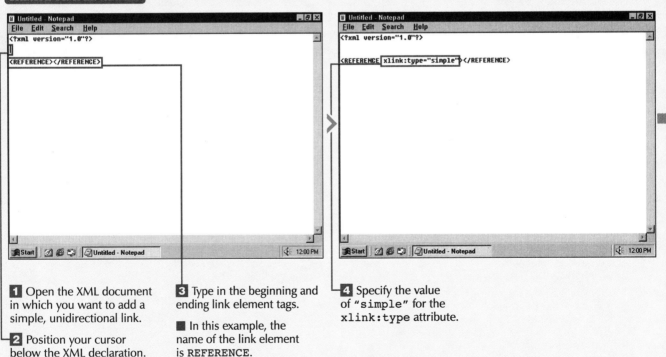

■1 Open the XML document in which you want to add a simple, unidirectional link.

■2 Position your cursor below the XML declaration.

■3 Type in the beginning and ending link element tags.

■ In this example, the name of the link element is REFERENCE.

■4 Specify the value of "simple" for the xlink:type attribute.

If the XML document in which you define an XLink contains a DTD, you must declare the XLink attributes like any other. For example, the following DTD syntax

■ Declares the REFERENCE element, including the xlink:type and xlink:href attributes

■ Predefines the type of the link as "simple" so that a value of xlink:type need not be included in the XML REFERENCE element

Example:

```
<?xml version="1.0"?>
<!DOCTYPE REFERENCE [
    <!ELEMENT REFERENCE (#PCDATA)>
    <!ATTLIST REFERENCE
        xlink:type CDATA #FIXED "simple"
        xlink:href  CDATA #REQUIRED
    >
]>
<REFERENCE
    xlink:href="bluprint.xml">XML Blueprints</REFERENCE>
```

The xlink:href attribute is sometimes referred to as the *locator attribute*.

The latest version of the XLink specification describes the xlink: attributes in detail. Go to www.w3.org/TR/xlink.

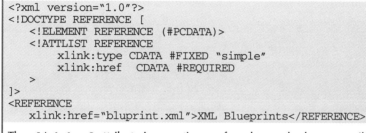

5 Specify the name of the target XML document for the xlink:href attribute.

■ In this example, the target XML document is bluprint.xml.

6 Type in link text.

■ In this example, the link text for the simple link is XML Blueprints.

DESCRIBE LINKS WITH *XLINK:ROLE* AND *XLINK:TITLE*

I n addition to the `xlink:type` attribute and the locator attribute `xlink:href`, a linking element may contain optional *semantic attributes*. These optional semantic attributes, which describe the function of linked resources for both human readers and XML processors, include

- `xlink:role`, which is an application-readable string describing the purpose of this link. If a value exists for this attribute, it is the responsibility of the XML processing application to access and process it appropriately.

- `xlink:title`, which is a human-readable string describing the linked document. If a value exists for this attribute, it is the responsibility of the XML processing application to access and display it appropriately.

Note: The XLink specification is still in draft form at the time of this writing, and no commercially available software fully supports the XML syntax described in this section. For this reason, XML links are currently practical only for prototyping efforts.

DESCRIBE LINKS WITH *XLINK:ROLE* AND *XLINK:TITLE*

```
Untitled - Notepad
File  Edit  Search  Help
<?xml version="1.0"?>

<REFERENCE
    xlink:type="simple"
    xlink:href="bluprint.xml">XML Blueprints</REFERENCE>
```

```
Untitled - Notepad
File  Edit  Search  Help
<?xml version="1.0"?>

<REFERENCE
    xlink:type="simple"
    xlink:href="bluprint.xml"

>XML Blueprints</REFERENCE>
```

1 Open the XML document to which you want to add a link description.

2 Position your cursor below the link element declaration, directly before the closing angle bracket (>).

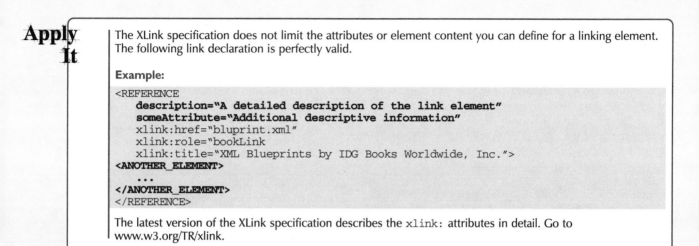

Apply It

The XLink specification does not limit the attributes or element content you can define for a linking element. The following link declaration is perfectly valid.

Example:

```
<REFERENCE
    description="A detailed description of the link element"
    someAttribute="Additional descriptive information"
    xlink:href="bluprint.xml"
    xlink:role="bookLink
    xlink:title="XML Blueprints by IDG Books Worldwide, Inc.">
<ANOTHER_ELEMENT>
    ...
</ANOTHER_ELEMENT>
</REFERENCE>
```

The latest version of the XLink specification describes the `xlink:` attributes in detail. Go to www.w3.org/TR/xlink.

-3 **Type an application-specific and application-readable role for the `xlink:role` attribute.**

■ In this example, the value assigned to `xlink:role` is `bookLink`.

-4 **Type in a human-readable title value for the `xlink:title` attribute.**

■ In this example, the value is `XML Blueprints by IDG Books Worldwide, Inc.`

SPECIFY LINK TRIGGERS

In addition to the required xlink:type and xlink:href attributes, a linking element may contain optional *behavior attributes*. One of these behavior attributes, xlink:actuate, describes when an XML link should be activated. Valid values for the xlink:actuate attribute include:

- **onLoad:** Tells the XML application to traverse the link immediately, as soon as it loads the link source document. Conceptually, this option is similar to the behavior of the HTML <IMG> tag.

- **onRequest:** Tells the XML application to traverse the link only after the user requests link activation.

- **undefined:** Tells the XML application that link activation must be performed by application-specific means.

Note: The XLink specification is still in draft form at the time of this writing, and no commercially available software fully supports the syntax described in this section. Because of this, XML links are currently practical only for prototyping efforts.

SPECIFY LINK TRIGGERS

```
Untitled - Notepad                                    _ 8 X
File  Edit  Search  Help
<?xml version="1.0"?>

<REFERENCE
    xlink:type="simple"
    xlink:href="bluprint.xml"
    xlink:role="bookLink"
    xlink:title="XML Blueprints by IDG Books Worldwide, Inc.">XML
Blueprints</REFERENCE>



Start    Untitled - Notepad                    12:00 PM
```

```
Untitled - Notepad                                    _ 8 X
File  Edit  Search  Help
<?xml version="1.0"?>

<REFERENCE
    xlink:type="simple"
    xlink:href="bluprint.xml"
    xlink:role="bookLink"
    xlink:title="XML Blueprints by IDG Books Worldwide, Inc."

>XML Blueprints</REFERENCE>



Start    Untitled - Notepad                    12:00 PM
```

1 Open the XML document to which you want to add a link description.

2 Position your cursor below the link element declaration, directly before the closing angle bracket (>).

Apply It

If the XML document in which you define an XLink contains a DTD, you must declare the XLink attributes like any other. For example, the following DTD syntax

■ Declares the REFERENCE element, including the xlink:type, xlink:href, xlink:role, xlink:title, and xlink:actuate attributes.

■ Predefines the type of the link as "simple" so that a value of xlink:type need not be included in the XML REFERENCE element.

Example:

```
<?xml version="1.0"?>
<!DOCTYPE REFERENCE [
    <!ELEMENT REFERENCE (#PCDATA)>
    <!ATTLIST REFERENCE
         xlink:type CDATA #FIXED "simple"
         xlink:href    CDATA #REQUIRED
         xlink:role    CDATA
         xlink:title    CDATA
         xlink:actuate CDATA
    >
]>
<REFERENCE
    xlink:href="bluprint.xml"
    xlink:role="bookLink"
    xlink:title="XML Blueprints by IDG Books Worldwide, Inc."
    xlink:actuate="onRequest">XML Blueprints</REFERENCE>
```

The xlink:actuate attribute may contain a value other than onLoad, onRequest, or undefined. In such cases, it is the responsibility of the XML processing application to access and interpret the value appropriately.

The latest version of the XLink specification describes the xlink:actuate attribute, including valid values, in detail. Check out www.w3.org/TR/xlink/#link-behaviors.

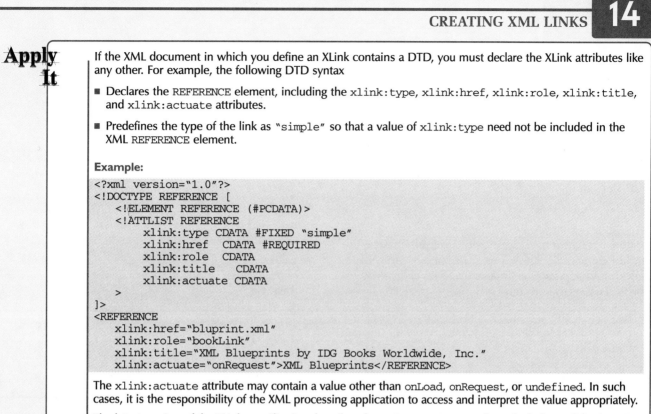

-3 Type in **xlink:actuate=**.

-4 Type in a value for the xlink:actuate attribute.

■ In this example, the value provided is onRequest, which specifies that the link be activated by user request.

SPECIFY LINK BEHAVIOR

Y ou can add an attribute to a link element to specify the way an XML link appears on activation.

In addition to the required xlink:type and xlink:href attributes, a linking element may contain optional *behavior attributes*. One of these behavior attributes, xlink:show, describes the way an XML link should appear when it is activated. Valid values for the xlink:show attribute include:

- **new:** Tells the XML application to open the link in a new window, frame, pane, or other relevant display context.

- **replace:** Tells the XML application to replace the current window, frame, pane, or other relevant display context with the activated link.

- **embed:** Tells the XML application to embed the activated link in the current window, pane, or other relevant display context.

- **undefined:** Tells the XML application that the link display must be performed by application-specific means.

Note: The XLink specification is still in draft form, and no commercially available software fully supports the syntax described in this section at the time of this writing. For this reason, XML links are currently practical only for prototyping efforts.

SPECIFY LINK BEHAVIOR

```
Untitled - Notepad
File  Edit  Search  Help
<?xml version="1.0"?>

<REFERENCE
    xlink:type="simple"
    xlink:href="bluprint.xml"
    xlink:role="bookLink"
    xlink:title="XML Blueprints by IDG Books Worldwide, Inc."
    xlink:actuate="onRequest">XML Blueprints</REFERENCE>
```

```
Untitled - Notepad
File  Edit  Search  Help
<?xml version="1.0"?>

<REFERENCE
    xlink:type="simple"
    xlink:href="bluprint.xml"
    xlink:role="bookLink"
    xlink:title="XML Blueprints by IDG Books Worldwide, Inc."
    xlink:actuate="onRequest"
>XML Blueprints</REFERENCE>
```

1 Open the XML document to which you want to add a link description.

2 Position your cursor below the link element declaration, directly before the closing angle bracket (**>**).

Extra

If you are familiar with HTML links, comparing HTML links to XML links can help you understand XML link behavior. For example, you can compare the value you specify for the `xlink:show` attribute of a link element to HTML constructs in terms of function:

VALUE FOR `xlink:show`	COMPARABLE HTML LINK BEHAVIOR
new	`<A ... target="_blank">`
replace	`<A ... target="_self">`
embed	`<IMG>`

The `xlink:show` attribute may contain a value other than `new`, `replace`, `embed`, or `undefined`. In such cases, it is the responsibility of the XML processing application to access and interpret the value appropriately.

The latest version of the XLink specification describes the xlink:show attribute, including valid values, in detail. Check out www.w3.org/TR/xlink/#show-Attribute.

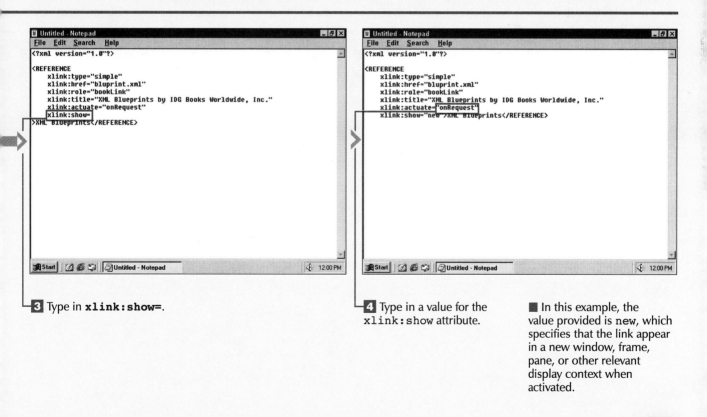

3 Type in `xlink:show=`.

4 Type in a value for the `xlink:show` attribute.

■ In this example, the value provided is new, which specifies that the link appear in a new window, frame, pane, or other relevant display context when activated.

ADD ABSOLUTE REFERENCES

Defining an absolute XPointer reference allows you to construct a link to a specific element inside a target document.

To define and reference an XPointer:

1. Define an XPointer by uniquely identifying a specific XML element. You identify XML data uniquely by using the ID attribute supported in DTDs.

2. Reference that XPointer inside an XML linking element using either *absolute* or relative XPointer syntax. An absolute reference identifies a specific element, regardless of where that element is declared in the XML document. A *relative* reference identifies a specific element in relation to other elements. The World Wide Web Consortium's XPointer working draft

at www.w3.org/TR/xptr describes complete XPointer syntax; in this example, you see the absolute id() keyword demonstrated. Here is the syntax:

```
<linkElement
xlink:href="xmlDocument#somePointer">
</linkElement>
```

linkElement is the name of the link element. *xmlDocument* is the URI of the target document. *somePointer* points to a predefined absolute XML id.

Note: Because the XPointer specification is still in working draft form, XPointer syntax may change by the time you read this. At the time of this writing, no commercially available software fully supports the syntax described in this section.

ADD ABSOLUTE REFERENCES

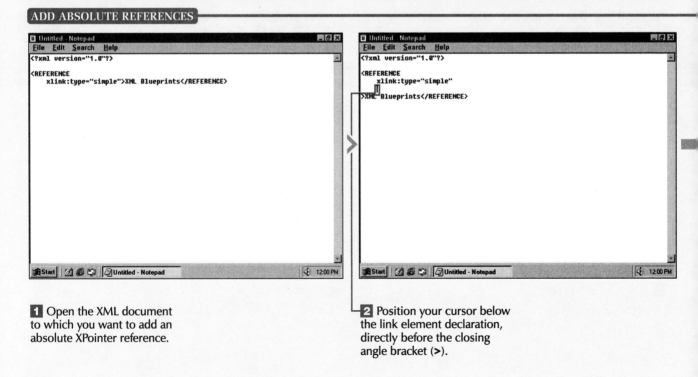

1 Open the XML document to which you want to add an absolute XPointer reference.

2 Position your cursor below the link element declaration, directly before the closing angle bracket (>).

Apply It

Below is the section of bluprint.xml that defines the XML pointer referenced in this task:

```xml
<?xml version="1.0"?>
<!DOCTYPE BLUEPRINT [
    <!ELEMENT BLUEPRINT (PAGE)*>
    <!ELEMENT PAGE (TITLE, DESC)>
    <!ATTLIST PAGE
        PAGENUMBER      ID  #REQUIRED>
    <!ELEMENT TITLE (#PCDATA)>
    <!ELEMENT DESC (#PCDATA)>]>
<BLUEPRINT>
<PAGE PAGENUMBER="page1">
  <TITLE>How to create an XLink</TITLE>
  <DESC>Covers the WWW3 recommendations; also includes examples.</DESC>
</PAGE>
<PAGE PAGENUMBER="page2">
  <TITLE>How to create an XPointer</TITLE>
  <DESC>Provides sample code for absolute and relative XPointers.</DESC>
</PAGE>
<PAGE PAGENUMBER="page3">
  <TITLE>Understanding XPath</TITLE>
  <DESC>Describes the role of XPath in the XPointer specification.</DESC>
</PAGE>
</BLUEPRINT>
```

The PAGENUMBER attribute of the PAGE element is declared as an attribute of type ID, which ensures that at runtime only one value of page2 will exist in this XML document. This is the element referenced in the code in this task.

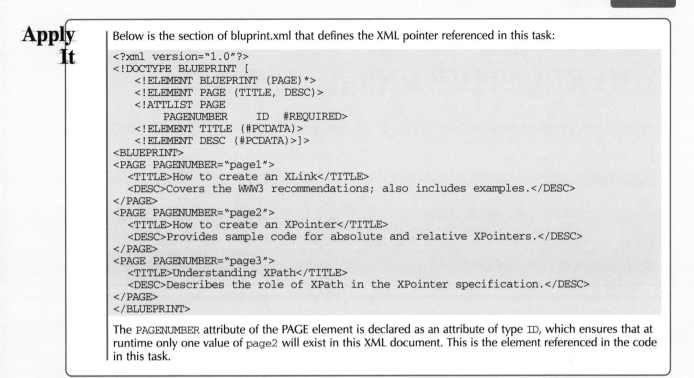

3 Type in the name of a document and associate it with the xlink:href attribute.

■ In this example, the name of the XML document to be linked to is bluprint.xml.

4 Append an absolute XPointer reference to the name of the XML document.

■ In this example, the XPointer reference is #xpointer(id('page2')), which links this XML document to an attribute of type ID containing a value of page2 declared in bluprint.xml.

ADD RELATIVE REFERENCES

This section shows you how to define a relative link to an element inside a target document.

Relative links provide much more flexibility than do absolute links. With relative links, you can link a document not just with a specific file (such as `some.xml`), but by position or some other criteria. For example, you can define a link from the first document in a list to the second document in that list.

Here is the syntax required to define a relative link:

```
<linkElement
xlink:href="xmlDocument#somePointer">
</linkElement>
```

`linkElement` is the name of the link element.

`xmlDocument` is the URI of the target document.

`somePointer` is a relative pointer to an XML element.

Note: Because the XPointer specification is still in working draft form, XPointer syntax may change by the time you read this. At the time of this writing, no commercially available software fully supported the syntax described in this section. For this reason, XML pointers are currently practical only for prototyping efforts.

ADD RELATIVE REFERENCES

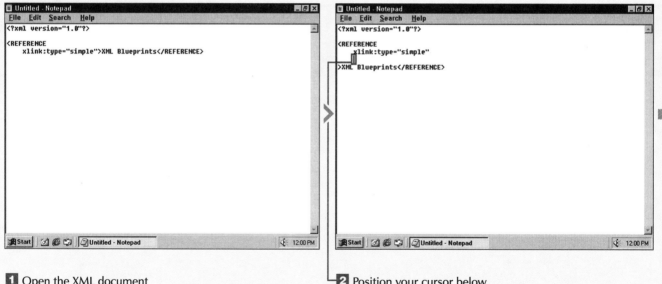

1 Open the XML document to which you want to add a relative XPointer reference.

2 Position your cursor below the link element declaration, directly before the closing angle bracket (**>**).

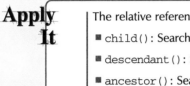

Apply It

The relative references defined in the current specification draft include

- `child()`: Searches through first-level child nodes
- `descendant()`: Searches through all child nodes
- `ancestor()`: Searches through parent nodes backwards, from the source element
- `preceding()`: Searches through both parent and sibling nodes backwards, from the source element
- `following()`: Searches through both child and sibling nodes declared after the source element
- `psibling()`: Selects the previously declared sibling
- `fsibling()`: Selects the next sibling declared after the source element

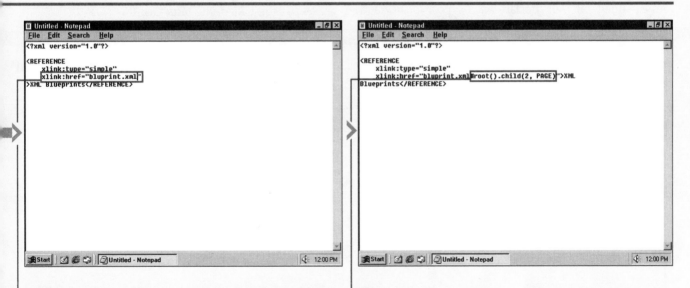

3 Type in the name of a document and associate it with the `xlink:href` attribute.

■ In this example, the name of the XML document to be linked to is `bluprint.xml`.

4 Append a relative XPointer reference to the name of the XML document.

■ In this example, the XPointer reference is `#root().child(2, PAGE)` which links this XML documer to the second PAGE element contained in the root element declared in bluprint.xml.

CREATE EXTENDED LINKS

You can associate multiple link sources with multiple link targets. Here is the syntax:

```
<linkElement
xlink:type="extended"
xlink:title="title"
xlink:role="role"
xlink:show="linkDisplayOption"
xlink:actuate="whenActivated">linkText</
linkElement>
```

title is a description of the extended link. *role* is application-specific text. *linkDisplayOption* describes the link display (new, replace, embed, or undefined). *whenActivated* is one of onLoad, onRequest, or undefined.

An extended link must declare one or more *locator* and *arc* elements.

Locators define the target URLs participating in the extended link:

```
<locatorElement
type="locator" href="documentTarget"
title="title" id="locatorId"/>
```

locatorElement specifies a locator for the extended link. *documentTarget* is the URL of the document target. *title* is a human-readable description of the locator. *id* is the internal name of this locator.

Arcs define traversal rules between two locators:

```
<arcElement
type="arc" from="fromURL" to="toURL" />
```

arcElement names this traversal rule (arc). *fromURL* is the URL of the source for this arc. *toURL* is the URL of the target for this arc.

CREATE EXTENDED LINKS

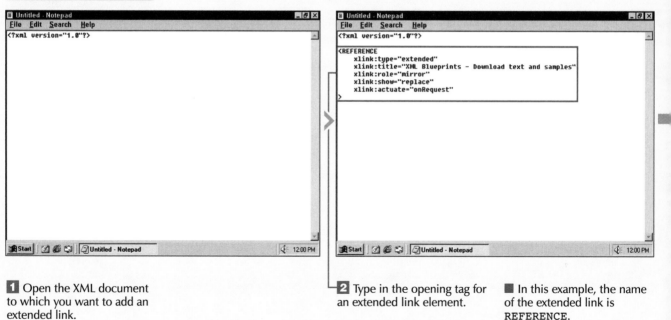

1 Open the XML document to which you want to add an extended link.

2 Type in the opening tag for an extended link element.

■ In this example, the name of the extended link is REFERENCE.

Extra

XML defines two types of links:

- Simple links: Similar to HTML links, simple XML links associate a single source with a single target. The first six sections in this chapter show you how to create a simple XML link.

- Extended links: Extended links allow you to associate multiple sources with multiple targets. This technology includes some potential benefits, such as flexibility in link traversal. In HTML-based applications, a user must traverse a chain of links one at a time. Using extended XML links, a user could choose at any time to visit any target the extended link declares.

Another potential benefit is separation of links from document content. Typically, you must physically modify an HTML document to correct a link to a missing or renamed document. In XML, document addresses can be stored separately from link elements, thus streamlining the application maintenance process.

Note: Because the specification is still in working draft form at the time of this writing, extended link syntax may change by the time you read this. Currently, no commercially available software fully supports the syntax described in this section; extended links are appropriate for prototyping efforts only.

```
Untitled - Notepad
File  Edit  Search  Help
<REFERENCE
    xlink:type="extended"
    xlink:title="XML Blueprints - Download text and samples"
    xlink:role="mirror"
    xlink:show="replace"
    xlink:actuate="onRequest"
>
<sourceSite
    xlink:type="locator"
    xlink:href="http://www.abc.com"
    id="sourceSite" />

<mirror2
    xlink:type="locator"
    xlink:href="http://www.def.com"
    id="mirror2" />

<mirror3
    xlink:type="locator"
    xlink:href="http://www.ghi.com"
    id="mirror3" />

<mirror4
    xlink=type="locator"
    xlink:href="http://www.jkl.com"
    id="mirror4" />
Start   Untitled - Notepad                          12:00 PM
```

```
Untitled - Notepad
File  Edit  Search  Help
    id="mirror3" />

<mirror4
    xlink:type="locator"
    xlink:href="http://www.jkl.com"
    id="mirror4" />

<go
    xlink:type="arc"
    xlink:from="sourceSite"
    xlink:to="mirror2" />

<go
    xlink:type="arc"
    xlink:from="sourceSite"
    xlink:to="mirror3" />

<go
    xlink:type="arc"
    xlink:from="sourceSite"
    xlink:to="mirror4" />

</REFERENCE>

Start   Untitled - Notepad                          12:00 PM
```

3 Type in one or more link locators.

■ In this example, four locators are defined: sourceSite, mirror2, mirror3, and mirror4.

4 Type in one or more arcs.

■ In this example, three arcs are defined, one each from the source to mirror2, to mirror3, and to mirror4.

5 Type in the closing link element tag.

VALIDATE LINK DECLARATIONS

You can create a document type definition, or *DTD*, to validate XML link and pointer declarations.

A DTD is a collection of semantic validation rules designed to constrain XML data values at application runtime. Here are some common data constraints:

- An XML value must exist.

- An XML value must match one of a handful of predefined strings.

- An XML value must not contain any special characters.

You define XML links and pointers as standard XML elements and attributes. To validate XML links and pointers, you can define

- An internal DTD: You can include a DTD inside the XML document that defines your XML links and pointers.

- An external DTD: You can define a DTD in a separate document and attach it to the XML document that defines your XML links and pointers.

VALIDATE LINK DECLARATIONS

```
Untitled - Notepad
File  Edit  Search  Help
<?xml version="1.0"?>


<REFERENCE
    xlink:href="bluprint.xml"
    xlink:role="bookLink"
    xlink:title="XML Blueprints by IDG Books Worldwide, Inc."
    xlink:actuate="onRequest"
    xlink:show="new"
>XML Blueprints</REFERENCE>


Start    Untitled - Notepad                        12:00 PM
```

```
Untitled - Notepad
File  Edit  Search  Help
<?xml version="1.0"?>

<!DOCTYPE REFERENCE [

]>

<REFERENCE
    xlink:href="bluprint.xml"
    xlink:role="bookLink"
    xlink:title="XML Blueprints by IDG Books Worldwide, Inc."
    xlink:actuate="onRequest"
    xlink:show="new"
>XML Blueprints</REFERENCE>


Start    Untitled - Notepad                        12:00 PM
```

1 Open the XML document to which you want to add a link-validating DTD.

2 Position your cursor between the XML declaration and the link declaration.

3 Type in the opening and closing < !DOCTYPE tags to begin the DTD declaration.

■ This example shows a DTD being created for the REFERENCE XML element.

Apply It

You can create an external DTD file and attach it to the XML document that declares your XML links. To declare an external DTD for the XML shown in this section, you can

■ Create a file containing the following DTD syntax:

```
<!ELEMENT REFERENCE (#PCDATA)>
<!ATTLIST REFERENCE
    xlink:type    CDATA #FIXED "simple"       xlink:href    CDATA #REQUIRED
    xlink:role    NMTOKEN       xlink:title    CDATA
    xlink:show    (new | replace | embed | undefined) #REQUIRED
    xlink:actuate (onLoad | onRequest | undefined)      #REQUIRED
>
```

■ Save the file (for example, some.dtd)

■ Create another file containing the following XML syntax:

```
<?xml version="1.0"?>
<!DOCTYPE REFERENCE SYSTEM "some.dtd">
<REFERENCE
    xlink:type="simple"       xlink:href="bluprint.xml"
    xlink:role="bookLink"     xlink:title="XML Blueprints by IDG Books Worldwide, Inc."
    xlink:actuate="onRequest"      xlink:show="new"
>XML Blueprints</REFERENCE>
```

The current working draft of the World Wide Web Consortium's XLink specification contains example DTD definitions for both simple and extended link elements. Go to www.w3.org/TR/xlink/.

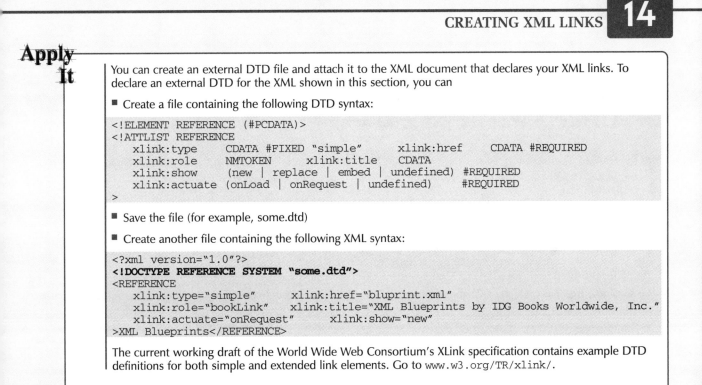

■4 Type in a data validation rule for the REFERENCE XML element.

■ In this example, the REFERENCE XML element is the link element.

■5 Type in data validation rules for the attributes associated with the link element.

■ In this example, link type is "simple"; link target is required; the link role spaces; link title character data; link display option must be new, replace, embed, or undefined; link activation option must be onLoad, onRequest, or undefined.

USING XML PRO 2.0

This section shows you how to create a simple XML file using Vervet Logic's XML authoring and editing tool, XML Pro 2.0.

XML Pro 2.0 is a graphical XML editor you can use to create, modify, and validate XML documents. Implemented in Java, XML Pro 2.0 features

- A clean, intuitive interface.
- Helpful wizards for creating XML elements and attributes.
- Validation support.

- The ability to switch between graphical tree layout and XML code views.
- Built-in help files, troubleshooting tips, and sample XML documents.

Version 2.0 contains no support for creating document type definitions, schemas, or style sheets.

A trial version is available on the companion CD and at www.vervet.com. This trial version is feature-complete, with two exceptions: You cannot save or print an XML document using the trial version. The full-fledged version of this product sells for around $150.

USING XML PRO 2.0

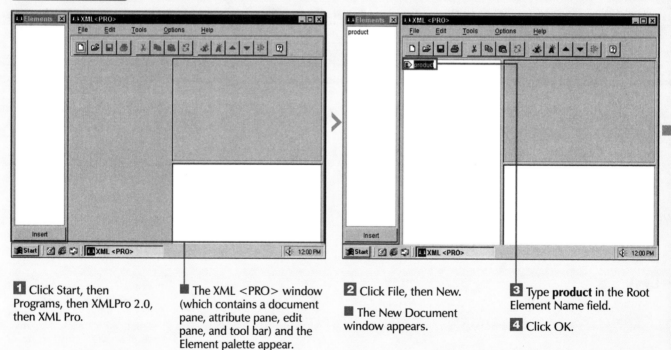

1 Click Start, then Programs, then XMLPro 2.0, then XML Pro.

■ The XML <PRO> window (which contains a document pane, attribute pane, edit pane, and tool bar) and the Element palette appear.

2 Click File, then New.

■ The New Document window appears.

3 Type **product** in the Root Element Name field.

4 Click OK.

Extra

XML Pro is a great tool for beginning XML developers, who can point-and-click their way to XML document creation. The interface is relatively intuitive (assuming you know a bit about XML) and well organized; you create elements and attributes using the Element Wizard and Attribute Wizard, respectively, and then organize those elements and attributes into a structured XML document.

However, that same interface makes creating long, text-intensive XML documents difficult and time-consuming. XML Pro doesn't allow developers to bypass the interface and enter tags and data directly; nor does it allow you to cut-and-paste large sections of text. And because XML Pro doesn't generate DTDs or schemas automatically, developers must code these separately. No explicit support for style sheets (cascading style sheets or XSL) is provided.

XML Pro's help facility is minimal. While the help covers all the basic functions of the tool, developers who aren't XML-savvy will have a hard time understanding why they might choose one option over another. For example, the File Operations⇨New help text tells readers that "Once you have selected New to create a blank document, you will be prompted to enter some information," and then displays the file creation dialog box. Users who aren't familiar with encoding, or don't know what a root element is (or why it must be specified in order to create an XML document), are left in the dark.

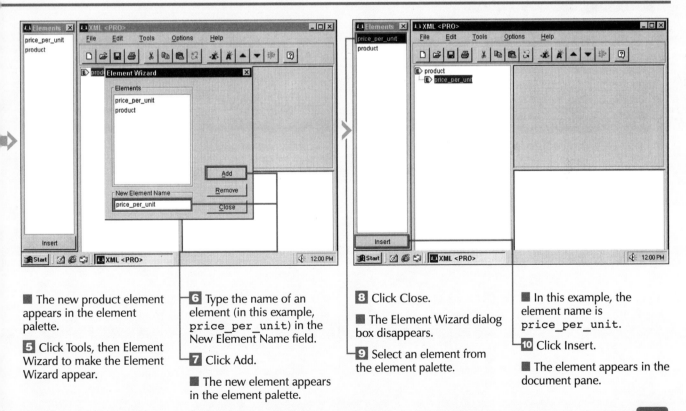

■ The new product element appears in the element palette.

5 Click Tools, then Element Wizard to make the Element Wizard appear.

6 Type the name of an element (in this example, `price_per_unit`) in the New Element Name field.

7 Click Add.

■ The new element appears in the element palette.

8 Click Close.

■ The Element Wizard dialog box disappears.

9 Select an element from the element palette.

■ In this example, the element name is `price_per_unit`.

10 Click Insert.

■ The element appears in the document pane.

USING XML PRO 2.0 (CONTINUED)

After you've defined an element, you can delete it right-clicking on the name of the element you wish to delete or change. (Make sure you right-click on the element name displayed in the XML Pro window, not the Elements window.) Right-clicking on a root element displays a menu with the following additional options:

- Add Element
- Add PCDATA
- Add Entity
- Add CDATA

- Add Comment
- Delete Element
- Move Element Up
- Move Element Down
- Expand Beneath
- Collapse Beneath

Once you're satisfied with the element, you can specify the element's type, associate a value with the element, and define attributes for the element, as shown in the steps on these pages.

USING XML PRO 2.0 (CONTINUED)

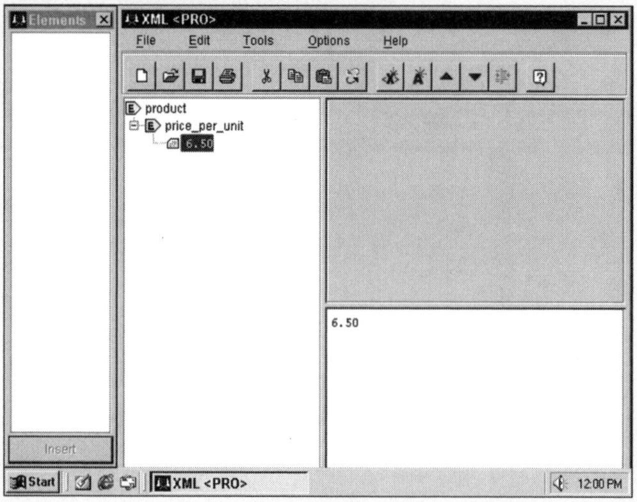

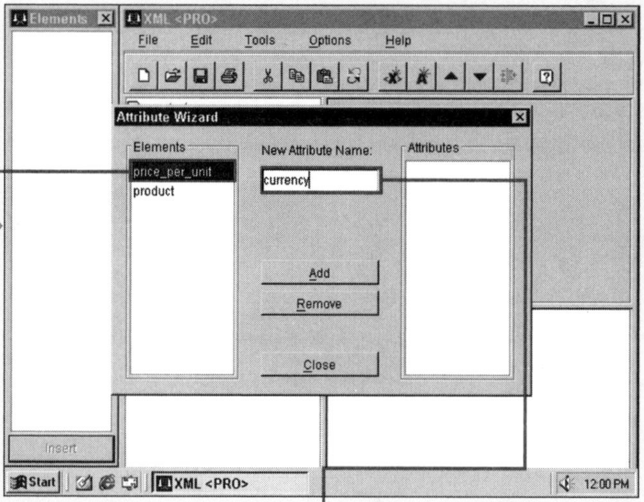

11 In the document pane, right-click an element (in this example, `price_per_unit`).

■ A pop-up menu appears.

12 Click Add PCDATA.

■ `<New PCDATA>` appears below the selected element.

13 Type a value (in this example, `6.50`) in the edit pane.

14 Choose Tools, then Attribute Wizard.

■ The Attribute Wizard appears.

15 Click an element for which you want to create an attribute.

■ In this example, the element name is `price_per_unit`.

16 Type the name of a new attribute (here, `currency`) in the New Attribute Name: field.

Extra

You can use the icons presented in the toolbar to perform the same editing tasks available through the pull-down menus. To see what task is associated with each icon, move your pointer over an icon and hold it there briefly until a pop-up description appears.

XML Pro 2.0 allows you to associate a DTD with an XML document by choosing Associate DTD from the Tools menu.

Because you must save and reload an XML document for the DTD association to take effect, however, this feature is not operational in the trial version of this product.

XML Pro 2.0 ships with four sample XML documents you can experiment with to become more familiar with the tool. To view these files, from the File menu, select Open to bring up the Load Document dialog box. Click the Examples folder to view four XML documents: catalog.xml, cd-collection.xml, hr.xml, and newspaper.xml. Select one of the four XML documents and click Open to load it into the document pane.

17 Click Add.

18 Click Close.

■ The Attribute Wizard disappears.

19 Click the name of an element (here, `price_per_unit`).

■ The `currency` attribute associated with that element appears in the attribute pane.

20 Type a value (here, USD) in the attribute field.

21 Click Tools, then View XML.

■ XML source code appears.

USING XML NOTEPAD 1.5

You can create a simple XML file using Microsoft's XML authoring and editing tool, XML Notepad 1.5.

XML Notepad is a graphical XML editor you can use to create, modify, and validate XML documents. Currently in beta, XML Notepad 1.5 features

- A simple interface
- Validation support
- The ability to switch between graphical tree layout and XML code views
- The ability to duplicate XML *nodes*, or selected portions of the XML tree

- The ability to search selectively through an XML document for a specified string
- A list of frequently asked questions and basic documentation

XML Notepad 1.5 does not support DTD creation. You cannot insert processing instructions in an XML document using this version of XML Notepad.

This product is available on the companion CD and at http://msdn.microsoft.com/xml/notepad/intro.asp.

USING XML NOTEPAD 1.5

1 Click Start, then Programs, then Microsoft XML Notepad, then Microsoft XML Notepad.

■ An untitled XML Notepad document (containing a toolbar, a document window, and editable element and attribute values) appears.

2 Double-click Root_Element in the Structure frame.

■ The Root_Element element is highlighted.

Extra

XML Notepad was designed to be a prototyping application: a quick-and-dirty way for developers to construct XML data sets that conform to Microsoft's document object model.

Still in beta form, XML Notepad does not allow developers to enter processing instructions, just elements and attributes. To create full-blown XML documents, users must massage the XML Notepad-generated file in another text editor (such as Notepad) or another XML editing environment. XML Notepad does not yet provide support for DTD creation or inclusion.

XML Notepad is a validating editor; when you select View and then Source from the main menu, not only is the generated XML source file displayed, but also a message stating either that the XML code is well-formed (according to the MSXML validating parser) or not.

3 Type the name of the root element you want to define.

■ In this example, the root element is named product, so product replaces `Root_Element`.

4 Double-click `Child_Element` in the Structure frame.

■ The `Child_Element` element is highlighted.

5 Type the name of a child element.

■ In this example, the name of the element to be defined as contained within the root is `price_per_unit`.

6 Type a value in the field in the Values frame opposite the previously defined element.

■ This example shows the value `6.50` associated with the `price_per_unit` element.

USING XML NOTEPAD 1.5 (CONTINUED)

XML Notepad offers a tutorial to help developers get up to speed quickly. To access this tutorial, either press F1 or click Help, then Contents and Index from the main XML Notepad menu. Topics covered include:

- Frequently asked questions concerning XML Notepad's implementation of the XML standard.

- Object model issues (including DOM implementation specifics).

- Creating and editing XML documents.
- Customizing your workspace.

After you've finished defining one or more elements, you can specify values for those elements and define any necessary attributes, as demonstrated in the following steps.

USING XML NOTEPAD 1.5 (CONTINUED)

7 Click Insert, then Attribute.

■ A small pink box appears in the Structure frame underneath the selected element (in this example, `price_per_unit`).

8 Type the name of an attribute in the Structure frame next to the pink box.

■ This example shows the `currency` attribute being defined.

Apply It

By default, XML Notepad uses the validating parser built into Internet Explorer 5 to validate an XML document as soon as you load that document into XML Notepad. To turn automatic validation off, from the Tools menu, choose Options to bring up the Options dialog box. Uncheck the check box next to Validate Document on Load.

XML Notepad does not include the following standard XML processing instruction when it generates a new XML document:

```
<?xml version="1.0"?>
```

Technically, this processing instruction is not required to exist in a valid XML document; however, including it is good programming practice.

You can rearrange XML elements and attributes by dragging and dropping them. To move an attribute from one element to another, in the Structure frame, click the icon of the attribute you want to move. Hold your mouse button down, drag the icon over the target element, and release the mouse button.

9 Type a value for the attribute in the field in the Values frame opposite the attribute name.

■ This example shows the USD attribute value being specified.

10 Click View.

11 Click Source.

■ The XML document source appears, complete with elements, attributes, and values.

USE XED 0.5

Y ou can create a simple XML file using the beta
version of XED, an XML authoring and editing tool
developed at the University of Edinburgh.

XED is an XML editor you can use to create XML
documents. Currently in beta, XED 0.5 features a text-
based interface that "fills in" correct XML syntax to help
you create well-formed documents. Unlike the
graphical drag-and-drop tools described earlier, XED

offers a powerful — if initially cryptic — editing
environment that will be familiar to users of the vi and
emacs editors.

You cannot create DTDs using XED, although you can
attach existing DTDs to your XML document.

This tool is available on the companion CD and at
`www.cogsci.ed.ac.uk/~ht/xed.html`.

USE XED 0.5

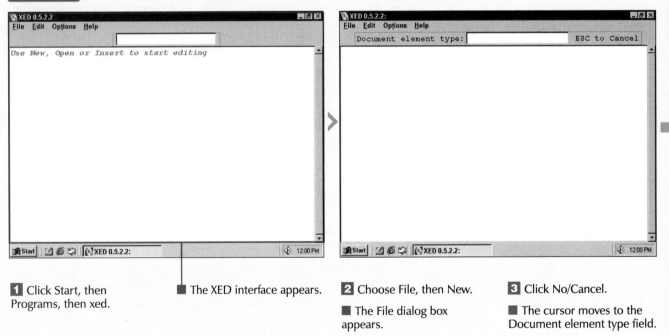

1 Click Start, then
Programs, then xed.

■ The XED interface appears.

2 Choose File, then New.

■ The File dialog box
appears.

3 Click No/Cancel.

■ The cursor moves to the
Document element type field.

Extra

XED can be confusing for users familiar with graphical point-and-click interfaces. Unlike more sophisticated code-generating development environments, XED is designed to aid developers who are comfortable typing XML code directly into a text editor but would like a little extra assistance. For these developers, XED "gets out of the way" of XML document creation but adds value through:

- Single-window presentation. This clean, simple interface allows developers to see their XML documents-in-process from one view only: the code view.

- Real-world editing capability, including support for cut-and-paste and multiple undo.

- Detailed error messages. Non-well-formed messages include line and character position to aid in bug-fixing.

XED is available for Solaris (UNIX) in addition to Windows.

4 Type the name of the element you want to define in the Document element type field.

■ This example shows the product element being defined.

5 Press Return.

■ The element appears in the document text.

6 Position your cursor between the element tags and press return.

7 Type a left arrow (<).

8 In the element menu that appears, select > **type-in**.

■ The cursor moves to the Element type field.

9 Type the name of another element (here, price_per_unit).

10 Press Return, and the element appears in the document text.

USING XED 0.5 (CONTINUED)

Clicking Help then Help Contents and Index displays an overview of the tool, a tutorial, and a line-by-line description of each menu implemented. Clicking Help then Summary help sheet displays a list of all the key commands and their functions; for example, pressing Home moves the cursor to the beginning of the edited text, End to the end of the edited text, and so on. (Developers familiar with UNIX editors such as vi and emacs will really appreciate this help sheet.)

After you've finished defining one or more elements, you specify values for those elements and define any necessary attributes in a similar fashion, as demonstrated in the steps on these pages.

USE XED 0.5 (CONTINUED)

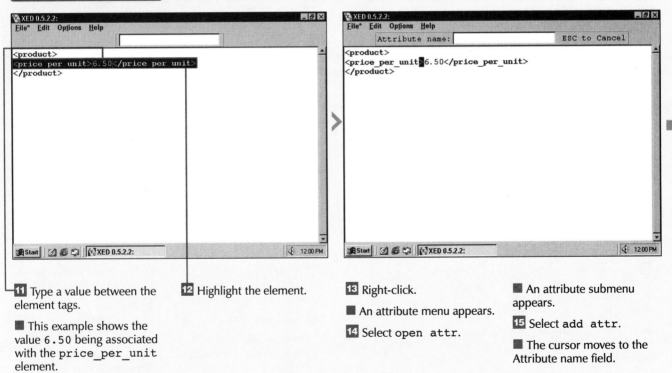

11 Type a value between the element tags.

■ This example shows the value 6.50 being associated with the price_per_unit element.

12 Highlight the element.

13 Right-click.

■ An attribute menu appears.

14 Select open attr.

■ An attribute submenu appears.

15 Select add attr.

■ The cursor moves to the Attribute name field.

Apply It

Highlighting any portion of a document and clicking the right mouse button pops up a menu of choices appropriate for that XML component.

XED is designed to work with command-line XML document processors. An XML document processor is a program installed on your computer that accepts XML source as input. A validating parser is an example of an XML document processor.

To configure XED to run a command-line processor, from the Options menu choose File Proc Command to bring up the File Processing Command dialog box. Type in the name of the processor and press Return.

To invoke the processor, choose Process File from the File menu.

You can interact with XED using shortcuts rather than standard point-and-click menu navigation. To see a list of the shortcuts available, choose Summary help sheet from the Help menu.

The best way to explore this tool is to begin typing XML syntax, as though you were using a simple text editor. XED pops up helpful menus automatically, based on the syntax you type in, to guide you through the document creation process.

---

16 Type the name of an attribute in the Attribute name field.

■ In this example, the name of the attribute being defined is currency.

17 Press Return.

■ The newly defined attribute appears in the document text.

18 Type a value for the attribute between the quotes.

■ In this example, the value being associated with the currency attribute is 6.50.

USING STYLEMAKER 1.4

You can create a simple cascading style sheet (CSS) element to use with your XML documents using StyleMaker 1.4, a style sheet editing tool developed by the Danere Group.

You can use StyleMaker's point-and-click interface to create and edit cascading style sheets visually. You can use the cascading style sheets you create to format and display XML data at runtime.

Note: Chapter 8 shows you how to attach a cascading style sheet to an XML document.

StyleMaker features include

- An icon-driven graphical interface.
- Several style sheet templates.
- The ability to switch between HTML code and WYSIWYG views.

StyleMaker does not currently support the creation of XML style sheets.

This tool is available on the companion CD and on the Web at www.danere.com.

USING STYLEMAKER 1.4

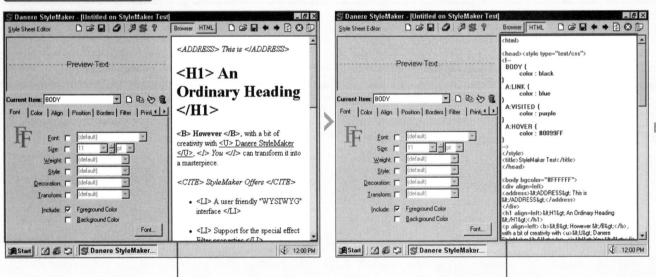

1 Choose Start, then Programs, then Danere StyleMaker v1.4, and then Danere StyleMaker.

■ The StyleMaker interface, which includes a browser button (to preview a style sheet as it appears in a browser) and an HTML button (to display a style sheet as HTML code) appears with a pre-loaded sample style sheet.

2 Click HTML.

■ The HTML code for the sample style sheet appears.

Extra

StyleMaker is a text-based cascading style sheet editor that is a good choice for developers new to cascading style sheets. StyleMaker prompts users to add appropriate configuration details (for example, size, weight, and decoration for a font style), and then allows them to test their effects immediately in the browser window. (StyleMaker also displays the generated CSS code.) StyleMaker ships with several pre-built CSS files with which users can experiment.

One of the perceived drawbacks of StyleMaker — the fact that it focuses exclusively on style sheets, unlike the many editors on the market that provide support for both HTML and cascading style sheets — makes it uniquely appropriate for use with XML.

Version 1.4 shipped in the summer of 1998, which was shortly after the last CSS standard recommendation by the World Wide Web consortium, so StyleMaker provides the most up-to-date CSS support possible.

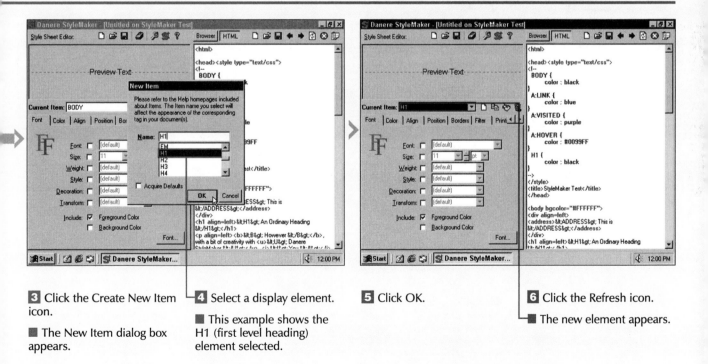

3 Click the Create New Item icon.

■ The New Item dialog box appears.

4 Select a display element.

■ This example shows the H1 (first level heading) element selected.

5 Click OK.

6 Click the Refresh icon.

■ The new element appears.

USE STYLEMAKER 1.4 (CONTINUED)

Instead of providing text menus, StyleMaker provides icon menus. For example, the first icon, which looks like a white sheet of paper, allows you to create a new style sheet. The second, which looks like an open file folder, allows you to open an existing style sheet; the third, which looks like a diskette, allows you to save a style sheet in progress; and so on.

Clicking on the yellow question mark (?) displayed midway across the main menu bar gives you access to StyleMaker's help menu.

After you've finished creating and naming a style sheet element, you can configure it by specifying its size, color, and so on, as demonstrated in the following steps.

USING STYLEMAKER 1.4 (CONTINUED)

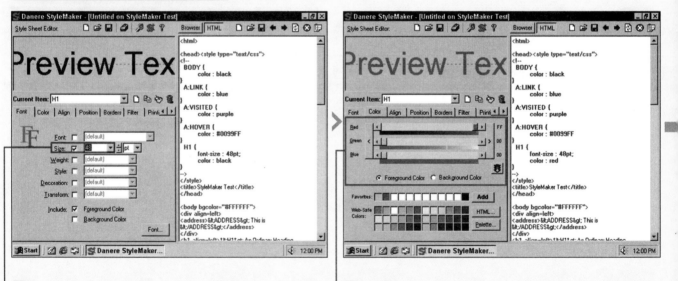

7 Configure the size of the newly defined element, if appropriate.

■ In this example, the size field is set to 48.

8 Configure the color of the newly defined element, if appropriate.

■ In this example, the foreground color is set to red.

Apply It

To use StyleMaker 1.4 for XML application development, you need to create style sheet elements that match the names of XML elements.

To create your own named style sheet elements, click the Copy Current Item icon to display the Copy Current Item dialog box and type the name of your XML element in the Name: field.

From the list on the right side of the dialog box, select the style sheet element that most closely matches the one you want to create and click OK.

Click the Refresh icon, and the newly created style sheet element appears in the editing window.

Finally, edit the newly created style sheet as appropriate.

9 Add text to the component for which you are defining a style rule, if appropriate.

■ In this example, the style rule will be applied to the text XML Blueprints.

10 Click the Refresh icon.

11 Click the Browser button to test the style rule.

■ The newly defined heading element, H1, displays XML Blueprints in large, red type.

WHAT'S ON THE CD-ROM

The CD-ROM included with this book contains many useful files and programs. Before installing any of the programs on the disc, make sure that a newer version of the program is not already installed on your computer. For information on installing different versions of the same program, contact the program's manufacturer.

SYSTEM REQUIREMENTS

To use the contents of the CD-ROM, your computer must be equipped with the following hardware and software:

- A PC with a 486 or faster processor.
- Microsoft Windows 95 or later.
- At least 16MB of total RAM installed on your computer (at least 16MB on Windows 95-equipped PCs and Mac OS computers with PowerPC processors).
- At least 300MB of hard drive space.
- A double-speed (2x) or faster CD-ROM drive.
- A sound card for PCs.
- A monitor capable of displaying at least 256 colors or grayscale.
- A modem with a speed of at least 14,400 bps.

INSTALLING AND USING THE SOFTWARE

For your convenience, the software titles appearing on the CD-ROM are listed alphabetically.

Author's sample files

For Mac and Windows 3.1/95/98/NT. These files contain all the sample code from the book. You can browse these files directly from the CD-ROM, or you can copy them to your hard drive and use them as the basis for your own projects. To find the files on the CD-ROM, open the D:\SAMPLE folder. To copy the files to your hard drive, just run the installation program D:\SAMPLES.EXE. The files will be placed on your hard drive at C:\QMFD.

StyleMaker

For Windows 95, 98, NT 4, 2000. Shareware. StyleMaker creates, manages, and edits cascading style sheets that you can apply to a single page or an entire Web site.

XED

For Windows 95, 98, NT 4, 2000. Free. This is a simple editor that automatically checks code for errors and suggests alternatives.

XML
Your visual blueprint for
building expert Web pages

XML Notepad
For Windows 95, 98, NT 4, 2000. Commercial version.
XML Notepad is a simple application for prototyping
small XML documents. From Microsoft.

XML Pro
For Windows 95, 98, NT 4, 2000. Trial. XML Pro
recognizes and organizes elements in your XML code
to make editing faster and easier. From Vervet Logic.

TROUBLESHOOTING

I tried my best to compile programs that work on most
computers with the minimum system requirements.
Your computer, however, may differ and some
programs may not work properly for some reason.

The two most likely problems are that you do not have
enough memory (RAM) for the programs you want to
use, or you have other programs running that are
affecting installation or running of a program. If you get
error messages like `Not enough memory` or `Setup
cannot continue`, try one or more of these
methods and then try using the software again:

- Turn off any anti-virus software.

- Close all running programs.

- In Windows, close the CD-ROM interface and run
  demos or installations directly from Windows
  Explorer.

- Have your local computer store add more RAM to
  your computer.

If you still have trouble installing the items from the
CD-ROM, please call the IDG Books Worldwide
Customer Service phone number: 800-762-2974
(outside the U.S.: 317-572-3342).

USING THE E-VERSION OF THE BOOK

You can view *XML: Your visual blueprint for building expert Web pages* on your screen using the CD-ROM disc included at the back of this book. The CD-ROM disc allows you to search the contents of each chapter of the book for a specific word or phrase. The CD-ROM disc also provides a convenient way of keeping the book handy while traveling.

You must install Adobe Acrobat Reader on your computer before you can view the book on the CD-ROM disc. This program is provided on

the disc. Acrobat Reader allows you to view Portable Document Format (PDF) files, which can display books and magazines on your screen exactly as they appear in printed form.

To view the contents of the book using Acrobat Reader, display the contents of the disc. Double-click the PDFs folder to display the contents of the folder. In the window that appears, double-click the icon for the chapter of the book you want to review.

USING THE E-VERSION OF THE BOOK

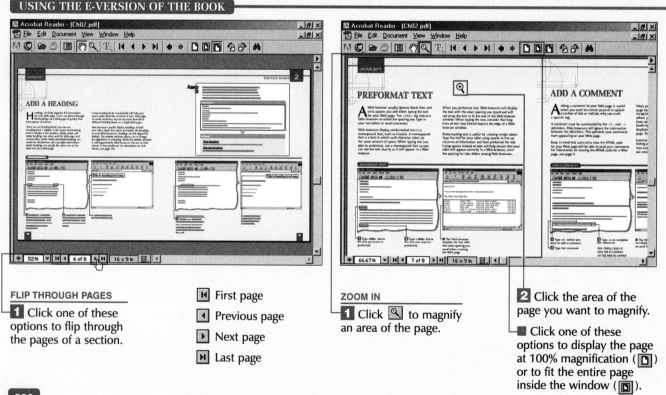

FLIP THROUGH PAGES

1 Click one of these options to flip through the pages of a section.

|◀| First page

◀ Previous page

▶ Next page

▶| Last page

ZOOM IN

1 Click 🔍 to magnify an area of the page.

2 Click the area of the page you want to magnify.

■ Click one of these options to display the page at 100% magnification (▣) or to fit the entire page inside the window (▣).

XML
Your visual blueprint for
building expert Web pages

Extra

To install Acrobat Reader, insert the CD-ROM disc into a drive. In the screen that appears, click Software. Click Acrobat Reader and then click Install at the bottom of the screen. Then follow the instructions on your screen to install the program.

You can make searching the book more convenient by copying the `.pdf` files to your own computer. Display the contents of the CD-ROM disc and then copy the PDFs folder from the CD to your hard drive. This allows you to easily access the contents of the book at any time.

Acrobat Reader is a popular and useful program. There are many files available on the Web that are designed to be viewed using Acrobat Reader. Look for files with the `.pdf` extension. For more information about Acrobat Reader, visit the Web site at **www.adobe.com/products/ acrobat/readermain.html**.

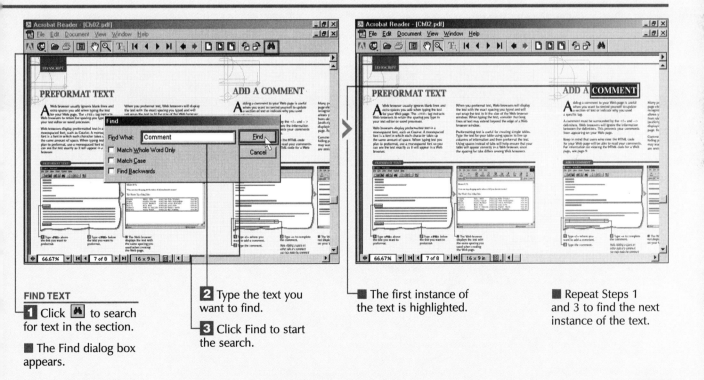

FIND TEXT

1 Click [🔍] to search for text in the section.

■ The Find dialog box appears.

2 Type the text you want to find.

3 Click Find to start the search.

■ The first instance of the text is highlighted.

■ Repeat Steps 1 and 3 to find the next instance of the text.

LICENSE AGREEMENT

XML
Your visual blueprint for
building expert Web pages

(b) IDGB AND THE AUTHOR OF THE BOOK DISCLAIM ALL OTHER WARRANTIES, EXPRESS OR IMPLIED, INCLUDING WITHOUT LIMITATION IMPLIED WARRANTIES OF MERCHANTABILITY AND FITNESS FOR A PARTICULAR PURPOSE, WITH RESPECT TO THE SOFTWARE, THE PROGRAMS, THE SOURCE CODE CONTAINED THEREIN, AND/OR THE TECHNIQUES DESCRIBED IN THIS BOOK. IDGB DOES NOT WARRANT THAT THE FUNCTIONS CONTAINED IN THE SOFTWARE WILL MEET YOUR REQUIREMENTS OR THAT THE OPERATION OF THE SOFTWARE WILL BE ERROR FREE.

(c) This limited warranty gives you specific legal rights, and you may have other rights that vary from jurisdiction to jurisdiction.

6. Remedies.

(a) IDGB's entire liability and your exclusive remedy for defects in materials and workmanship shall be limited to replacement of the Software Media, which may be returned to IDGB with a copy of your receipt at the following address: Software Media Fulfillment Department, Attn.: *XML: Your visual blueprint for building expert Web pages*, IDG Books Worldwide, Inc., 10475 Crosspoint Blvd., Indianapolis, IN 46256, or call 800-762-2974. Please allow three to four weeks for delivery. This Limited Warranty is void if failure of the Software Media has resulted from accident, abuse, or misapplication. Any replacement Software Media will be warranted for the remainder of the original warranty period or thirty (30) days, whichever is longer.

(b) In no event shall IDGB or the author be liable for any damages whatsoever (including without limitation damages for loss of business profits, business interruption, loss of business information, or any other pecuniary loss) arising from the use of or inability to use the Book or the Software, even if IDGB has been advised of the possibility of such damages.

(c) Because some jurisdictions do not allow the exclusion or limitation of liability for consequential or incidental damages, the above limitation or exclusion may not apply to you.

7. U.S. Government Restricted Rights. Use, duplication, or disclosure of the Software by the U.S. Government is subject to restrictions stated in paragraph (c)(1)(ii) of the Rights in Technical Data and Computer Software clause of DFARS 252.227-7013, and in subparagraphs (a) through (d) of the Commercial Computer–Restricted Rights clause at FAR 52.227-19, and in similar clauses in the NASA FAR supplement, when applicable.

8. General. This Agreement constitutes the entire understanding of the parties and revokes and supersedes all prior agreements, oral or written, between them and may not be modified or amended except in a writing signed by both parties hereto that specifically refers to this Agreement. This Agreement shall take precedence over any other documents that may be in conflict herewith. If any one or more provisions contained in this Agreement are held by any court or tribunal to be invalid, illegal, or otherwise unenforceable, each and every other provision shall remain in full force and effect.

LICENSE AGREEMENT

GNU GENERAL PUBLIC LICENSE

Version 2, June 1991

Copyright (C) 1989, 1991 Free Software Foundation, Inc.

59 Temple Place - Suite 330, Boston, MA 02111-1307, USA

Everyone is permitted to copy and distribute verbatim copies of this license document, but changing it is not allowed.

Preamble

The licenses for most software are designed to take away your freedom to share and change it. By contrast, the GNU General Public License is intended to guarantee your freedom to share and change free software—to make sure the software is free for all its users. This General Public License applies to most of the Free Software Foundation's software and to any other program whose authors commit to using it. (Some other Free Software Foundation software is covered by the GNU Library General Public License instead.) You can apply it to your programs, too.

When we speak of free software, we are referring to freedom, not price. Our General Public Licenses are designed to make sure that you have the freedom to distribute copies of free software (and charge for this service if you wish), that you receive source code or can get it if you want it, that you can change the software or use pieces of it in new free programs; and that you know you can do these things.

To protect your rights, we need to make restrictions that forbid anyone to deny you these rights or to ask you to surrender the rights. These restrictions translate to certain responsibilities for you if you distribute copies of the software, or if you modify it.

For example, if you distribute copies of such a program, whether gratis or for a fee, you must give the recipients all the rights that you have. You must make sure that they, too, receive or can get the source code. And you must show them these terms so they know their rights.

We protect your rights with two steps: (1) copyright the software, and (2) offer you this license which gives you legal permission to copy, distribute and/or modify the software.

Also, for each author's protection and ours, we want to make certain that everyone understands that there is no warranty for this free software. If the software is modified by someone else and passed on, we want its recipients to know that what they have is not the original, so that any problems introduced by others will not reflect on the original authors' reputations.

Finally, any free program is threatened constantly by software patents. We wish to avoid the danger that redistributors of a free program will individually obtain patent licenses, in effect making the program proprietary. To prevent this, we have made it clear that any patent must be licensed for everyone's free use or not licensed at all.

The precise terms and conditions for copying, distribution and modification follow.

TERMS AND CONDITIONS FOR COPYING, DISTRIBUTION AND MODIFICATION

0. This License applies to any program or other work which contains a notice placed by the copyright holder saying it may be distributed under the terms of this General Public License. The "Program", below, refers to any such program or work, and a "work based on the Program" means either the Program or any derivative work under copyright law: that is to say, a work containing the Program or a portion of it, either verbatim or with modifications and/or translated into another language. (Hereinafter, translation is included without limitation in the term "modification".) Each licensee is addressed as "you".

    Activities other than copying, distribution and modification are not covered by this License; they are outside its scope. The act of running the Program is not restricted, and the output from the Program is covered only if its contents constitute a work based on the Program (independent of having been made by running the Program). Whether that is true depends on what the Program does.

1. You may copy and distribute verbatim copies of the Program's source code as you receive it, in any medium, provided that you conspicuously and appropriately publish on each copy an appropriate copyright notice and disclaimer of warranty; keep intact all the notices that refer to this License and to the absence of any warranty; and give any other recipients of the Program a copy of this License along with the Program.

    You may charge a fee for the physical act of transferring a copy, and you may at your option offer warranty protection in exchange for a fee.

XML:
Your visual blueprint for
building expert Web pages

2. You may modify your copy or copies of the Program or any portion of it, thus forming a work based on the Program, and copy and distribute such modifications or work under the terms of Section 1 above, provided that you also meet all of these conditions:

a) You must cause the modified files to carry prominent notices stating that you changed the files and the date of any change.

b) You must cause any work that you distribute or publish, that in whole or in part contains or is derived from the Program or any part thereof, to be licensed as a whole at no charge to all third parties under the terms of this License.

c) If the modified program normally reads commands interactively when run, you must cause it, when started running for such interactive use in the most ordinary way, to print or display an announcement including an appropriate copyright notice and a notice that there is no warranty (or else, saying that you provide a warranty) and that users may redistribute the program under these conditions, and telling the user how to view a copy of this License. (Exception: if the Program itself is interactive but does not normally print such an announcement, your work based on the Program is not required to print an announcement.)

These requirements apply to the modified work as a whole. If identifiable sections of that work are not derived from the Program, and can be reasonably considered independent and separate works in themselves, then this License, and its terms, do not apply to those sections when you distribute them as separate works. But when you distribute the same sections as part of a whole which is a work based on the Program, the distribution of the whole must be on the terms of this License, whose permissions for other licensees extend to the entire whole, and thus to each and every part regardless of who wrote it.

Thus, it is not the intent of this section to claim rights or contest your rights to work written entirely by you; rather, the intent is to exercise the right to control the distribution of derivative or collective works based on the Program. In addition, mere aggregation of another work not based on the Program with the Program (or with a work based on the Program) on a volume of a storage or distribution medium does not bring the other work under the scope of this License.

3. You may copy and distribute the Program (or a work based on it, under Section 2) in object code or executable form under the terms of Sections 1 and 2 above provided that you also do one of the following:

a) Accompany it with the complete corresponding machine-readable source code, which must be distributed under the terms of Sections 1 and 2 above on a medium customarily used for software interchange; or,

b) Accompany it with a written offer, valid for at least three years, to give any third party, for a charge no more than your cost of physically performing source distribution, a complete machine-readable copy of the corresponding source code, to be distributed under the terms of Sections 1 and 2 above on a medium customarily used for software interchange; or,

c) Accompany it with the information you received as to the offer to distribute corresponding source code. (This alternative is allowed only for noncommercial distribution and only if you received the program in object code or executable form with such an offer, in accord with Subsection b above.)

The source code for a work means the preferred form of the work for making modifications to it. For an executable work, complete source code means all the source code for all modules it contains, plus any associated interface definition files, plus the scripts used to control compilation and installation of the executable. However, as a special exception, the source code distributed need not include anything that is normally distributed (in either source or binary form) with the major components (compiler, kernel, and so on) of the operating system on which the executable runs, unless that component itself accompanies the executable.

If distribution of executable or object code is made by offering access to copy from a designated place, then offering equivalent access to copy the source code from the same place counts as distribution of the source code, even though third parties are not compelled to copy the source along with the object code.

4. You may not copy, modify, sublicense, or distribute the Program except as expressly provided under this License. Any attempt otherwise to copy, modify, sublicense or distribute the Program is void, and will automatically terminate your rights under this License. However, parties who have received copies, or rights, from you under this License will not have their licenses terminated so long as such parties remain in full compliance.

5. You are not required to accept this License, since you have not signed it. However, nothing else grants you permission to modify or distribute the Program or its derivative works. These actions are prohibited by law if you do not accept this License. Therefore, by modifying or distributing the Program (or any work based on the Program), you indicate your acceptance of this License to do so, and all its terms and conditions for copying, distributing or modifying the Program or works based on it.

6. Each time you redistribute the Program (or any work based on the Program), the recipient automatically receives a license from the original licensor to copy, distribute or modify the Program subject to these terms and conditions. You may not impose any further restrictions on the recipients' exercise of the rights granted herein. You are not responsible for enforcing compliance by third parties to this License.

7. If, as a consequence of a court judgment or allegation of patent infringement or for any other reason (not limited to patent issues), conditions are imposed on you (whether by court order, agreement or otherwise) that contradict the conditions of this License, they do not excuse you from the conditions of this License. If you cannot distribute so as to satisfy simultaneously your obligations under this License and any other pertinent obligations, then as a consequence you may not distribute the Program at all. For example, if a patent license would not permit royalty-free redistribution of the Program by all those who receive copies directly or indirectly through you, then the only way you could satisfy both it and this License would be to refrain entirely from distribution of the Program.

If any portion of this section is held invalid or unenforceable under any particular circumstance, the balance of the section is intended to apply and the section as a whole is intended to apply in other circumstances.

It is not the purpose of this section to induce you to infringe any patents or other property right claims or to contest validity of any such claims; this section has the sole purpose of protecting the integrity of the free software distribution system, which is implemented by public license practices. Many people have made generous contributions to the wide range of software distributed through that system in reliance on consistent application of that system; it is up to the author/donor to decide if he or she is willing to distribute software through any other system and a licensee cannot impose that choice.

This section is intended to make thoroughly clear what is believed to be a consequence of the rest of this License.

8. If the distribution and/or use of the Program is restricted in certain countries either by patents or by copyrighted interfaces, the original copyright holder who places the Program under this License may add an explicit geographical distribution limitation excluding those countries, so that distribution is permitted only in or among countries not thus excluded. In such case, this License incorporates the limitation as if written in the body of this License.

9. The Free Software Foundation may publish revised and/or new versions of the General Public License from time to time. Such new versions will be similar in spirit to the present version, but may differ in detail to address new problems or concerns.

Each version is given a distinguishing version number. If the Program specifies a version number of this License which applies to it and "any later version", you have the option of following the terms and conditions either of that version or of any later version published by the Free Software Foundation. If the Program does not specify a version number of this License, you may choose any version ever published by the Free Software Foundation.

XML:
Your visual blueprint for
building expert Web pages

10. If you wish to incorporate parts of the Program into other free programs whose distribution conditions are different, write to the author to ask for permission. For software which is copyrighted by the Free Software Foundation, write to the Free Software Foundation; we sometimes make exceptions for this. Our decision will be guided by the two goals of preserving the free status of all derivatives of our free software and of promoting the sharing and reuse of software generally.

NO WARRANTY

11. BECAUSE THE PROGRAM IS LICENSED FREE OF CHARGE, THERE IS NO WARRANTY FOR THE PROGRAM, TO THE EXTENT PERMITTED BY APPLICABLE LAW. EXCEPT WHEN OTHERWISE STATED IN WRITING THE COPYRIGHT HOLDERS AND/OR OTHER PARTIES PROVIDE THE PROGRAM "AS IS" WITHOUT WARRANTY OF ANY KIND, EITHER EXPRESSED OR IMPLIED, INCLUDING, BUT NOT LIMITED TO, THE IMPLIED WARRANTIES OF MERCHANTABILITY AND FITNESS FOR A PARTICULAR PURPOSE. THE ENTIRE RISK AS TO THE QUALITY AND PERFORMANCE OF THE PROGRAM IS WITH YOU. SHOULD THE PROGRAM PROVE DEFECTIVE, YOU ASSUME THE COST OF ALL NECESSARY SERVICING, REPAIR OR CORRECTION.

12. IN NO EVENT UNLESS REQUIRED BY APPLICABLE LAW OR AGREED TO IN WRITING WILL ANY COPYRIGHT HOLDER, OR ANY OTHER PARTY WHO MAY MODIFY AND/OR REDISTRIBUTE THE PROGRAM AS PERMITTED ABOVE, BE LIABLE TO YOU FOR DAMAGES, INCLUDING ANY GENERAL, SPECIAL, INCIDENTAL OR CONSEQUENTIAL DAMAGES ARISING OUT OF THE USE OR INABILITY TO USE THE PROGRAM (INCLUDING BUT NOT LIMITED TO LOSS OF DATA OR DATA BEING RENDERED INACCURATE OR LOSSES SUSTAINED BY YOU OR THIRD PARTIES OR A FAILURE OF THE PROGRAM TO OPERATE WITH ANY OTHER PROGRAMS), EVEN IF SUCH HOLDER OR OTHER PARTY HAS BEEN ADVISED OF THE POSSIBILITY OF SUCH DAMAGES.

END OF TERMS AND CONDITIONS

INDEX

Special Characters

XML:
Your visual blueprint for
building dynamic Web pages

XML:
Your visual blueprint for
building expert Web pages

XML:
Your visual blueprint for
building expert Web pages

XML:
Your visual blueprint for
building expert Web pages

INDEX

XML:
Your visual blueprint for
building expert Web pages

XML:
Your visual blueprint for
building expert Web pages

INDEX

INDEX

XML:
Your visual blueprint for
building expert Web pages

INDEX

XML:
Your visual blueprint for
building expert Web pages

W

INDEX

XML:
Your visual blueprint for
building expert Web pages

with these two-color Visual™ guides

The Complete Visual Reference

For visual learners who want an all-in-one reference/tutorial that delivers more in-depth information about a technology topic.

"Master It" tips provide additional topic coverage

ORDER FORM

IDG BOOKS ®

TRADE & INDIVIDUAL ORDERS

Phone: **(800) 762-2974**
or **(317) 572-3993**
(8 a.m.–6 p.m., CST, weekdays)
FAX : **(800) 550-2747**
or **(317) 572-4002**

EDUCATIONAL ORDERS & DISCOUNTS

Phone: **(800) 434-2086**
(8:30 a.m.–5:00 p.m., CST, weekdays)
FAX : **(317) 572-4005**

CORPORATE ORDERS FOR 3-D VISUAL™ SERIES

Phone: **(800) 469-6616**
(8 a.m.–5 p.m., EST, weekdays)
FAX : **(905) 890-9434**

Qty	ISBN	Title	Price	Total

Shipping & Handling Charges

	Description	First book	Each add'l. book	Total
Domestic	Normal	$4.50	$1.50	$
	Two Day Air	$8.50	$2.50	$
	Overnight	$18.00	$3.00	$
International	Surface	$8.00	$8.00	$
	Airmail	$16.00	$16.00	$
	DHL Air	$17.00	$17.00	$

Subtotal _____

CA residents add
applicable sales tax _____

IN, MA and MD
residents add
5% sales tax _____

IL residents add
6.25% sales tax _____

RI residents add
7% sales tax _____

TX residents add
8.25% sales tax _____

Shipping _____

Total _____

Ship to:

Name _____

Address _____

Company _____

City/State/Zip _____

Daytime Phone _____

Payment: □ Check to IDG Books (US Funds Only)
□ Visa □ Mastercard □ American Express

Card # _____ Exp. _____ Signature _____

maranGraphics™